The Quieted Voice

Robert L. Hilliard and Michael C. Keith
With a Foreword by Robert W. McChesney

The Quieted Voice

The Rise and Demise of Localism in American Radio

Southern Illinois University Press
Carbondale

Copyright © 2005 by the Board of Trustees,
Southern Illinois University
All rights reserved
Printed in the United States of America
08 07 06 05   4 3 2 1

Library of Congress Cataloging-in-Publication Data
  Hilliard, Robert L., date.
  The quieted voice : the rise and demise of localism
in American radio / Robert L. Hilliard and Michael
C. Keith.
      p. cm.
  Includes bibliographical references and index.
  1. Radio broadcasting—United States. 2. Local mass
media—United States. I. Keith, Michael C., date.
II. Title.
HE8698.H55 2005
384.54'0973—dc22
ISBN 0-8093-2673-6 (cloth : alk. paper)
ISBN 0-8093-2674-4 (pbk. : alk. paper)   2005005648

Printed on recycled paper. ♻

The paper used in this publication meets the minimum requirements of American National Standard
for Information Sciences—Permanence of Paper for
Printed Library Materials, ANSI Z39.48-1992. ∞

These are dark days for local radio. The number of independent stations falls every year. . . . Big business is killing radio's democratic promise, severely limiting the number of voices that can be heard.

—Robert Worth, *New York Times*

Loss of Localism undercuts the public service mission of the media, and this can have dangerous consequences.

—Ted Turner, *Washington Monthly*

Don't you see that the whole aim is to narrow the range of thought.

—George Orwell, *1984*

Contents

Foreword ix
 Robert W. McChesney
Preface xiii

1. **The Pendulum Swings**
   Radio's Local Roots and National Ambitions 1
2. **An Act of Local Substance**
   Regulating for the Public 24
3. **Acting in the Local Interest**
   Localism and the National Networks 43
4. **Changing the Broadcast Landscape**
   Radio Reinvents, Television Dominates, and an Act Reforms 55
5. **In Whose Best Interest?**
   Diversity, Localism, and Consolidation 69
6. **Lights Through the Smoke Screen**
   Ownership Deregulation and Local Opposition 88
   Appendix 6.1
   The Growing Concentration of Media Ownership 106
   Appendix 6.2
   FCC Sets Limits of Media Concentration 123
   Appendix 6.3
   Statement of FCC Commissioner Michael J. Copps on Media Consolidation
       and Diversity 132
7. **Disharmony in the Air**
   Downsizing Music Playlists 140
   Appendix 7.1
   Senate Testimony on Radio Deregulation 148
   Appendix 7.2
   An Analysis of Radio Deregulation 154
8. **New Audio Media and Localism**
   The Impact of Satellite and Internet Radio 170
9. **Tuning the Alternatives**
   Community Radio and Pirate Broadcasts 185
10. **What, If Not Local?**
    Globalism, Localism, and Public Interest 200

Notes 217
Suggestions for Further Reading 233
Index 235

Foreword

Over the past quarter-century, a very impressive body of scholarship and popular writing has chronicled the severe problems with the content generated by the U.S. media system. The recent tradition was launched by sociologists like Gaye Tuchman and Herbert Gans to media scholars like Edward S. Herman and Noam Chomsky to journalists like Ben H. Bagdikian. Organizations like Fairness and Accuracy in Reporting, which have mushroomed over the past decade, are examples of the growth of media criticism in our political and intellectual culture. All of this work was built upon a long-standing U.S. tradition of radical media criticism that went back a good century.[1] By radical criticism, I do not necessarily mean left-wing, although much of it was and is, but rather radical in the precise definition of the word, meaning getting to the root. The current wave of press criticism is not devoted to highlighting how negligent owners and practitioners are botching their jobs and should be replaced, but, to the contrary, how the current media system makes it rational for intelligent and talented people to generate content of dubious social value. The solution, therefore, lies in changing the system to make it rational to produce socially desirable content.

Understood this way, this radical media criticism can be distinguished from the so-called conservative critique of the "liberal" media, which argues that because many journalists vote for Democrats, the news is heavily biased to favor left-wing positions. This analysis of journalism fails to survive serious scholarly analysis, but it enjoys a clear prominence in the United States because it serves the political ends of the very wealthy and powerful organized political right.[2] The point of this criticism from the right is not to change the media system structurally but to limit what autonomy journalists enjoy from the prerogatives of owners and have them report more sympathetically on conservatives. It has been, by all accounts, a smashing success and one of the key factors in explaining the victory of George W. Bush in the 2004 U.S. presidential election.

In addition, there is a clear practical political dimension to the new wave of media criticism. It has logically led to the formation of an energetic media reform movement in the United States, a movement that is attempting to draw informed citizens into the policymaking process such that government regulations and subsidies work for the public rather than powerful media corporations. The contemporary media reform movement exploded on the scene in 2003 as millions of Americans from across the political spectrum rose up to oppose the Federal Communications Commission's plans to relax long-standing media ownership rules. The effects of such rules changes would have been a dramatic increase in media concentration and the virtual elimination of local media ownership except along the margins. The popular revolt was successful in contributing to several Congressional votes overturning aspects of the FCC's rules changes, and then, ultimately, to a 2004 court decision to throw the FCC's changes out entirely.

But the issue is being revisited in Washington in 2005–2006, and the fight should prove to be intense. The stakes are very high.

It is in this context that we can appreciate the singular importance of this new volume by Robert Hilliard and Michael Keith. Their study goes directly to arguably the two most sensitive areas in the media system today, the two areas that most thoroughly demonstrate the corruption and banality of the status quo: radio broadcasting and localism.

Radio broadcasting is living testament to the absurdity of the claim that ours is a "free market" media system. The entire system is based upon government grants of scarce monopoly licenses to commercial interests. The government grants these valuable licenses at no charge and then enforces the license holder's monopoly access to the scarce channel. In exchange, the license holder is supposed to serve the "public interest"—that is, act in a manner that is not entirely profit-driven—to justify why they, more than some other concern, should receive this lucrative government-granted monopoly use of scarce and valuable public property.

In the case of radio broadcasting, the most logical public service for the medium was to provide local content. Radio is arguably the least expensive of all our media in which to produce high-quality content. Therefore, while it is unrealistic to expect every mid-sized city to have its own major film studio or TV network, it is economically feasible to expect every community to have several commercially viable, locally based radio stations. Radio is in fact the ideal local medium.

Commercial interests that own our radio stations have long chafed at the notion of "public interest" obligations for self-evident reasons. As the FCC has never taken a license away from a profitable broadcaster for failing to serve the public interest, commercial interests have learned they could forgo doing anything substantive and instead simply use PR to proclaim their vast service to the public. The localism that emerged in radio over the course of U.S. history—and as Hilliard and Keith demonstrate, it was at times substantial—was due, more than anything else, to strict ownership rules that maintained a high degree of local ownership and competition. These ownership rules were never popular with the largest radio-station-owning firms that wanted to get bigger so they could face less competition and have greater profits.

When the largest media conglomerates—firms like Viacom and Clear Channel—were able to have radio ownership rules eliminated at the national level and greatly relaxed at the local level, it produced a frontal assault on what remained of localism in U.S. radio broadcasting. Local news and content were too expensive to produce, so they were gutted for standardized fare, and commercialism raged on. Hilliard and Keith chronicle this distressing demise. Ironically, the proponents of relaxing ownership rules called this rule change "deregulation," but it was nothing of the kind. Deregulation would imply that all the channels would be opened up for competitive usage, something possible with digital broadcasting but impossible for traditional broadcasting. This type of deregulation might mean that the existing radio giants would lose their market power, and they had zero interest in anything along those lines. Instead, they simply wanted to be able to gobble up more government-created and -enforced monopoly broadcast licenses, to have more monopoly power. They call that "deregulation," but it really means "re-regulation strictly to serve a handful of corporate interests with no concern for the public."

What has happened in radio is taking place across the U.S. media system. Firms get larger and larger, markets get less competitive, and local ownership and local content declines. In community after community, there is only a smidgen of local news, and it is often embarrassingly bad. Defenders of the status quo state that there is no need to worry because the Interact will set us free with its zillions of Web sites. But while we can go online to read French and Italian newspapers and read blog after blog of pontificators, we still cannot go online to find fresh and well-researched journalism on Decatur, Illinois, or Springfield, Massachusetts, or thousands of other communities. The Internet might distribute quickly and inexpensively what already exists, but it does not have the capacity to build local media out of thin air. That requires explicit policies to achieve that end.

If we want radio broadcasting to serve local communities, if we want more localism in our media—and it is clear that most Americans of all political persuasions desperately want this—it can be done. What is required are policies to encourage it. And this requires an informed and organized citizenry prepared to do what is necessary to accomplish the task. This superb book by Hilliard and Keith is an important tool to assist citizen understanding and involvement.

—*Robert W. McChesney*

Preface

The media, including broadcasting, do not exist in a vacuum. They are integral to the world they live in—they not only are impacted by the political, social, economic, environmental, scientific, and other aspects of their society but have a profound impact on the lives of all the people they reach.

We have tried, in all of our books—jointly and individually—to take a practical approach to the media. That is, we have attempted to show the interaction between media and society. For example, our book *Waves of Rancor: Tuning In the Radical Right* was the first to describe how extremist groups are using the media to foment hate and violence. Our book *Dirty Discourse: Sex and Indecency in American Radio* deals with a continuing key controversial issue in America: censorship and the First Amendment. Even our history of American radio and television, *The Broadcast Century and Beyond*, includes a time line that relates broadcasting's development to concurrent national and international events.

In this book, *The Quieted Voice*, we deal with a world phenomenon, conglomeration, including its impact on American media, specifically radio. We attempt to show that the short-term financial gains from consolidation in radio have resulted in the demise of local radio services to individual communities, concomitantly resulting in the not-so-long-term possible demise of radio itself—a case of killing the goose that lays the golden eggs. We also attempt to show that consolidation has, at the same time, resulted in the erosion of a key aspect of American democracy: the freedom of Americans to receive a diversity of information, opinions, and ideas, as opposed to the control of such information by a few corporate or governmental entities as is the case in most of the rest of the world.

Our thesis is that, in light of increased competitive distribution systems providing the programming and services once associated with terrestrial radio, more and more listeners are turning away from traditional radio. We believe that one thing that might save radio as we have known it is a return to localism.

Satellite radio and Internet radio have both become significant competitors and are growing at an exponential pace while terrestrial radio has been losing both audiences and advertising revenue. Some experts believe that iPods are an even bigger threat to terrestrial radio than satellite radio. And low-power local radio, which was vigorously opposed by the industry and its National Association of Broadcasters, has increasingly provided local services and used local talent that have largely disappeared from conglomerate-owned stations.

As this preface is being written, in January 2005, corporate radio and the NAB appear to have realized what their support of conglomeration and the deregulation of radio ownership have wrought. Industry claims that programming from central sites to stations hundreds of miles away provides a station's community with adequate local services has not fallen on ears turned to other services that provide at least as much community-oriented services and music aligned to particular interests and tastes.

In early 2005, the radio industry launched a $28 million advertising campaign to defend radio against competition from satellite radio, Internet radio, iPods, and file sharing. Appearing in the spots are some of the contemporary era's best-known musical artists supporting the ads' tag line: "Radio—you hear it here first." But it may well be a case of too little, too late.

As "old" radio hands, we hope radio as we have known it survives. But we believe it can only do so with a change in policy by Congress, the Federal Communications Commission, the radio industry, and the NAB. By reversing deregulation and creating once again a diversity of locally owned and operated stations, and by reestablishing the localism that marked radio for so many decades, terrestrial radio may become competitive again.

We wish to acknowledge the contributions of a number of colleagues, friends, and strangers. First and foremost we thank Robert McChesney, whose foreword reflects his eloquent commitment to the media's responsibilities to a democratic society and to diversity and localism in media programming. His comments set the tone for this book. We appreciate, too, the generosity of scholars and practitioners in the industry who responded to our request for ideas and comments, including Lee Abrams, Mike Adams, Jay Allison, Michael Brown, Lynn Christian, Rollye Cornell, Valerie Geller, Donna Halper, Christopher Maxwell, Allen Myers, Sean Ross, Ed Shane, and Christopher Sterling. We also wish to express our appreciation to Jenny Toomey and the Future of Music Coalition for permission to reprint appendixes 7.1 and 7.2. We thank, too, Karl Kageff and the excellent staff at Southern Illinois University Press for their work in seeing this book through to its production.

The Quieted Voice

.

1 The Pendulum Swings

Radio's Local Roots and National Ambitions

Radio began as a local phenomenon, bringing information, then education, music and the arts, culture and entertainment to the communities in which radio stations were located. As technological advances permitted increased transmitter power and antenna height, radio station signals began to reach other communities and across state lines. Less than a decade after the first radio station with a regular schedule went on the air in 1920, regional and ultimately national networks expanded radio into a national phenomenon.

But just as is happening now in the first decade of the twenty-first century and happened in the 1950s decade of the twentieth century, radio in its infancy faced a trauma that required an extreme makeover. Because radio was not regulated in its early years of the 1920s—licenses were granted by the Department of Commerce to virtually anyone who wanted one—frequencies and power clashed, resulting in chaos on the airwaves, with interference among stations' broadcast signals running rampant. In what may seem ironic today, broadcasters begged the government to establish regulations to solve the problem. Finally, Congress passed the Radio Act of 1927, which set up a Federal Radio Commission (FRC). The FRC immediately revoked all licenses and reassigned frequencies on a non-interference basis. Some stations, principally those previously operated noncommercially by colleges and universities, were forced off the air. Commercial operators, with their growing political leverage, got the most and best frequencies. Radio was on a new playing field.

As television has done since the last half of the twentieth century, radio networks back then dominated the evening hours of the American public, with drama, sitcoms, comedy, music, variety shows, documentaries, news, interviews—the entire panoply of information, education, and entertainment. Throughout the 1930s, as radio networks grew, radio became less local and more national. By the early 1950s, radio's principal listening audience was tuned to the three major national radio networks, NBC, CBS, and ABC, and to a fourth essentially news and music network, the Mutual Broadcasting System.

Even though radio had made the transition from local to national, outside of the prime-time network schedules and some daytime programs, principally soap operas, much of the programming, even on network-affiliated stations, was local. Not only was there a sense of responsibility on the part of the mostly locally owned and operated stations to serve the needs of their immediate communities, but by targeting local audiences they also were able to serve the needs of local merchants seeking local business—concomitantly enhancing the stations' advertising revenues. Stations that were network affiliates sold commercial time not already filled with national ads on network programs to local advertisers, and independent stations added much-needed local spot revenue to national advertiser spots sold by their station representative firm.

Many radio stations, including network affiliates, opened their studios and airtime to local productions that dealt with and served the interests of the local communities. One of the authors of this book performed on such a radio program in Cleveland, Ohio, in the late 1940s, *The Ohio Story*, which told in docudrama form key stories from the history of the state and area; and in the early 1950s, he wrote, produced, and directed a similar series, *The Delaware Story*, on a Wilmington, Delaware, station.

Although many stations were owned and operated by networks and multiple-station owners, each owner was limited to just a handful of stations. As late as the 1970s, Federal Communications Commission regulations limited multiple ownership to the so-called rule of sevens—a maximum of seven TV stations, seven AM radio, and seven FM radio for any one owner.

In the 1950s, along came television and frightened radio right off its national tuffet. Within a few years after the establishment of national television networks in 1951, virtually all the talent that had for years been on prime-time radio had moved to prime-time television. The dramas, the sitcoms, the music and variety stars—virtually everything and everyone, with the exception of soap operas for a few years—disappeared from radio. Radio networks as the country had known them since the late 1920s were gone, the public now tuned to prime-time television from seven to eleven P.M. every evening. Radio appeared to be dead and, indeed, was pronounced comatose by many observers and critics. Many radio stations went off the air. What could radio do? It clearly could not compete with prime-time television. It was left with few options. It could still do news, although international and national news became the province of television networks. It could still do music, although it could not duplicate the live music offered by television.

Reinventing to Survive

Radio, for decades serving the public with national programming, no longer could do so. It either had to disappear or somehow reinvent itself to survive. It did the latter. It took its only viable option: it became local again. Although the radio networks tried to reinvent themselves, as well, by providing short-term (a half-hour here, an hour there) and long-term (a block of several hours) specialized programming one or more days a week to its affiliates, radio was essentially local. Much of the news became local. Music was aimed at local interests and needs, with stations vying to determine and serve the music preferences of the demographics of their respective signal areas. After a while, rather than compete with each other for the broad demographics of a mutual market, competing stations aimed programming at specific audience segments in the community, with narrower and narrower formats, finding that even a small but loyal slice of the audience pie was a profitable way to match potential advertisers with the specific demographics of likely customers.

The public seemed to be happy: television for national programming and radio for locally oriented news, music, and, eventually, talk shows. Radio, left for dead in the early 1950s, had resurrected itself into an increasingly burgeoning media service and bottom-line as a local provider. Its voice was stronger than ever. After several decades, however, radio found itself once again in a dilemma. In the latter years of President Jimmy Carter's administration and through President Ronald Reagan's years in office, the White House, Congress, and the Federal Communications Commission (FCC) cooperated with the increasingly powerful media giants and relaxed the government restrictions on conglomerate ownership of the media. In their noteworthy 1980 study of the state of radio in the age of television, Peter Fornatale and Joshua Mills were already lamenting the decline of localism: "We are deeply concerned about the increasing use of automated formats provided by consultants; however efficiently they are produced, they cut deeply into local input. Banning automation is outlandish, but we believe it is reasonable to require any station using more than twelve hours of such programming daily to carry several shows a week of locally produced material. We are equally concerned about how few stations leave decisions on what music to play to their own on-air personnel. We feel there is social value in diversity."[1]

In interpreting the Communication Act of 1934's requirement that stations operate in the "public interest, convenience, or necessity," the FCC had implemented the principle of diversity. Specifically, the act states that the purpose of its enactment is "to make available, so far as possible, to all the people of the United States, without discrimination on the basis of race, color, religion, national origin, or sex, a rapid, efficient, nation-wide, and world-wide wire and radio communication service with adequate facilities and reasonable charges."[2] In applying the principle of diversity—that is, to prevent any one owner or a few owners from dominating the information and ideas available in any given community—the FCC had limited both national and local ownership of stations. Over the years, the FCC enacted regulations designed to prevent too much concentration of power over peoples' minds and emotions in any given community or in many communities.

In a 1998 review of its ownership rules, the FCC stated, "First, in a system of broadcasting based upon free competition, it is more reasonable to assume that stations owned by different people will compete with each other, for the same audiences and advertisers, than stations under the control of a single person or group. Second, the greater the diversity of ownership in a particular area, the less chance there is a single person or group can have an inordinate effect, in a political, editorial, or similar programming sense, on public opinion."[3] In announcing the ownership review, FCC chair William Kennard said, "Broadcast remains the way that most Americans get vital information about their local community."[4]

Deregulation began slowly under Carter and accelerated under Reagan. Restrictions on the number of stations that could be owned nationally, both in television and radio, and that could be owned locally by any one entity were gradually relaxed and reached what appeared to be the point of no return under President Bill Clinton's administration. The Telecommunications Act of the 1996, passed by a Republican Congress and endorsed and signed by a Democratic White House, eliminated virtually all restrictions on monopoly ownership of television and radio stations as well as cable systems, telephone companies, and other communications services.

Uniting for Profit

The effect on radio was immediate. Radio was completely deregulated. One owner could own as many radio stations throughout the country as they could buy, beg, or bulldoze. In the larger markets, one owner could own as many as eight radio stations. A consolidation frenzy ensued. The richest and most powerful radio station owners became even more rich and powerful. One owner, Clear Channel, acquired ownership of about one-tenth of all radio stations in the United States within a few years. Comparatively few locally owned stations remained in any given community. In 2003, the FCC went even further in deregulating the media, eliminating in practice virtually all restrictions.

Well, one must ask, so what? Why is consolidation (or conglomeration) a problem that merits the writing and publishing of a book and, more important, the time you are taking to read it? Media conglomeration in the United States is not an isolated phenomenon. It is part of the globalization of many industries and services throughout the world. Because the media are part of the globalization process, they usually tell us of the advantages of conglomeration and not of its disadvantages. Most of us are not aware of how global and national consolidation has affected us locally. Jerry Mander, director of the International Forum on Globalization, provides one perspective. He says that although signs of the "instability and unfairness" of globalization are everywhere, the media has been negligent in reporting them to us. When they are reported, the media fail to show us that the problems are rooted in globalization itself. Mander says that the media tend to treat the global companies with a touch of glamour, not explaining the real meaning of terms such as downsizing, efficiency, and competition—which, in fact, "usually mean replacing workers with machines . . . keeping wages down . . . eliminating middle management jobs, spreading anxiety from the cities to the suburbs."[5]

Critic Neal Lawrence applies this conclusion to local U.S. radio stations that are taken over by conglomerates.

> What typically happens is that the new guys come in and ruthlessly clean house. They fire longtime and popular air personalities so they can hire people at less cost, trim back news departments, abandon local autonomy in program decisions and eliminate budgets earmarked for community service. They often bring multiple stations under one roof and share air personnel. Aside from ruining staff morale, then shortchange the listener . . . smaller suburban and outlying rural signals are often

"moved in" toward larger and more lucrative urban markets as broadcast companies search for new properties. The result has been a loss of local service to the stations' "community of license" and an excessive concentration of stations in the already congested larger urban areas. Many rural communities across the Heartland have seen their hometown radio station abandon most or all of its local content. In many cases, entire rural regions are without any local radio.[6]

On the PBS public affairs program *Now,* host Bill Moyers in 2003 introduced the subject of media consolidation by referring to the "shrinking world of the mass media." He noted that in two decades the fifty owners of the United States' major media outlets had shrunk to six. "How a handful of companies came to exercise such control over the media is one of the astonishing stories of our time. And one of the most unreported. Big companies don't encourage the journalists who work for them to write about them. So while two-thirds of today's newspaper markets are monopolies, you don't find many newspapers writing about . . . monopolies. But there are real consequences to what's happening . . . real consequences for democracy and consumers."[7] The program dealt with the impact of consolidation on radio.

To some people, the issue of radio consolidation may seem minor compared to larger world concerns. But to many more people, such consolidation is simply an extension of global industry conglomeration as a whole. It is no longer controversial that whoever controls the media—principally radio and television and more recently the Internet—has the most powerful influence over people's minds and emotions. In other words, whoever controls the media controls the politics of any given country or region. The increasing growth and power of mega-companies, including in the United States the military-industrial complex that Republican president Dwight Eisenhower warned us about almost a half-century ago, punctuates the struggle in the United States and in the world between those who represent the public or consumer interests and those who represent the corporate ideologies and interests. To many people, it is a struggle to maintain the essence of democracy: power emanating from the people and their local communities against power centralized in and dictated by a few of the wealthiest corporate owners. We must all ask ourselves whether the consolidation of radio is destroying local community service and threatening the democratic process. Exploring this question is the underlying purpose and theme of this book.

Views Pro and Con

Ted Turner, former owner of one of the largest media conglomerates, has written

Today, media companies are more concentrated than at any time over the past 40 years, thanks to continual loosening of ownership rules by Washington. The media giants now own not only broadcast networks and local stations; they also own the cable companies that pipe in the signals of their competitors and the studios that produce most of the programming. . . . Healthy capitalist markets turn into sluggish oligopolies, and that's what is happening in the media today. Large corporations are more profit-focused and risk-averse. They often kill local programming because it's expensive, and they push national programming because it's cheap—even if their decisions run counter to local interests and community values.[8]

Frank A. Blethen, publisher of the *Seattle Times,* has said, "Bad things happen when media conglomerates swallow up independent voices: Quality is diminished, local news and investigative journalism disappear, differing points of view vanish, community service becomes an afterthought, and jobs are eliminated. All are sacrificed in an incessant drive for ever-higher profits."[9]

Conglomerate owners will tell you that by pooling the resources of many stations and thereby cutting costs, they can bring the public better programming and more efficient operations, thus serving the community more advantageously. With a large number of stations being operated from distant conglomerate headquarters, it is indeed more cost effective to feed common programming to most, if not all, of the conglomerates' stations. By centralizing many management as well as programming operations, conglomerates do not need as many personnel in individual stations. Staffs are reduced, in some cases drastically. Automated and semi-automated operations took over in many cases. From the point of view of the conglomerates, this is clearly a winning situation for economic productivity. Media giant Clear Channel's former radio division head, Randy Michaels, has stated that "consolidation, the collision of deregulation and technology is going to create the most powerful and the most positive change for radio. We've created lower cost to the consumer and at the end of the day the standard of living in this country is rising in direct proportion to efficiencies we are creating."[10]

David Field, the president and CEO of Entercom Communications, has said that the allegation that consolidation has led to less innovation and creativity in programming "is pure unadulterated garbage. There are critics with business agendas or political agendas that benefit from thrashing the radio industry, and that have asserted a handful of myths. . . . The fact is, like virtually every other company in the industry that I'm aware of, all of our stations are pressed today for innovation more than ever. . . . Many others demonstrate that the industry remains a vibrant and dynamic source of new programming."[11]

Is a monopolistic win for corporate media a win for the local station and community as well? With consolidation, local needs and programming become secondary to profits. Local programming needs frequently have been ignored, not necessarily out of ill will or even neglect but because it is not cost-efficient and because corporate officials in a far-off state are not likely to know much about a given station's community needs and interests. Many local people who worked in the local radio station, some for years or even for entire careers, have been fired, their knowledge of and commitment to the local community lost to the station. As one writer put it, deregulation "has led to a radio situation that's sort of akin to what McDonald's did to the food situation. Instead of a hit-or-miss local diner, there was a place spread across the nation that offered a uniform product. . . . Gone in the last few years are [local radio station owners], to be replaced by businesses that have their hearts elsewhere."[12] The voice of local radio appears to be quieted once more, this time to such a degree that it seems likely not to regain it, as it did a half-century ago.

Media critic and author Lawrence Soley addressed the issue in an affidavit in a court case involving local radio. Soley detailed key reasons for what he called the "decline in community programming." He cited the FCC's deregulation of radio, the consolidation of radio station ownership, the growth of satellite radio, the elimination by the FCC in 1978 of low-power community radio stations, and the decline in minority ownership. He concludes that the pressures of cost and the profit line within the new consolidated environment of the radio industry will cause more and more stations to seek programming from outside sources. He notes that there are "far too many stations with very little local content or identification. Whether live local, satellite/network or live assist, there is a continuing need to identify with, and to provide companionship for, the local listener. All too often, we're not hearing it. Too many operators are succumbing to a 'set it and forget it' mentality, and failing to provide enough local elements to bond with the local listener."[13]

The National Lawyer's Guild Committee on Democratic Communications asked the following questions in a 1998 position paper, two years after passage of the Telecommunications Act of 1996.

> Does the present media system, in which broadcasting is the primary channel of communication, information and dialogue for our democracy, meet this Constitutional and Legislative mandate [diversity and the Communications Act of 1934]? Are there a broad spectrum of views and opinions available to the people of the United States? Do people hear about choices other than Clinton or Dole? Is the view that the economy is not so rosy for the one-third of American children living below the poverty line up for discussion? Does anyone who thinks the war on (some) drugs isn't such a hot idea have an audience? Is a media system which grants access to only a narrow range of view Constitutional? Is a media system where the price of a soapbox is millions and millions of dollars Constitutional? Are recent developments, such as the Telecommunications Act of 1996, moving it closer or further away from complying with the dictates of First Amendment?[14]

Add to these questions critical issues in the world in which we are living today. Are dissident and alternative views to those of the government, the corporate sector, and the generally accepted majority being presented by the media? Should they be? The questions continue to be asked as conglomeration increases. Add to these questions ones concerning local issues in your own community. How would pro-industry sources respond? How would pro-consumer sources respond?

In its less than a century of existence, radio has gone from local to national to local and national again. This time, however, practitioners in the field—station managers, program directors, disc jockeys, news and sales personnel, and others who on a daily basis have tried to provide their communities with what they believe is the best programming services possible—see few, if any, saving graces of consolidation or much hope for the future of local radio. Let us examine some of their concerns and then look in more detail at why and how radio has gotten to the place where it is today.

Striking Sour Notes

In 2002, as consolidation grew apace, the Broad Artists Coalition, consisting of organizations representing the key programming element of radio—music—wrote to the FCC about its concerns.[15] "Radio is a public asset," the coalition stated, "not private property." It noted that since 1934, the federal government, through the Federal Communications Commission, has overseen the regulation and protection of this public asset to create a communications medium that serves the public interest. Unlike other businesses, radio stations have acquired their distribution mechanism—the airwaves—without any expenditure of capital. The public owns the airwaves. Owners of broadcast stations were given access to the broadcast spectrum by the government for free. The quid pro quo for free use of the public bandwidth required that broadcast stations serve the public interest in their local communities.

However, it has become clear that both recording artists and citizens are negatively impacted by legislation, regulatory interpretations and by a number of standardized industry practices that fail to serve the public interest. We call on the Federal Communications Commission (FCC) to undertake a comprehensive review of the following aspects of the radio industry that are anti-artist, anti-competition, and anti-consumer.

Among the requests made by the coalition were the following: "an investigation of the impact of recent unprecedented increases in radio ownership consolidation on citizens and the music community . . . an examination of the way vertical integration of ownership in broadcasting . . . decreases fair market competition."

In one section of its letter, the coalition addressed the "impact of widespread industry consolidation."

The federal government must also examine the impact of loosened ownership caps on the listening public. Until 1996, the Federal Communications Commission regulated ownership of broadcast stations so any company could own no more than two stations in any one market and no more than 40 stations nationwide. When Congress passed the Telecommunications Act of 1996, the restrictions governing ownership of radio stations evaporated. Now, radio groups own numerous stations around the country and exercise unreasonable control over the airwaves. For example, in 1996 there were 5133 owners of radio stations. Today, for the Contemporary Hit Radio/Top 40 formats, only four radio stations groups—Chancellor, Clear Channel, Infinity and Capstar—control access to 63 percent of the format's 41 million listeners nationwide. For the country [music] format, the same four groups control 56 percent of the format's 28 million listeners.

A year after receiving this letter, the FCC enacted rules that facilitated consolidation even more, exacerbating the problems seen by the coalition and quieting even further the voice of local radio.

In a study entitled "Radio Programming Diversity in the Era of Consolidation," Professor Todd Chambers stated,

> The golden age of radio might actually be gone. In this era of consolidation, radio management decisions include issues of voice-tracking, branding, and programming synergies within local clusters. Technology and infrastructure upgrades have enabled radio companies to transform the notion of localism by distributing on-air talent across several markets via voice tracking. For example, a local disc jockey may actually be broadcasting from a different market hundreds of miles away and it might have even been previously recorded. In addition to the issue of voice-tracking, there have been recent questions about the autonomy of local radio stations. Soon after the September 11 tragedy, industry news sources reported that Clear Channel Communications circulated a memorandum to its radio program directors listing songs that might be insensitive to play on the radio. On one hand, the list of songs highlighted the effectiveness of a large corporation to communicate sympathy across the country where the majority of its media properties operate. On the other hand, the mere suggestion that corporate dictates programming decisions characterized the company as one where efficiencies come before diversity in content.[16]

Chambers notes that television "forced radio to become a more specialized and local medium serving the needs of a local audience" and that radio transformed itself from a "national network to a local fragmented system," with radio formats continuing "to be more specialized as broadcasters search for the format niche that will deliver large audiences of listeners in demographic and lifestyle groups that advertisers are looking to reach." The results of Chambers's study "confirmed the assumption that there have been negative effects of ownership concentration," that "as the degree of concentration increases, the number of overall plays and the number of gold song titles decreases in that market," and that "markets with more competition played a wider variety of radio formats."[17]

The Digital Beat, an Internet publication that tracks media trends, stated that "when the Telecommunications Act of 1996 was passed, most discussion focused on its potential ramifications on telephone and television services, but it is perhaps radio that has changed most dramatically since the landmark Act. Over the past few years, unprecedented consolidation has led to the creation of corporate radio giants that are enjoying record advertising revenues, while nearly crushing the diversity and localism that have long been hallmarks of American radio."[18] In noting that "localism radio has strayed far from its deep local roots," *The Digital Beat* quotes from an article by Marc Fisher in the *American Journalism Review:* "A tidal wave of consolidation generated by the Telecommunications Act of 1996's loosening of ownership limits has put most big- and medium-market stations under the control of a handful of huge corporations, which have shown little interest in paying for local newsgathering." Fisher also notes that just one of the two available national news services "provide not only traffic and weather reports, but also the newscasts on virtually all the stations in town." Andrew Jay Schwartzman, longtime head of the public interest Media Access Project, adds that "the local angle just gets lost completely."

Brent Staples, in a *New York Times* article, lamented "the death of American radio."

> The mega companies that acquire a hundred stations each must squeeze every cent out of every link in the chain. They do this by dismissing the local staff and loading up squalling commercials and promotional spots that can take up as much as 30 minutes per hour during morning "drive time." The corporate owners then put pressure on their remaining rivals—and often force them to sell out—by promoting national advertising packages that allow commercials to be broadcast on several stations, or all over the country, at once. Disc jockeys are often declared expendable and let go. Where they remain in place, they are figureheads who spin a narrow and mind-numbing list of songs that have been market-tested to death, leaving stations that sound the same from coast to coast. . . . By standardizing music and voices around the country, radio is slowly killing off local music cultures. . . . Independent radio even 25 years ago was as important to a civic landscape as city hall or the local sports star who made good. The disc jockeys (or "on-air personalities," as they came to be called) embodied local radio to the public.[19]

Writing in *Billboard* magazine, Doug Reece said, "The 1996 Telecom Act . . . has blighted the radio industry by creating an environment where independent broadcasters could no longer compete." Reece quoted Americans for Radio Diversity president Jeremy Wilker: "The mega-media corporations coming in and buying up stations have destroyed radio localism and the community that it used to bring."[20] One typical example of conglomerates replacing local programming with distant multi-station programming occurred in the Duluth-Superior market when Clear Channel dropped local talk radio shows on its just-purchased stations and substituted a sports program from one of its stations in the Minneapolis–St. Paul market.[21]

Not long after passage of the Telecommunications Act of 1996, *USA Today* noted that consolidation was taking radio from a "kitchen-table culture of mom-and-pop businesses to one at home in the boardrooms of the nation's largest companies." It also noted that the changes were "hurting the diversity of content for listeners" and "turning a business with deep local roots into one that's more distant." The chair of the FCC at the time, William Kennard, stated that "the fundamental economic structure of the industry is changing from one of independently owned operators to something akin to a chain store."[22] A case in point is Akron, Ohio. In the five years following passage of the Telecommunications Act of 1996, its key stations were taken over by Clear Channel and Infinity, which standardized the stations' programming. Former broadcaster and Akron deputy mayor David Lieberth said that "radio is no longer a place for diverse viewpoints. . . . Local radio is a thing of the past." By 2003, 70 percent of the radio programming in the Akron area came from a distant radio conglomerate.[23]

Maintaining diversity of viewpoints is to many critics a key to maintaining a democratic society. The Benton Foundation summarized this concern as follows: "A robust democracy is dependent on open and accessible forums for debate, forums in which the widest range of views can be expressed. For much of this century [twentieth century], communities around the nation have depended on radio as a vital venue for discussion, as well as an outlet for local music and community viewpoints."[24]

In the summer of 2004, the United Church of Christ's Office of Communication—which had taken a key leadership role in the 1960s and 1970s in combating racism in programming and employment in radio and television networks and stations throughout the country—announced a campaign to hold broadcasters accountable for carrying programs in the public interest, especially in that presidential election year. A consortium of public policy, grassroots, and media-reform groups joined in the campaign. The director of the church's Office of Communication, former FCC commissioner Gloria Tristani, deplored the coverage of election campaign issues as being at an all-time low and asked citizen groups to meet with their local station executives to get them to pledge to carry a minimum of two hours a week of electoral coverage. Tristani stated, "Our democracy is grounded in an informed citizenry. It is time for broadcasters to truly serve the public and cover the issues [that the public] is concerned about—whether it's the reasons for going to war, how environmental policies will affect their community, who will pay for a loved one's medications or how we will pay for the burgeoning federal deficit."[25]

Local Intent

While the concern of this book is the quieted voice of local radio, it is worth noting that consolidation and the loss of local services is endemic in broadcasting as a whole: Conglomerates that own television and radio stations strengthen their overall profits by standardizing both media and conglomerates that principally own only radio or television properties reinforce each other in their consolidation practices. Less than two years after the passage of the Telecommunications Act of 1996, the Media Access Project and the Benton Foundation analyzed the effects of consolidation on television. In a joint report entitled "What's Local about Local Broadcasting?" they found the following: (1) Of 13,250 hours of programming in five markets by forty commercial TV stations, only 0.35 percent (one-third of one percent) dealt with local public affairs; (2) in three of the five markets, not a single station presented any local public affairs; (3) 35 percent of the stations presented no local news, and 25 percent of the stations carried neither local news nor local public affairs; during the most heavily viewed hours of 6 p.m. to midnight, only two stations presented any local public affairs programming for a total of only two hours. The report stated the basis for local programming in broadcasting: "Local programming is the keystone commitment of America's broadcasting system and the basis for the licensing scheme under which every broadcaster operates. The nation has hundreds of commercial [TV] broadcasters in place not to rebroadcast national programming, but to be responsive to the interest, convenience, and necessity of the communities they serve. The compact between local broadcasters and their communities—that a broadcaster receives a license to act as a public trustee of the public interest—is expressed in both court rulings and Federal Communications Commission policy."[26]

While there is disagreement between the industry and those representing listeners and consumers as to whether local service is being implemented under radio consolidation, there is no disagreement as to the need for localism as the cornerstone of radio broadcasting. Media researcher John Armstrong notes that some skeptics characterize the FCC's apportionment of channels among communities in order to serve local needs as a fiction and claim that the commission's policies really serve to "squelch competition and program diversity. Nonetheless, localism, as both a description and a justification, is closely associated with the system of locally-based radio and television outlets that has dominated the United States broadcasting system for most of the twentieth century."[27] Consumer media watchdog groups such as the Media Access Project and industry groups such as the National Association of Broadcasters (NAB) rarely agree on much, but both advocate the importance of localism. In a marketing guide for local broadcasters, the NAB says, "It is at the local level that the industry's true impact as a community service provider can best be seen and understood. It is at the local level that stations are working to serve the public interest."[28] The Broadcast Industry Council issued a special report for broadcasters on community services, declaring, "Broadcasters also can play a critical role in drawing attention to successful community programs and in promoting communitywide discussions."[29]

Viewing Localism from Far and Near

What do the people on the front line—that is, the people working in radio today—think? In preparing this book, we asked some practitioners in the field, some professors of media, and some critics and experts in specific communities several questions on the role of local radio and the impact of consolidation. All agreed on the importance of local radio. There was not unanimous agreement, however, on the role consolidation is playing in eroding local programming and local service. Our first question was, "Is localized radio programming still of value in an increasingly globalized media culture?"

Valerie Geller of Geller Media believes that "localized communication of *any* kind is of value to the audience, providing it is quality programming that is truthful and relevant to the lives of the listeners, with new information, that entertains, inspires and informs the public. Audiences still want to know 'what is happening in their own backyards, or how does a big news story affect *us* here.' A city that has had a call center close down due to international outsourcing may feel differently about the President's speech [supporting outsourcing] than a town that has not." Mike Adams, chair of the Department of TV-Radio-Film-Theatre at San Jose State University in California, agrees. He notes that "in the Bay Area of Northern California (San Jose, San Francisco, Oakland), 'local' radio serves the local Indian, Asian (Vietnamese, Chinese), Latino and Fillipino communities, and many smaller groups. We are a true 'melting pot' and radio is affordable and makes sense." Sean Ross, vice president of music and programming at Edison Media Research, states that "the larger issue is whether radio is still a news and information resource for the audience and that answer is yes. Even in an environment where news had long disappeared from many music stations, listeners were still looking to radio to keep them connected in the wake of 9/11."

Professor and author Donna Halper emphatically believes that local radio programming is important "more so now than ever." As she puts it, "Global media have led to syndication of certain announcers and shows in market after market. That may be okay for music (although I question where it's good to do away with 'local hits'), but with talk shows and shows about current issues, I believe it is essential for local communities to have some kind of voice and be able to express themselves. Also, it's important for there to be accountability—if you don't like what a syndicator is doing, it can take months for your complaint to be addressed, whereas if it's a programmer in your own community, you stand a better chance of relaying your feedback and getting some response."

Christopher Sterling, author of communication books and professor of communications at George Washington University, believes that localized programming should be of value, "but in fact is less relevant all the time because of the lack of *real* local, programs on the vast majority of stations. Put another way, localism *should* be alive, but isn't, because it does not pay—and yet the industry continues to wave high and hard the flag of that (local) service it no longer provides." National talk show host Rollye Cornell says

Since the advent of television, radio's biggest assets were it ability to be local and live. From the service aspect, more than the entertainment factor, there is an absolute need for a local, immediate media source, and nothing can fill it better than local radio. Whether that locally oriented content can be done successfully at a distance is a current debate. Regarding entertainment: For a long time the prevailing logic, particularly with talk radio, was that to be successful, a show needed to be local. Rush Limbaugh single-handedly proved this axiom false. In order to succeed, a radio show needs to be relatable, and while local content can go far to that end, it is not absolutely necessary. Relatability is not necessarily linked to geography. But from the standpoint of service—using radio as a utility—from inclement weather and school closing news to warnings of hazardous conditions (ranging from inconvenient traffic tie-ups to truly threatening toxic spills), nothing fulfills the public's need to know better than well-programmed local radio. Clearly this is not the kind of content that would be under the entertainment umbrella, but for stations with reputations of being on the scene whenever there is a scene locally, a solid listener base is always assured. (This explains the very high cume [unduplicated listeners], though often low time, spent listening to many all-news outlets.) So, is localism necessary for entertainment? No. But to uphold the conditions under which the license was granted in the first place, absolutely. And more than that, for listener loyalty and recall, nothing beats being an immediate source of community news in a crisis.

Jay Allison, director of public broadcasting station WNAN on Nantucket Island, Massachusetts, says that local programming is, "of course," still of value, and "more than ever." He explains that "at our station, we feel our mission, in a way, is to create neighborliness. Our listeners are strangers to one another, connected only by the fact that they are listening to our station and that we all share a connection to place. We want to build on those two affinities." Christopher Maxwell, manager of another noncommercial station, Radio Free Richmond, carries his "of course" affirmation a step further. "We will still have geographically localized needs. Democracy happens at the precinct level. Purchases and those decisions happen at the metro level or even household level. People will still need something that is interactive and reflects what is going on in their area. Democracy is run by those who show up, so if you have a radio station that alerts you to 'show up' in some fashion at places where your values may be challenged, then that radio station is providing a valuable service." Professor Michael Brown of the University of Wyoming believes that localized radio programming "is a valuable source of local information and local advertising. The local information is at most risk. None of our local commercial stations have much of a news presence. Any local radio news comes from the university's NPR affiliate. The only commercial station with a strong local presence is actually a Clear Channel AM station that is primarily about sports."

Ed Shane, president of Shane Media, notes some examples (in Houston, Texas) of how KUHF, the NPR affiliate, provided the locality with important information about the schools and the school board that was not available elsewhere, except in the *Houston Chronicle*. Shane says, "I feel that radio should serve the public's need for this information, not just the public's desire or interest." Shane supports the concept of "psychographic localism" as differentiated from geographic localism. "The shared experience of radio," he states, "links people in widely separated localities into communities of like-minded individuals. . . . Psychographic localism created a sense of shared community of the so-called 'Golden Age of Radio' . . . shows [that] were national in their distribution yet entirely local in the listener response."

We then asked each of these respondents whether they thought radio consolidation was a principal threat to local radio. Lynn Christian, former senior vice president of the National Association of Broadcasters and the

Radio Advertising Bureau, agreed that local programming was still of value and added that, in addition to consolidation, "the Internet, localized sections of major metropolitan newspapers, local TV and special community cable channels are also increasing threats to local community service, or 'localization,' by locally operated radio stations." Jay Allison believes consolidation is a principal threat because "globalization is expensive and greed drives consolidation and globalization." Sean Ross, however, thinks concentration is

> less the threat than the catalyst. Radio was already on the way to becoming less local and less information driven even before deregulation. The fragmentation of radio formats had already convinced many operators of music stations that they couldn't compete as a news source, while the syndication of Howard Stern and other big name morning shows was already spreading. While it's tempting to believe that consolidation equals cost savings equals less localism, there are also a lot of radio stations paying as much for a syndicated morning show as they would for a local one. Those stations believe that they can't compete with superior out-of-town talent unless they use a national or regional show.

Donna Halper, on the other hand, believes that consolidation has had a highly negative effect on local information and ideas in programming, that

> it has permitted the right wing conservative takeover of the discourse in our society. It has made it seem that "everyone agrees" when in fact other viewpoints just are not represented. With giant conglomerates calling the shots (and several of these companies have well-documented ties to the current [2004] Republican administration), the public may be misinformed and not even realize it, since the same untruths and exaggerations are repeated in city after city by Rush Limbaugh or Michael Savage or whoever. And as for music, we all saw what happened when it was perceived that the Dixie Chicks had questioned the war on Iraq— their songs were dropped by at least one chain of 42 stations (Cumulus) and, I am told anecdotally, many Clear Channel stations dropped them as well. Now, the Dixie Chicks, whether one likes their politics or not, have many hit songs; yet, for a while they were banned by corporate fist. Corporate fist also dictated that certain anti-war songs not be played. I find trends like this terrifying. The more that large conglomerates can dictate what gets played and what points of view are acceptable, the less we have a democracy.

Christopher Maxwell is also concerned with the concentration of power over programming content. While he states that consolidation is not, in itself, necessarily a threat to localization, it becomes

a problem when reinforced by chicken-shit fraidy-cat programmers hiding behind their Excel spreadsheets to cry and moan that "radio is a mature medium" and that there is no new programming that's proven. Well, of course, if it's new it's not yet proven. They are just defending their laziness. But as long as there are at least a half-dozen really competitive possibilities for an area—the more signals the better—then even the big companies will have to respond to that competition. The real threat here is that radio stations mostly pursue the same audience, the same advertisers and underwriters who all have the same set of values that are not necessarily the same values as those of the listeners. And anything that reduces the smaller competitors from providing a real escape point from the big guys dramatically decreases the value of the broadcast band. That is the principal threat to localization. Tied in with that threat is the increased cost of advertising on radio that shuts out the smaller stores in a locality; again, as long as the conglomerates have a half-dozen or more real competitors, they can crank up the price of advertising only so much. What marketplaces need are a half dozen low-power FM stations each, whose programming is not duplicating anything heard on the Big Boys. We need an escape path for the smaller "underwriter" and for alternative music and views.

In a similar vein, Mike Adams points out that although minority groups in the Bay area have access to low-power AM stations, "the powerful AM and FM channels are still Infinity and Clear Channel, programming mostly 'white-people's' radio."

Several of our interviewees stressed the bottom line—money—as a corollary of the threat of consolidation. Christopher Sterling, for example, does not think radio concentration is the biggest threat to localism, although he believes it contributes to its erosion. He says that it is "hard to be local in hundreds of places if you are providing increasingly centralized program production, recording, and re-use—not to speak of voice tracking, which pretends to be local." He believes that "the prime cause of the decline of localism is the same as with all other major program trends in radio and television—economics. It's all about money. Local programs lack the appeal of national shows, and cost the station more to produce (in most cases). This is an old story. Localism remains on television as it still pays (e.g., hours of 'local' news)."

Rollye Cornell also cites economics as the principal cause:

When a company pays a significant amount for a radio station, in many cases much more than some would argue its obvious cash flow would demand, economy of scale is essential. The buying frenzy which occurred after the passage of the Telecommunications Act of 1996 led a handful of broadcasters to quickly secure as many facilities as possible, the theory being that early acquisitions would be key to creating a strong base from which to operate. Since the number of radio stations plus the power each has and the frequency on which each broadcasts is part of a very tightly controlled spectrum, he who hesitated would be lost, or so it was believed. Therefore, if stick value was not reflective of advertising revenues at the time, the belief was that down the road it would be seen as a bargain. Until that time came, operating the facilities at a profit—or at least not as a loss—was the immediate challenge. There are only two ways to increase cash flow: one is to bring in more revenue, the other is to cut costs. Increasing revenue is not a guaranteed proposition, cutting costs is. Of course, there comes a point when no further cuts are possible, but with a national chain of radio stations, much consolidation can be done before that time. Not only can payroll be saved on a number of positions by co-locating previously competing stations (thus one receptionist, one traffic person, etc., rather than six or seven), but through today's technology many functions can handled outside the local marketplace as well. The on-air sound can be executed in a number of outsourced ways, from the success of national talk shows like Rush Limbaugh's to individual voice tracking geared specifically for a market. Today it is not unusual for the news department of a cluster in a large market to handle on-air reports for clusters in smaller markets, some of which none of the personnel may have ever visited. The advent of concentration allows for this kind of consolidation of resources. The economics of concentration demands it. For most of these mega-groups, doing otherwise would be financially fatal.

Michael Brown comes to a similar conclusion, that "concentration means the bottom line becomes most important (as opposed to passion for the media and connection to the community), and the bottom line can be improved by centralizing production. There are still opportunities for local advertising, but the money generated doesn't necessarily stay in the community." Valerie Geller notes that

consolidation of radio unfortunately has become just another arm or element of what is happening in business all over the United States and throughout the world. Obviously, when you have programming that comes from a single source, far away from a community, delivered via satellite, you lose local flavor. It's cost effective for owners. If you only pay one on air talent to service hundreds of stations, it makes sense from that perspective. But the day-to-day local programming suffers. Arguably, if consumers (listeners) and advertisers hugely supported local shows with ratings results, the same way they come out in droves to support national programming, that might be one way to continue to hang on to local hosts and local news at local stations. In the early days of radio, programming came from a network and there were only a couple of prime networks. Soap operas, variety shows, news, music programming, westerns, comedies, all came out of a single source. This trend is actually circling around back to that concept. Under the major owners, commercial radio right now is about profit and demonstrating growth for shareholders and stockholders. The pressure on local broadcasters for profit is extreme. If radio in the United States, as in other countries, were more about genuine public service and not so focused on profit, we would not be having this discussion about the "loss" of local radio.

Ed Shane explains that "the availability of syndication, network programming, and voice tracking from other stations in the same chain offers operators the opportunity to cut costs, thereby adding an asset value. As costs are cut, so are services, and often that means services to the local community, because personnel are not available to interact with members of the public or to attend news related events. Remote voice-tracking tends to rely on generic content instead of specific local content . . . and undermines the sense of locality."

Lee Abrams, chief programmer for XM satellite radio, contributes a different point of view, reflecting the purpose and recent growth of satellite radio. "Local radio," Abrams states, "has been dead for 25 years. Other than the *true* local stations, mostly big AMs like WGN or KMOX, local radio is primarily satellite fed, voice tracked from remote locations or syndicated. The definition of 'local' is changing. In XM satellite radio's case, local means 48 states. Music downloading is only the tip of the iceberg. The bigger problem is that contemporary music has run out of creative steam. Media concentration threatens the future of *terrestrial* radio."

The Importance of Being Local

The question of localism in radio, although appearing to reach a crisis point in the first decade of the twenty-first century, has been a continuing issue for the previous decade, especially since the passage of the Telecommunications Act of 1996. Its importance is reflected in the many articles and forum reports in the *Journal of Radio Studies (JRS)*. Some examples from *JRS* are described below.

In a 1995–96 article, Gregory Newton wrote, "The economics of the industry provide substantial pressure against predominantly geographical local program production and distribution. The Commission [FCC] has, in fact, noted the tension and the desirability of an audience-centered localism policy as a means of fostering diversity and meeting the public interest. However, the FCC has left programming choices increasingly to the marketplace in the wake of the deregulation inquiry, and still relies on policies of geographic localism (exemplified by licensing and ownership provisions)."[30] Any media observer believes that program diversity becomes a seriously endangered concept when a single owner (individual or corporation) acquires and ultimately operates eight stations in the same market.

> Because bottom-line concerns invariably occupy the thoughts of the most enlightened broadcast executive, the nature of the air product will naturally be predicated on the basis of financial viability and marketability. That is, a format will be devised or duplicated if there is a sizeable enough audience to interest advertisers, especially those with deep pockets. In other words, if you can make money programming four classic rock stations in the same city, then why not program (bunch) four classic rock stations? Indeed, can there be a greater variety of radio programming formats and features from which to choose when virtually a handful of radio groups own the majority of stations in the country?[31]

In a 2000 issue of *JRS*, Duncan Brown wrote, "Three years after the passage [of the Telecommunications Act of 1996], many of the promises made by the act's supporters—increased competition, protection against monopoly power, greater consumer choice, and lower prices—remain unfulfilled for most users of many telecommunications services. And yet one consequence of the Act was already very clear. The relaxation of radio station ownership limits promulgated by the Act had produced massive restructuring of the broadcast radio industry in the United States. There had been a tidal wave of mergers and acquisitions with the emergence of a small number of 'megagroups.'"[32]

The radio industry, however, has taken a diametrically opposite view. At the National Association of Broadcasters (NAB) annual Radio Show in 2004, NAB president and CEO Edward O. Fritts stated that, in fact, there was no better business than local radio. He said, "We've helped establish a stable regulatory framework that protects your licenses and allows you to better serve listeners." He noted the NAB's role in protecting commercial radio stations from interference by restricting the addition of more low-power FM radio stations. He described the work of the NAB on behalf of the radio industry: "We work to bring broadcasters together with industry leaders and new technology. . . . [We] make sure that new technologies actually work in the real world." He stressed radio's local commitment: "NAB is your voice in the nation's capitol. . . . For your part, you are the tangible voice of your communities. You serve them in good times and in bad, day in and day out. I want to commend all of you for what you do in your communities each and every day. . . . I believe in my bones that there is not a better business in America than local radio."[33]

While the FCC has continued, through 2004 and into 2005, unequivocally to support the growth of consolidation, it has done so on the basis of political ideology. With the Republican control of the White House and both houses of Congress through 2008, there is little question that consolidation and industry monopoly will be given even more official government support. FCC commissioner Michael Copps, who with another Democratic member of the commission voted against the FCC's 2003 three-to-two decision to further relax media ownership regulations, has accused the FCC of putting the interests of the conglomerates above that of diversity and local needs and concerns. He has stated that the Republican-controlled commission is responsible for the "Clear Channelization" of radio. "We are skirting dangerously close to taking the public interest out of the airwaves," Copps has said. "Step by step, rule by rule, bit by bit, [the current Commission] has allowed the dismantling of a whole variety of public interest protections and flashed the green light for more consolidation. . . . Anything with the name 'independent' on it seems to be on the endangered species list. But there is so much more creativity across America than the lowest common denominator entertainment from Madison Avenue."[34]

How did radio reach this point, where, for the third time in its existence, it faces an extreme makeover?

2 An Act of Local Substance

Regulating for the Public

The first station on the air with a regular schedule of programs tried hard not to be local. In 1920, KDKA, Pittsburgh, owned by the Westinghouse corporation, sought widespread publicity as it prepared to unveil its new station, hoping that newspaper accounts would convince as many far-flung potential listeners as possible to buy its radio receivers—its principal reason for putting a station on the air. Transmitters, at the time, were one hundred watts in power, which limited the signal range to about twenty to forty miles depending on the height of the transmitting antenna. Westinghouse wanted the widest range of customers and reportedly gave or lent receivers to its higher-level employees, VIP friends and acquaintances, and organizations such as country clubs within the maximum range of its signal, including communities across the state line in Ohio. (It should be noted that there is some disagreement among media historians as to whether KDKA actually was the first U.S. station on the air with regularly scheduled programming. Some arguments have been made for the University of Wisconsin's WHA, which operated with regular reports from before World War I and through it. Other arguments have been made for WWJ, Detroit, which was operated as an amateur station financed by the *Detroit News,* which, like Westinghouse, had an aggressive public relations component. Across the border, in Montreal, Canada, radio station CFCF was on the air before any of its United States counterparts. Neither the U.S. nor Canada have uncontested claims to the first station anywhere; that honor belongs to the Netherlands, which is considered to have begun radio operations in 1919.)[1] In any event, radio in the early years of the 1920s was local, necessarily so because of the technological limits of the broadcast signal.

Within a few years, advances in transmitter power and the placement and height of antennas made it possible for radio stations to reach well beyond the boundaries of their communities. Soon stations with five hundred watts, fifteen hundred watts, and the maximum thirty thousand watts and by the end of the decade with fifty thousand watts were sending signals far beyond their studio sites. A peculiarity of AM signals is its ability at dusk to bounce off an atmospheric phenomenon called the Kennelly-Heaviside layer (named after its discoverers) and carry back to earth. Some stations' signals, therefore, could be heard hundreds of miles away and, when conditions were right, more than halfway across the country. (Listeners today who experiment with their radio dial can pick up many stations from afar. On the East Coast, for example, on almost any night one can hear stations from Cincinnati, Chicago, Detroit, Boston, Washington, DC, and Montreal, among others. Some stations in America's Midwest stretch all the way to the West Coast.) But, although the radio signal no longer was locally limited, programming and service still remained local in principle and execution.

Peter Orlik, in his book *The Electronic Media,* says, "From the beginning, electronic mass media in the United States have reflected local rather than national orientations. While European countries were building highly centralized state systems to distribute national programming exclusively, the United States was allowing a host of individual stations and operators to serve their local communities in their own ways. Some of these stations later voluntarily joined to share programs (to network), but individual responsibility and decision making remained at the local level."[2] This concept is reinforced in Gregory Newton's article, "Localism in Radio" in the *Encyclopedia of Radio.*

> The concept of "localism," or serving a specific community, has always been central to the practice of radio programming and to government policies concerning broadcasting in the United States. In contrast to much of the rest of the world, American radio stations were allocated to local communities and licensed to serve audiences defined by the boundaries of these communities. The Federal Communications Commission (FCC) has described its radio allocation priorities as (1) providing a usable signal from at least one station to everyone and diversified service to as many persons as possible, and (2) creating sufficient outlets for

local expression addressing each community's needs and interests. That system of license allocation remains the foundation of American broadcasting.[3]

The notion of localism in early broadcasting emanated from the initial concepts of communication as civilization developed families, groups, tribes, and community organizations such as towns and states. Before electronic inventions, all communication of an immediate, oral nature was local. The Greek marketplace or agora and the Roman forum, where the entire population of the area theoretically communicated with each other and was communicated to, were bases for communication among citizens of later communities. The epitome of democracy was embodied in free (unhindered) local exchange. The rhetoric of communication during the early days of radio in the United States "reflected utopian notions of radio as a tool to enhance local democracy."[4]

By the time the first radio network was established in 1926, there were almost six hundred radio stations on the air and millions of radio receivers had been sold throughout the United States, mainly on the East Coast. This new network, the National Broadcasting Company (NBC), was formed by the Radio Corporation of America, General Electric (GE), and Westinghouse. (GE left the radio station business not long afterward and it wasn't until 1986 that it returned, ironically, as the owner of NBC. The irony increased a year later when GE sold the NBC radio network, retaining the TV network.) In 1927 a second network was established, which adopted the name Columbia Broadcasting System the following year. NBC shortly thereafter established a second network, and called its two branches the Red Network and the Blue Network. The latter was sold off by FCC edict in 1943 to become the American Broadcasting System (ABC).

While the growth of the networks meant that local stations that were affiliated with networks would now air principally national programming in prime time, they did not lose their local flavor or commitment. Even the early commercials were local. In fact, the first commercial was aired in 1922 (is it possible that radio executives did not understand the income potential from radio advertising until two years after stations went on the air?) as a ten-minute talk on WEAF, the NBC flagship station in New York City, by an executive of the "Queensboro Corporation extolling the virtues of buying an apartment in a new suburban development called Jackson Heights—today a highly urbanized area." As we pointed out in a previous work, "These first paid advertisements resulted in the sale of apartments, and advertising as the support base for American broadcasting was born."[5]

This commercial, like many others to follow it, was local, and even though regional and national companies touted their products and services on radio, the thrust of the commercials most often took on a local flavor, oriented to the demographics and needs and interests of the local audience's potential buyers. In some cases, multiple ads were prepared for different sections of the country and specific markets and communities. Even today, with increasing centralization of all programming, this specialization remains true of advertising. Local stations employ station representative firms that serve national and regional sellers of a given station's available commercial-spot times. While most stations retain a sales staff for local advertisers, it would be too expensive to maintain national and regional sales personnel as well. The commercial ad survival for most radio stations is still local.

Early programming made direct use of the locality itself. Jeffrey L. Stein has described such programming in Iowa: "Early broadcasters took advantage of the public's curiosity by creating programming designed to encourage audience participation. These programs, generally called 'man on the street' programs, typically aired during the midday hour and featured an announcer with a live microphone at a public gathering place—a department or discount store, a hotel lobby, or a busy sidewalk. The announcer would encourage those passing by to stop and chat before live microphones, often offering prizes as incentives." Stein summed up this aspect of the localism of radio: "From their earliest days as a curiosity—a way to fill time, promote the station, and give citizens a chance to watch radio in action—to today's chance for listeners to call and offer opinions or ask questions of expert guests, these programs help the station fulfill the congressional mandate of all stations: 'to serve the public interest, convenience, and necessity.' Whether by the old 'man on the street' programs, or telephone call-in shows, the unique interaction between broadcasters and their audience remains alive and well."[6]

Too Many, Too Few

But even as radio grew in the early 1920s and networks were being formed, the industry was facing a crisis. During that early period, the federal government licensed stations through the Department of Commerce. There were virtually no requirements for licensing, such as specific channel assignments or restrictions on transmitter power or antenna height. Anyone with the resources to put a station on the air anywhere could do so. For example, a license-seeker in Boston could take the night train to Washington, DC, arrive in the morning and go from Union Station to the

Department of Commerce and file an application, few questions asked. After lunch, that individual could return to the Commerce Department, pick up the approved license and take a train back to Boston. Theoretically, the next day they could have a station on the air. What did this mean for broadcasting? It meant that many people were speculating on the new communication craze and stations were springing up everywhere.

But the limitation on the number of usable available channels (just three by 1923) resulted in chaos on the air. Someone might have station operating in a community with a relatively clear signal until someone else put up a station on the same frequency with higher power and antenna height, drowning out the signal of the first station. Multiply that situation by many stations in many cities and interference reigned. The late Erik Barnouw appropriately titled the first volume in his definitive history of broadcasting *A Tower in Babel*.

Broadcasters were unhappy. The public was unhappy. The government and the Department of Commerce, including Secretary of Commerce Herbert Hoover (later to become president) were unhappy. To try to solve the problem, Hoover called a series of national radio conferences. While they prompted proposed legislation in Congress, Congress took no action. Within the industry there was dissension. For example, when David Sarnoff, then head of RCA, announced that his company was considering building a series of fifty-thousand-watt stations throughout the country, local station owners with lower power were afraid that Sarnoff would conglomerate them out of business; at one of Hoover's radio conferences, they got the attendees to oppose monopolies in broadcasting. Some historians have noted that Hoover, a strong ideological conservative, appeared to have favored the larger corporations at the expense of the smaller stations. Interestingly, that was exactly eighty years prior to the concerns of many groups today, as this book is being written, about current monopolies in broadcasting.

Yet Hoover himself, at the first radio conference in 1924 and in congressional hearings, warned against the kind of monopolization that he later appeared to support or at least permit. He declared,

> It is inconceivable that the American people will allow this new-born of communication to fall exclusively into the power of any individual group or combination. Great as the development of radio distribution has been, we are probably only at the threshold of the development of one of the most important of human discoveries bearing on education, amusement, culture, and business communication. It cannot be thought that any single

person or group shall ever have the right to determine what communication may be made to the American people. . . . The fundamental thought of any radio legislation should be to retain possession of the ether in the public and to provide rules for orderly conduct of this great system of public communication by temporary permits to use the ether. It should be kept open to free and full development, and we should assure that there can be no monopoly over the distribution of material.[7]

This view was reiterated by the Radio Broadcasters Society of America, an organization of independent stations, which affirmed that if radio broadcasting

is put into the hands of a trust, into the hands of a monopoly—if a monopoly is not stopped now and they get control in this country—it might well be that some official of the monopoly company, sitting in the quiet of his executive office, surrounded and protected and away from the public, where he can not be seen, will issue the fiat that only one kind of religion shall be talked over the radio; that only one kind of politics shall be talked over the radio; that only one candidate can give messages to the people; that only one kind of soap can be advertised.[8]

As chilling as this warning appeared to be at the time, it became more chilling eight decades later when, in 2003 and 2004, monopoly owners in fact did keep off the air individuals and material that disagreed with the policies of the current administration: Clear Channel's banning from its stations the Dixie Chicks after the musical group publicly disagreed with President George Bush on his war on Iraq, and the Disney Corporation's refusal to distribute Michael Moore's Golden Palm–winning film *Fahrenheit 911* because it was also critical of Bush's policies, amid comparable actions by other conglomerate companies.

Whether some of those who spoke against monopoly in radio were sugar-coating their pro-monopoly actions is a matter of debate. As Lawrence Soley points out in his book, *Free Radio,* the government, through the U.S. Navy, controlled radio communication through World War I. After the war the government turned over this monopoly to the Radio Corporation of America (RCA) through its control of patents. Through agreements with General Electric, Westinghouse, and AT&T, RCA controlled virtually all the equipment necessary for radio operation. Soley states that "in effect, the RCA companies were given complete control over broadcasting, except when it concerned 'amateur' broadcasting, which the patent agreements excluded."[9]

Hoover did try to do something about the interference problem. He did get some stations to agree to share frequencies and airtime and to limit transmitting power, but this was essentially a hit-or-miss self-regulation by persuasion. The Zenith Radio Corporation sued the government for what it felt were undue restrictions imposed by Hoover and won. That meant that the government, through the Department of Commerce, had no legal right to impose any considerations on anyone who wished to build and operate a radio station. Immediately, the situation got even worse, with the biggest and most powerful stations, the counterpart of today's conglomerates, switching channels and poaching on any frequency in any market with stronger signals, overwhelming the signals of the weaker operators.

Unlike the Congress of the late 1990s and early 2000s, the government at that time tried to do something about the big devouring the little. In 1927 it passed a bill sponsored by Republican representative Wallace White Jr. of Maine and Democratic senator Clarence Dill of Washington. This was the Radio Act of 1927, which established a Federal Radio Commission (FRC) to establish rules and regulations for radio licensing and operations that would first and foremost eliminate the chaos on the airwaves and provide for the orderly growth of the new medium. The problems that promoted the 1927 act were described effectively by Orestes Caldwell, one of five commissioners named to the FRC, in a speech shortly after his appointment.

Many stations jumped without restraint to new wave lengths which suited them better, regardless of the interference which they might thus be causing to other stations. Proper separation between established stations was destroyed by other stations coming in and camping in the middle of any open spaces they could find, each interloper thus impairing reception of three stations—his own and two others. Instead of the necessary 50-kilocycle separation between stations in the same community, the condition soon developed where separations of 20 and 10 kilocycles, and even eight, five, and two kilocycles, existed. Under such separations, of course, stations were soon wildly blanketing each other while distracted listeners were assailed with scrambled programs. . . . Heterodyne interference between broadcasters on the same wave length became so bad at many points on the dial that the listener might suppose instead of a receiving set he had a peanut roaster with assorted whistles. Indeed, every human ingenuity and selfish impulse seemed to have been exerted to complicate the tangle in the ether.[10]

Acting in the Public's Interest

What did this have to do with localism? The Radio Act of 1927 established an entirely new playing field. The FRC had the power to go far beyond the regulation of interference, although that was the principal issue that led to its establishment. As noted in Christopher Sterling and John Kittross's *Stay Tuned,* the FRC was given the authority to

1. Classify stations.
2. Prescribe the nature of service to be provided.
3. Assign frequencies.
4. Determine power and location of transmitters.
5. Regulate apparatus used.
6. Make regulations to prevent interference.
7. Set up zones of service (coverage areas).
8. Make special regulations concerning chain (network) broadcasting when necessary.[11]

One thing the FRC was not able to do—nor was the subsequent Federal Communications Commission, which replaced the FRC in 1934—was to censor any programming. In fact, although censorship was forbidden, both the FRC and the FCC could exert efforts in other areas of regulation and through "friendly persuasion" that did have an influence on programming decisions. This influence, in turn, could affect localism in terms of content. What, in fact, was the FRC's stance on localism in those early days, and what impact did the FRC have on localism as radio moved into its heyday as America's most popular source of information and entertainment?

The very fact that the government established regulatory jurisdiction over radio and a commission to implement that jurisdiction with rules and regulations concomitantly established principles that became cornerstones of the argument between those who claim that the airwaves belong to the people and those who claim that any regulation vitiates radio operators' First Amendment rights: scarcity principle and the diversity principle. The scarcity principle argues that there are a limited number of frequencies available for radio (and, later, television and other media distribution methods that use the airwaves) and that therefore the government must protect this resource on behalf of the public it represents. This differs from newspapers, at the time the major source of information, over which the government has not claimed regulatory control. The argument is that anyone with enough money can set up a newspaper because there is ostensibly no limitation on the number of printing presses available. The only restriction on newspapers is in the general antitrust and other acts that apply to all businesses. No regulatory legislation is specifically aimed only at newspapers. The diversity principle states that the power of the media is so strong that if one entity controls a substantial portion the broadcast and print media in any one locality, that entity has a substantial impact on the beliefs and even actions of the public in that area.

In most of the world today, there is no question that radio and television, not newspapers, are the most powerful forces for affecting the minds and emotions of the people. For example, in a revolution or coup, what is the first target for a takeover? Not the universities, not the government buildings, not the treasury, not even the airfields, but the radio and/or television stations. In most countries today, the government itself owns and operates the broadcast stations or, if it permits private ownership, those owners are either closely allied with the ruling power or the government retains ultimate decision-making power over all programming. An extreme example is provided by Germany under Hitler: control over the political process is facilitated when the people in a country are convinced to think as one mind, with local differences or needs submerged into the national agenda, and any dissent from the beliefs or actions of the country's leader considered subversive. In interpreting the democratic tenets of the United States, limits were eventually placed on station ownership in hopes of increasing diversity of viewpoints. These limits encompassed how many stations one entity could own throughout the country (multiple-ownership rule) and in one market or community (duopoly rule), and included ownership of different media, such as a daily newspaper and a broadcast station in the same market (cross-ownership rule). As noted in chapter 1, the Telecommunications Act of 1996 and subsequent FCC rulings in 2003 vitiated these scarcity and diversity principle protections.

Monopoly Versus Diversity

Those favoring the elimination of antimonopoly regulations cite the advancement of communications technology as a key factor in making the scarcity and diversity principles no longer relevant. With the development of cable, satellite, and the Internet, proponents of eliminating ownership limits claim that there no longer is scarcity of sources of information and entertainment. In addition, they believe that these myriad sources also provide a great diversity of ideas and opinions, further making ownership regulations unnecessary. Consumer advocates address this argument by pointing out that conglomerate media owners especially, and most broadcast station owners in general are, by the very nature of their ownership of media, monetarily wealthy and prominent in their communities, whether local or national. They usually are part of the elite, members of corporate boards, arts and sports organizations, country clubs, and, in their position, management executives. To them, the world they are living in appears to be the best of all possible worlds. They are happy with the status quo and see no public value in social, political, or economic change. Dissent is disruptive. Therefore, this counterargument goes, although there may be a greater number of outlets and greater diversity in the means of media distribution, there is little if any diversity in the attitudes of the owners of these media outlets, and the greater number of outlets any one entity owns, the less and less diversity of information and entertainment content there is. Those who support this latter view support the retention of as much localism as possible in the media, including radio.

These contrary attitudes developed over the years, exacerbated in 1927 with the charge given to the new Federal Radio Commission. The problem, however, was not new. A study by Derek W. Vaillant in the *American Quarterly* used Chicago as a demonstration. He points out that throughout the 1920s, including the period before the FRC, local radio stations that had not affiliated with any network or chain, as they were then called,

> used music and cultural affairs programs to entertain, inform and serve communities of ethnic, immigrant, middle- and working-class listeners. . . . Local broadcasting promoted face-to-face community life among its audiences, whether encouraging listeners to participate in programs as talent or guests, support ethnic institutions and causes, attend church, vote for local politicians, patronize local businesses, support organized labor, or even cut loose at neighborhood dance halls. . . . The airwaves became a neighborhood as well as a metropolitan stage, and many listeners tuned to independent stations swelled with pleasure and pride at hearing music and cultural programs that acknowledged and validated their particular languages, histories, and cultural backgrounds for both the designated group and the larger audience to hear.[12]

(Vaillant's study principally examines the racial and ethnic entities that were not served by Chicago radio in those days, in contrast to the excellent contributions local radio had made to some other groups. His apt description is embodied in his use of the term "the sound of whiteness.")

Vaillant describes the crisis that occurred in 1927 when the new FRC eliminated many licenses, reassigned others, changed power limits, and established other requirements that forced existing radio stations in the city to compete with each other for the licenses that would be allocated to Chicago. They did so by trying to show that they, individually, most effectively served the new criteria of the public interest, convenience, or necessity. "Local broadcasters took to the airwaves to rally public support . . . competing with well-funded and politically connected network lobbyists. . . . These [independent] operators presented their stations as producing an electronic public culture of pluralism in which ethnic, local, and 'American' themes coexisted. Network representatives dismissed this ideal-type and argued for a market-driven model in which heavily capitalized, centralized producers should supply a national market with programs created for mass appeal." Notwithstanding the eventual adoption—as we have today—of the market-driven model, Vaillant concludes that at least in the 1920s and 1930s, "local, independent radio operators . . . were far more significant in establishing the social and cultural identity of radio than has been previously acknowledged."[13]

Chicago was also the subject example of a 1926 congressional debate on potential monopoly effects leading up to the passage of the Radio Act the following year. Senator James Couzens of Michigan was concerned about what he considered to be virtually carte blanche transfers of licenses in the Chicago market without protections against undue concentration of ownership and questioned the solicitor of the Department of Commerce, Stephen B. Davis, about it. Couzens suggested that under the policy being followed at that time, a single company "could monopolize the whole district by buying up stations." Davis responded that he had no evidence that that was happening. Couzens pushed further: "If priority is ignored in that case then the apparatus controls the situation, and anyone who buys the apparatus can control the situation." Davis answered that

> we have felt this way about it, Senator, that the license ran to the station rather than to the individual. In other words, we have never felt it wise to adopt a policy under which we would say to an individual, "yes, go in and build the station at whatever cost there may be. If you die it is worth nothing. If you change your mind and want to quit broadcasting it is worth nothing. If you get into business trouble it is worth nothing to your creditors. It has only got a refuse value." We take the position that inasmuch as these licenses are only 90-day licenses anyway [by 2005 license terms had been extended to eight years, with renewals virtually automatic], that the license ran to the apparatus; a man can transfer his apparatus, and if there is no good reason to the contrary we will recognize that sale and license the new owner of the apparatus.

Couzens then responded, "It seems to me, then, it is up to Congress to provide some means whereby no single interest can control the broadcasting of the district."[14]

This question of monopoly control in broadcasting became a key issue in Congress's consideration of legislation introduced to regulate radio. In a prospectus for a study of localism in broadcasting, John Armstrong, citing historian Donald Godfrey, states that "when Congress was formulating a regulatory regime for radio in the 1920s, broadcasting was defined in large part by what it should *not* be: a monopoly. . . . The danger of monopoly was one of the prime concerns expressed in Congressional debates over the Radio Act of 1927. Legislators believed that a system of geographically dispersed broadcast outlets would be a safeguard against monopolies of business, ideas or culture."[15]

In a 1926 House of Representatives debate on the issue, Luther A. Johnson of Texas expressed the feelings of many others in and out of Congress:

> As a means of entertainment, education, information, and communication it [radio] has limitless possibilities. The power of the press will not be comparable to that of broadcasting stations when the industry is fully developed. If the development continues as rapidly in the future as in the past, it will only be a few years before these broadcasting stations, if operated by chain stations, will simultaneously reach an audience of over half of our entire citizenship, and bring messages to the fireside of nearly every home in America. They can mold and crystallize sentiment as no agency in the past has been able to do. If the strong arm of the law does not prevent monopoly ownership and make discrimination by such stations illegal, American thought and American politics will be largely at the mercy of those who operate these stations.[16]

Mapping the Airwaves

Given the strong concerns by many members of Congress about the dangers of monopolies in radio, how did the Radio Act of 1927 and the Federal Radio Commission deal with the struggle between localism and market-driven networking and consolidation? How did the FRC's actions establish a legacy for the FCC seven years later and for the present policy on localism and conglomeration?

On the surface, the act and the FRC appeared to affirm the principle of localism as opposed to monopoly. The Radio Act of 1927 initially divided the country into five broadcasting zones, ostensibly to assure an equity if not equality of assignments for regions and localities. The FRC was directed as follows: "In considering applications for licenses and renewals of licenses, when and in so far as there is a demand for the same, the licensing authority shall make such a distribution licenses, bands of frequency, of wave lengths, periods of time of operation, and of power among different States and communities as to give fair, efficient and equitable service to each of the same."[17] Many critics have interpreted this section as supporting the principle of localism. Alan Stavitsky has written that "the 1927 Act, which made only passing reference to networks, established a system of broadcast regulation based upon the licensing of individual stations."[18] Many members of congress reinforced their belief that the act should protect local, independent stations. For example, representative Ewin Davis of Tennessee wrote to the FRC that "chain programs should undoubtedly be made available . . . yet they should not be given such assignments of wave lengths and power as will prevent the satisfactory broadcasting and reception of independent stations."[19]

The "zone" approach was abandoned by the Federal Communications Commission in 1936, but the language for "a fair, efficient and equitable distribution of radio service to each state and community" was retained, recognizing that "localism was . . . undeniably a powerful concern in Congress."[20] But, as historian Erik Barnouw stated in the first volume of his trilogy on the history of broadcasting, *A Tower of Babel*, there were no provisions in the Radio Act addressing the issue of networks and their potential for controlling the medium, and the possibility of centralization, or, as we call it today, consolidation or conglomeration, remained real and imminent.[21]

In spite of the all the talk about independent stations, however, one of the first acts of the FRC was to reauthorize most of the commercial stations licenses, especially those that were owned by or affiliated with one of the fledgling networks. Many of the smaller local stations and most of the noncommercial stations operated by colleges and universities—which had been pioneers in establishing radio—were put off the air. In effect, the FRC's actions reflected the wishes of radio's big three at the time, RCA, General Electric, and Westinghouse. It was a seminal example in the field of communications of what has become a not-so-tongue-in-cheek dictum in Washington: that regulatory agencies are controlled by those they are supposed to regulate. Analyses by some critics like Thomas Hazlitt suggest that the use of the chaos on the air for establishing federal regulation over radio may have been a ploy between the powerful broadcasters and the government to allocate the best frequencies to the leading radio companies while restricting or eliminating frequencies for their competitors, and at the same time giving the government some measure of control over this new medium that had such powerful potential to affect the political thinking and climate in the United States.[22]

After the FRC had begun its work, Representative Davis's concerns deepened, and in 1928 he got Congress to adopt what was called the Davis Amendment to the Radio Act, designed to protect local, independent stations from being overrun by larger network stations. This amendment required the FRC "to work out means for assigning equal numbers of stations and equal amounts of power and air time to each of the country five zones." Application of this requirement resulted in the removal of 109 stations that appeared to be causing the most ifterference and the issuance in 1928 of FRC General Order 40, described as follows in the FRC's 1928 annual report.

> General Order No. 40, issued yesterday by the Federal Radio Commission, supplies the official basis for an adjustment in the assignment of the country's broadcasting facilities, under a plan which it is believed will provide an improved standard of radio reception generally. . . . The plan calls for full-time assignments for 100-watt stations equaling in number the total of all other classes of broadcasters put together. Of the 74 channels made available for high-grade reception, 34 will be assigned for regional service, permitting 125 full-time positions for this type of station, and 40 channels will be assigned to stations with minimum power of 5,000 watts and a maximum to be determined. . . . On these 40 channels only one station will be permitted to operate at any time during night hours, thus insuring clear reception of the station's program up to the extreme limit of its service range.[23]

Presumably, this order would result in much more interference-free reception throughout the country and would reflect congressional intention that such reception would be equal in all the communities in the United States. John Armstrong cites historian Susan Smulyan's determination that "the amendment's core supporters were rural and southern legislators who questioned the centralized system that was already emerging," and they enacted the Davis Amendment "as a bulwark for local, rural culture against encroachment by elite, urban East coast radio fare provided by the emerging networks." Clearly, the passage of this amendment indicated support of localism in radio, albeit for what some might consider political and social rather than unbiased informational principles. Armstrong goes on to say that one of Smulyan's significant implications is "the Davis Amendment, reflecting a desire to protect rural culture, helped establish the 'local service' doctrine. This influentiad theory held that as many communities as possible should have their own broadcast outlets."[24]

Some regulators and many politicians continued to endorse the principle of localism in radio for a variety of reasons, ranging from community application of states' rights beliefs by conservatives to consumer protection from monopolistic control of ideas, information, culture, and economics by liberals. Other regulators and politicians supported the growth of networks and the concept of centralized management control and programming as a logical outgrowth of the capitalistic marketplace practices that marked America's industrial development. It goes without saying that the radio networks were not only beneficiaries but practitioners of the latter approach. Over the next seven years, until the FRC was replaced by the FCC, there would be a continuing struggle between centralization and localism. The stations themselves, including those that were gwned bq gr affiliated with the three networks (two owned by NBC), thrived on the basis of their local service coupled with the attractiveness of network programming.

As Derek Vaillant points out (albeit with the caveat that local programming, like national programming, was oriented principally to the white majorities in the community of service), "Local radio operators championed a competing model of localism, whose electronic public culture consisted of the voices and music of dozens of different [local] ethnic groups." He explains that "local, independent radio operators . . . were far more significant in establishing the social and cultural identity of radio than has been previously acknowledged. Their blueprint for broadcasting contained cultural features salient to understanding American culture in the 1920s and the critical role of radio in everyday life. . . . In the 1920s and 1930s local broadcasters controlled the nature of ethnic representation on air as means of counterbalancing the assimilating pressures of commercial advertising, Americanization campaigns, and the 'homogenous' fare of 'chain' and early network broadcasting." Vaillant makes clear the special services local stations brought to their listeners: "In ways that had not been possible before in real time, radio enabled listeners to aurally 'visit' parts of the city they had never seen, or never would see, at minimal risk to their persons or reputations. Listeners could sample forbidden urban spaces and sounds . . . radio supplied aural access to urban musical spaces without the associated costs or unpredictable prospects of a face-to-face encounter with strangers that might occur at the actual venue. . . . One listened and moved on with a twirl of a knob, without concern about any permanent record of one's participatory 'presence.'"[25]

Historian Susan Douglas describes the dichotomy between media localism and centralization as a theory reflective of America's struggle between a national culture and cultural diversity, between individualism and collectivism.

> Radio has given full expression to these distinctly American tensions while necessarily exacerbating them. This stems, in part, from a fundamental contradiction that characterizes radio. There is a rift between the inherent technical properties of radio and the economic system in which it was—and is—imbedded. The deeply personal nature of radio communication—the way its sole reliance on sound produces individualized images and reactions; its extension of a pre-commercial, oral tradition; its cultivation of the imagination—all work in stark contrast to the needs of its managers, who seek homogenized responses, and need a like-minded audience instead of idiosyncratic individuals.[26]

A Free and Vital Source

The stock market crash of 1929 and the subsequent economic depression that devoured America for over a decade was a death blow to many businesses—but turned out to be a boon for radio. Entertainment venues disappeared. Only those relatively few people who escaped the collapse of the stock market and the long lines of unemployed—the huge number of jobs lost was not approached again until 2003—could afford to go to stage shows, nightclubs, and vaudeville theaters. Even when some top vaudeville acts and other entertainers from the Keith's and Orpheum circuits took to the road in buses to try to reach audiences, they found that people simply didn't have the money to attend their ad hoc performances. As one star performer, Charles "Cow-Cow" Davenport, told one of this book's authors many years ago, "They didn't have money to pay for tickets, so we let them in for food, for bread and corn and chickens. But our buses wouldn't run on chickens and we just had to give up."

Films fared much better. With "talkies" having made their debut in 1927, the number of attendees increased. While large city movie palaces charged a quarter or more for admission, one could buy a ticket in smaller movie houses in cities and small towns for a dime. Yet even that was difficult for more and more people. A loaf of bread or a bottle of milk cost a nickel during the Depression, and ten cents could buy a lunch or a scrumptious pie for Sunday dinner. Families on welfare (it was called "relief" then) in New York City sustained a family of four on $14 a week.

Most people turned to the one source of entertainment that was free: radio. They could hear at no cost the stars they had read about or seen in films. It was, in fact, the growth of the networks that lured stars to radio. Most saw no reason to perform for just a local audience at little compensation prior to the growth of networks. But when they could obtain national exposure and the monetary rewards resulting from the networks' national advertising incomes, their attitudes changed.

Although magazines such as *Liberty* and the *Saturday Evening Post* retained their hold on the American public, keeping their cost at two cents an issue was becoming more and more difficult, and some of their feature story subjects could now be found on radio. Newspapers were still omnipresent, with many competing papers in any given city. In New York City, for example, two cents for the *Daily News* or *Daily Mirror* was still doable, as was the five cents for their Sunday editions with the prized comic sections. But for many people, what may have been a daily purchase of two or three newspapers now became one or none. Radio became a key source of news and information as well as of entertainment. In the 1930s, radio became the medium that reached the mass of America, surpassing movies, newspapers, and magazines.

But while Americans were being exposed to a national culture and national news, they were also being exposed to and especially served by radio's presentation of local news and public affairs, local celebrities, human interest stories about local people, local advertisements from local merchants and services, local sports, local performers on the local radio stations—including announcers who, in some localities, became celebrities themselves—and participation by the station's management and personnel in local organizations and affairs. The local station became the extended proverbial hot stove in the local general store and the radio receiver each listener's personal cracker barrel.

Radio therefore developed in the late 1920s and early 1930s with a dual role: service to the local community concomitant with the rapid growth of national networks. By 1934 and the demise of the Federal Radio Commission to make way for the Communications Act of 1934 and the Federal Communications Commission, the networks had become a dominating force in American broadcasting. Reasons for their growth have been suggested by a number of media historians; some of the principal reasons offered are

- agreements made among key industry players to divide up the responsibility and opportunity to develop and exploit the new technology;
- the audience demand for more expensive productions, which only the networks could afford;

- the development of a system of financing based on national advertising, which called for national programming;
- regulatory decisions made in radio's formative years that inadvertently prompted the formation of national networks.[27]

One piece of evidence of the strength of the radio networks and their owners, RCA and the Columbia Broadcasting System, was their control of the availability of television for the general public in the United States. By 1934, seven years had passed since the first public test of television in the United States. The first drama on an experimental station had been produced in 1928. By 1931, eighteen experimental TV stations were operating in a number of cities. The technology, while not perfect, nevertheless was adequate. The FRC—under pressure, some critics have maintained, from the networks—refused to allocate sufficient frequency space for television stations to move from local "experimental" status to regular widespread broadcasting. Some historians have suggested that because David Sarnoff, in command of NBC's two radio networks, and William Paley, head of CBS, were making great profits for their radio networks, they wanted to wait for a more opportune economic time to introduce television. They also allegedly wanted more time to solidify their control over television, which they knew would to a greater or lesser degree supplant radio.

From the government's standpoint, new communications legislation was needed for more efficient regulation. First, there were new technologies since the 1927 act that fell under the general rubric of communication, including television and what later became facsimile transmission via telephone. Second, the FRC was considered inadequate insofar as radio regulatory function alone was fragmented among a number of different federal agencies; for example, the Department of Agriculture was involved with stations serving farm needs, the Department of State oversaw stations with signals into foreign countries, and the Interstate Commerce Commission had a hand in the regulation of interstate telephone and telegraph operations. Further, the FRC had been established as a temporary body, and it was clear that a permanent commission was necessary for effective regulation, in terms of the act, of all services that "rely on wires, cable, or radio as a means of transmission."[28] Members of the FRC and, given the passage of bill in Congress and its support by President Franklin D. Roosevelt, legislators and the executive branch, supported the change to a permanent commission. The National Association of Broadcasters, on behalf of its member stations and the radio networks, strongly opposed the change because they feared it would give the government a stronger role in the regulation of their industry.[29]

On July 1, 1934, however, in spite of that opposition, the Communications Act of 1934 went into effect, beginning a new era in American broadcasting.

3 Acting in the Local Interest

Localism and the National Networks

The Communications Act of 1934, aside from centralizing the regulation of the known panoply of communication technologies under one agency, extended and broadened the charge and even much of the language of the Radio Act of 1927 and the responsibilities of the Federal Radio Commission. The new Federal Communications Commission (FCC) had both advantages and disadvantages compared with its predecessor, the FRC. In the previous seven years, radio had grown tremendously, advertising had become the economic staple of its operations, and networks had expanded quantitatively and in terms of power. Their power included virtual dictatorial control over their affiliates as well as owned and operated stations, tremendous influence in Congress and in the executive branch of the federal government and in their counterparts on the state and local levels, and what many considered a cozy relationship with the FCC through network lobbyists, representatives of individuals, and through broadcasting's official lobbying organization, the National Association of Broadcasters (NAB). The FCC was subject to tremendous outside pressure, from within and without the government.

The FCC's early rulings continued the FRC's favoring of large corporate broadcasting entities. For example, some members of Congress, concerned by the FRC's virtual elimination of noncommercial stations in order to accommodate more commercial stations, asked the FCC to study the possibilities of reserving channels for nonprofit local stations for educational purposes. In 1935, the FCC reported back to Congress, Lawrence Soley notes in *Free Radio,* that "existing commercial stations provide ample educational programming and that no special frequencies needed to be assigned for noncommercial purposes."[1] The FCC's assessment was not valid, and it would take continued lobbying by educational and civic groups and pressure by members of Congress before the FCC finally reserved, years later, frequencies for local noncommercial stations.

Soley states several reasons why he believes FCC commissioners then and still today are so likely to create regulations that will benefit corporate over nonprofit, local, or experimental broadcasters. One is because commissioners frequently "come from telecommunications industries—the very industries that the FCC is supposed to police." Another reason is that "commissioners who prove to be loyal supporters of corporate interests are rewarded with high-paying industry jobs after leaving the FCC." A third reason is that the strong lobbying of, personal contacts with, and campaign contributions by the broadcasting industry to politicians assures that legislators of every political stripe are beholden to broadcasters. A fourth reason is that the media's control of news and information, strengthened greatly by the elimination of the Fairness Doctrine by the Reagan administration in 1987, permits the industry to slant the news and to editorialize for or against any legislation or regulation affecting it without having to present opposing or alternative information or views.[2]

Enhanced Power

The FCC was given an advantage over the FRC in that the 1934 act gave it stronger regulatory powers not only over more areas of communication, but over more aspects of licensing, operations, and by implication even programming. Within a few years, the FRC took action against stations for programming such as astrology, advertisements for contraceptives, horse racing information, patent medicine commercials, and programs with personal advice the FRC considered misleading.[3]

The FCC early on got involved in the issue of indecency on the air—an issue that has reappeared in national concern even as this is being written (see the authors' *Dirty Discourse: Sex and Indecency in American Radio*). Probably the case that had the most impact not only at the time but for future FCC considerations was a 1937 appearance on a popular weekly radio show, headlined by ventriloquist Edgar Bergen and his "dummy," Charlie McCarthy, of Hollywood sex symbol Mae West. In a sketch about the Garden of Eden, quite innocuous in terms of actual language and content, Mae West's "come up and see me some time" voice inflections gave special meaning to an otherwise unobjectionable line of dialogue. In the social milieu of that period, the skit was considered by much of the public, the industry, and even Congress as shocking—probably more so than any subsequent programming for almost seventy years, up to Janet Jackson's "wardrobe malfunction" during the 2004 Super Bowl and the crackdown on Howard Stern prompted by the Jackson event. In 1937, the FCC only reprimanded NBC for the Mae West incident. NBC, however, banned West from the airwaves. In 2004, the FCC's fine against some the stations carrying Stern's program prompted Clear Channel, which carried Stern on a number of its stations, to drop him from its network. Networks and stations carrying Howard Stern continue to be fined by the FCC.

Although the FCC was not given the authority to license networks or otherwise regulate them (except in instances of monopoly, as will be discussed shortly), the FCC did have the power to affect network practices through its licensing and regulation of local stations, including network affiliates and owned and operated stations. FCC action regarding networks has been sporadic throughout its history and usually the result of a dramatic occurrence or intense public pressure. It wasn't until 1961, when President Kennedy appointed Newton Minow chair of the FCC, that the agency established an Office of Network Study to determine what should and could be done about network practices deemed not in the public interest.

Fritz Messere, in his article on regulation in the *Encyclopedia of Radio*, notes that the FCC had two main charges: to make most effective use of the available radio spectrum and to see that stations operated in the public interest, convenience, or necessity. Localism was deemed a key criterion for radio, even with the concomitant growth of networks.[4]

> Encouraging localism became [one of] the fundamental principle[s] for the Federal Communications Commission. This regulatory policy proved useful for several reasons. First, the agency inherited a commercial structure for broadcasting based almost entirely on advertising revenues. Local radio stations affiliated with national network program suppliers frequently found their broadcast scheduled manipulated by the same networks who provided stations with high quality programming. Stations without affiliation looked to local community sources for program inspiration. However, both network and local programs were being provided to listeners via a local licensee assigned to serve a geographical area. Although the FCC had very limited control over national networks, it discerned that its power to regulate was essentially the power to control local stations, the stations' relationships with network program suppliers, and the stations' relationships with the community of license.[5]

Mandating Localism

A number of critics have interpreted the 1934 act as a mandate for maintaining and strengthening the concept and practice of localism in radio. Among the FCC prerogatives under the act are the allocation of broadcast frequencies to specific geographical areas of the United States, the licensing of specific stations on specific frequencies, and the determination of the maximum allowable power (and, therefore, signal reach) for each station. All of the above are predicated on any given station serving the public interest, convenience, or necessity. For several decades, the FCC interpreted this procedure on an intermittent basis, presumably applying it to guarantee the independence and growth of local station service to the local community— while at the same time allowing if not encouraging the growth of networks and groups stations owners. Political winds in the country at any given time determined whether the FCC (and other government agencies) leaned toward the industry or toward consumers. A case in point is the FCC's 1965 Policy Statement on Comparative Broadcast Hearings. These hearings were held during America's counterculture revolution, the burgeoning of its civil rights movement, and the stirrings of the movement for equality for women. The FCC was operating under the liberal legacy of a President John Kennedy– appointed commission and mandate. Comparative broadcast hearings were held when two or more entities were competing for the same channel or frequency. The 1965 policy statement affirmed the public interest principle by stating that a station must provide "the best practicable service to the public" and that assignments must result in "maximum diffusion of control of the media of mass communication."[6] The policy statement set forth six principal criteria in decision making, among which were localism, integration of station ownership with the local management of the station, and programming service oriented to the community.[7] To some degree, these concepts were applied in the years between the passage of the 1934 act and 1965, and to a greater degree from 1965 until the end of the 1970s, when FCC chairman Charles Ferris, a Democrat appointed by President Jimmy Carter, opened the door to deregulation, which then grew exponentially under his successor, Mark Fowler, a Republican appointed by the next president, Ronald Reagan.

One of the most comprehensive legal analyses of localism was a 2001 article in the *Federal Communications Law Journal* by Washington, DC, communications attorneys David M. Silverman and David. N. Tobenkin. Using the "main studio rule" (discussed further below) as a base, they maintain that "localism, the communication law policy that requires spectrum licensees to serve the needs of local communities, represents a bedrock concept in the Communications Act of 1934 . . . and the Federal Communications Commission's . . . jurisprudence."[8] They use a definition of localism by Robert Copple: "Early in its history of broadcast regulation the Commission assumed that local broadcast stations would be the electronic version of the community newspaper. The perception was that like the local newspaper, the local broadcast station would significantly contribute to local participatory democracy and would operate 'as a kind of latter-day Mark Twain, who understands the needs and concerns of his community in an imaginative and sensitive way.'"[9]

Silverman and Tobenkin note, further, that to implement the localism implications of the 1934 act, over the years the FCC enacted regulations "limiting the power of networks over local affiliates," "limiting ownership of multiple radio or television stations, both within a market and nationwide," "requiring nonduplication protection for locally received network and sports programming," "requiring non-entertainment programming and barring excessive commercialization," and "requiring formal ascertainment procedures and the keeping of program logs." They note that most of the rules pertaining to localism have been eliminated or eased over the years, frequently by court decision, as imposing an undue burden upon broadcasters. They also contend, however, that the courts did not "reject the Commission's localism policy, but rather the means used to achieve it."[10]

The "main studio rule" was a key part of localism regulation, stemming most particularly from a 1939 FCC rule that "the term 'main studio' means, as to any station, the studio from which the majority of its local programs originate, and/or from which a majority of its station announcements are made of programs originating at remote points." Subsequent paragraphs of the main studio rule reinforced the concept of localism. According to Silverman and Tobenkin, industry considered the main studio requirement to be a hindrance to the development of broadcasting.

PAR. 3.30 STATION LOCATION.

(a) Each standard broadcast station shall be considered located in the state and city where the main studio is located.

(b) The transmitter of each standard broadcast station shall be so located that primary service is delivered to the city in which the main studio is located, in accordance with the "Standards of Good Engineering Practice," prescribed by the Commission.

PAR. 3.31. AUTHORITY TO MOVE MAIN STUDIO.

The licensee of a standard broadcast station shall not move its main studio outside the borders of the city, State, district, Territory, or possession in which it is located without first making written application to the Commission for authority to so move, and securing written permission for such removal. A licensee need not obtain permission to move the main studio from one location to another within a city or town, but shall promptly notify the Commission of any such change in location.[11]

Later on, in 1946, the FCC promulgated similar main studio rules for television stations, requiring that main studios be located as near the center of the given city as practicable and/or in a location that provided the maximum service to the area served.[12]

Silverman and Tobenkin cite a 1950 FCC "Report and Order" as the principal guide to localism as defined by the main studio rule. Radio transmission was defined as "the opportunity which provides for the development and expression of local interests, ideas, and talents for the production of programs of special interest to a particular community. . . . A station often provides service to areas at a considerable distance from its transmitter but a station cannot serve as a medium for local self expression unless it provides a reasonably accessible studio for the origination of local programs."[13]

In 1952, the FCC promulgated essentially the same rule for television: "The accessibility of the broadcast station's main studio may well determine in large part the extent to which the station 1) can participate and be an integral part of community activities and 2) can enable members of the public to participate in live programs and present complaints or suggestions to the station."[14] Silverman and Tobenkin conclude that these 1950 and 1952 FCC rules establish clearly the commission's concern with maintaining localism through "assurance that stations provide service to everyone, not just to those who live in major metropolitan areas," that stations "generate locally oriented programming," that stations use "local residents in the production of programming," that stations be encourage to participate "in community activities," and that there be a "facilitation of community residents' complaints or suggestions to station personnel."[15]

During the 1980s, as deregulation became the byword of regulatory agencies under a Republican administration (a former Republican chair of the FCC called it "unregulation"), the main studio rule was abated to the extent that "main studios had to be *capable of* originating and transmit-

ting programming even though they were not required to actually originate any programming" (emphasis added).[16]

In Local Decline

Silverman and Tobenkin point out that through the years, the FCC has lib-
eralized or eliminated most of the key regulations related to localism,
including rules pertaining to percentages, types and, ascertainment of
programs designed to serve a local community, and they conclude that,
"on the whole, localism is viewed by many observers as a policy in decline."[17] They consider it an obsolete rule and believe even its remaining
vestiges should be eliminated entirely or be rewritten in a more precise
and limited form. Their analysis and conclusions concerning the programming aspect of localism, once a key part of radio's local voice, reflect what
has happened over the years to localism as a whole.

Probably the most significant regulatory action for localism, or, perhaps more accurately, against conglomeration, was the FCC's 1941 chain
broadcasting rules. In the late 1930s, the FCC responded to Congress's growing concern over the growth and power of the radio networks. As more
efficient use was made of available radio frequencies, the numbers of stations grew and so did the numbers of network affiliates, concurrently
increasing the power and impact of the networks. In 1926, an engineering study showed that the AM band could accommodate 331 stations; in
1939, the FCC declared that the 764 AM stations on the air had saturated
the band; and by the early 1980s, more than 4,000 AM stations could fit
into the band. In addition, by 1940 the new FM service was proven to be
remarkably effective, with twenty experimental stations on the air that
demonstrated much better audio quality than AM, albeit limited to a
shorter range than comparable AM power because of the former's point-
to-point signal. FM had first been demonstrated by its inventor, Edwin
Howard Armstrong, in 1935, and the FCC eventually authorized forty channels for its operation to begin in 1941.

By 1939, almost two-thirds of the American public were getting news
and information from radio, although newspapers still continued as the
primary source of news for most of the public. In fact, newspapers had a
huge amount of control over all news received by Americans inasmuch
as, by 1940, they owned or controlled more than a third of all radio stations. In one hundred cities, newspapers also owned the town's only radio station. This concentration of power prompted President Franklin D.
Roosevelt to ask the FCC to investigate the effect of such cross-ownership.[18]
(The subsequent rule barring cross-ownership began to be vitiated in the

1980s, and in 2004, as this is being written, it was on the verge of being totally eliminated by the FCC.)

Chains of Power

Between the radio networks and the newspapers, Americans, then as now, had little access to alternative or independent news and information. Congress had no regulatory authority over newspapers, but through the Communications Act of 1934 it did over broadcasting, and in 1938 it pressured the FCC into investigating the implications of growing monopolies in radio, specifically in "chain broadcasting" and in general in the entire broadcasting industry. The result was the most significant regulatory action concerning conglomeration—and, by implication, localism—until the Telecommunications Act of 1996. In 1940, the FCC issued a preliminary report on its findings, and in 1941, after hearings on this report, it issued its *Report on Chain Broadcasting*.

World War II, which began in Europe in 1939 and which the United States would enter in 1941 following the Japanese attack on Pearl Harbor, prompted many Americans, in and out of Congress, to become especially concerned about the concentration of media power. Such concentration was a key tool in the rise of fascism and Nazism, with German radio, newspapers, and film controlled either directly by the government or by companies sympathetic to the government, allowing for no alternative or, especially, dissenting views. Although shortly after entering the war the United States used radio, newspapers, and film for its own propaganda purposes through the cooperation of those media rather than by government takeover, in early 1941 the concept of diversity was still honored. Critic Patrick Burkart notes writer Jacques Ellul's arguments in his 1959 book *Propaganda: The Formation of Men's Attitudes*: "Ellul argued that propaganda is a condition of modern progress because propaganda is the way symbols become common currency and support progressive political and social movements. But if wielded by an evil state, propaganda can be misused in lying campaigns, exerting secret, nefarious, and manipulative effects on society. Ellul notes a tendency for propaganda to become one of the most repressive institutional characteristics of modern state systems and warns [the public] to be vigilant and critical of manipulative media campaigns."[19]

According to Sterling and Kittross, the most important regulations in the *Report on Chain Broadcasting* were

- Network affiliation contracts would be limited to a single year for both parties—previously, stations had been bound to networks for five years, but the networks were bound for only one year.

Affiliations could no longer be exclusive—an affiliate could use programs from other networks or sources.

- Networks could no longer demand options on large amounts of station time because the FCC believed that stations—that is, licensees—should be in charge of and responsible for their own program content and arrangement.
- An affiliate could reject any network program that in its view did not meet the public interest, convenience, or necessity and could not sign away that right in its affiliation contract.
- Networks would have no control over a station's rates for other than network programs.
- No license shall be issued to a standard broadcast [AM] station affiliated with a network organization which maintained more than one network except where such networks operated at different times or covered substantially different territory.[20]

Essentially, the new rules were aimed at NBC, whose two networks gave it a distinct advantage over its competitors, CBS and the Mutual Broadcasting System (MBS). Although MBS supported the ruling, insofar as it was the smallest of the four networks and at most disadvantage, CBS joined with NBC in angry denunciation of the order. Not only was CBS also immediately affected by the new restrictions on network control of its affiliates, but the principle restricting the growth of any network, quantitatively or otherwise, might well affect its own future. In the immediate short run, the rule changes meant NBC had to sell one of its two networks, either the Red or the Blue.

CBS joined NBC in bringing suit against the FCC in federal court. The networks contended that the new rules would weaken broadcasting as whole, threaten the continuation of the nation's favorite network programs, and give the government undue control of the media in violation of the First Amendment. The network even played the nationalism card, warning that in a world at war the networks might be paralyzed if called upon to serve the national interest.

As the suit was going through a rocky judicial road up to the Supreme Court, the country did become a party to World War II. The FCC added fuel to the networks' presumed pyre by enacting a "duopoly" rule that prevented one owner from owning two broadcast stations (at that time, two AM radio stations) in the same market and by moving ahead with its investigation of cross-ownership (which eventually also was barred several decades later). In 1942, the Department of Justice (DOJ) filed antitrust suits against NBC (and its parent company, RCA) and CBS. MBS supported the DOJ. NBC and CBS appealed the FCC rules to the Supreme Court, which adjudicated the case. In a 1943 decision in *National Broadcasting Company et al. v. U.S. Department of Justice,* the networks' suit against the FCC's rules changes, the Supreme Court supported the FCC in its general mandate to regulate stations in their relationship with networks, saying that in doing so the FCC did not violate station or network First Amendment rights, and that the chain broadcasting rules, including the requirement that NBC give up one of its networks, were constitutionally valid. The decision was written by Justice Felix Frankfurter. He and Justice William Douglas became known as the two most consumer-oriented and antimonopoly (and, to many, most liberal) justices on the Supreme Court: both, in general, favored regulation in the public interest. Frankfurter, in applying the scarcity principle and duopoly concern to networks, wrote,

> Suppose, for example, that a community can, because of physical limitations, be assigned only two stations. That community might be deprived of effective service in any one of several ways. More powerful stations in nearby cities might blanket out the signals of the local stations so that they could not be heard at all. The stations might interfere with each other so that neither could be clearly heard. One station might dominate the other with the power of its signal. But the community could be deprived of good radio service in ways less crude. One man, financially and technically qualified, might apply for and obtain the licenses of both stations and present a single service over the two stations, thus wasting a frequency otherwise available to the area.[21]

The antitrust suit by the Justice Department was then dropped as NBC and CBS complied with the new rules. Shortly after the Supreme Court decision, NBC (RCA) sold its Blue Network, which, two years later, became the American Broadcasting Company (ABC). From a financial standpoint, at least, the networks' fears were exaggerated. Even after the sale of the Blue Network, NBC's revenues increased. Between 1940 and 1945, gross revenues of the networks and their affiliates almost doubled, and revenues of independent stations more than doubled.[22]

Localism Championed

The concept of localism was given another big boost in 1946 with the FCC's issuance of a document entitled "Public Service Book." It got its nickname because when the FCC's public information office issued the report to the public, it happened to have blue paper available for the report's cover. The "Blue Book" was not a set of rules or regulations, but a policy statement of what the FCC would look for when stations' licenses came up for renewal. It contained four main sections and a summary. The focus was on programming and its content, which once again set off cries of First Amendment rights by broadcasters and others. Part one of the report stressed the importance of local programming and the need to have more programming in general as opposed to the increasing amounts of advertising on radio. Parts two and three noted the FCC's consideration of local programming and local ownership in cases where there were two or more applicants for a frequency, and the kinds of programming that would fulfill a station's public service obligations to its community. Such programming might include unsponsored educational and cultural programs—programs that met the needs of local civic, minority, and other unserved or underserved segments of the community, and programs that experimented with the unique aesthetic and artistic possibilities of the radio medium. Part four dealt principally with the economics of radio. The summary reiterated key points of the earlier parts of the policy statement, with an emphasis on local programming, public affairs programming, and less advertising as considerations in seeking license renewals. Although the Blue Book continued to be a bone of contention between broadcasters and the FCC and between proindustry and proconsumer advocates for years to come, it succeed in establishing a base for future FCC actions promoting localism and for broadcasting's own self-examination, which included reinforcing the National Association's Code of Ethics, a voluntary code to which most stations subscribed in principle, if not always in fact.

License terms then were for three years, a short enough time to persuade stations to adhere to FCC and policy recommendations. Renewal of licenses wasn't a virtually automatic process as it is today (2005). It wasn't until the 1980s that radio license terms were expanded to seven years and in the Telecommunications Act of 1996 to eight.

One result of the chain broadcasting rules and the Blue Book criteria was the growth of small stations throughout the country. According to Susan Douglas, "Between 1946 and 1951, the number of small stations, between 200 and 1,000 watts, increased by 500 percent. And their proliferation coincided with the collapse of network radio and the explosive rise of small, independent record companies. . . . The geography of sound began to change as music played on many small radio stations reflected more local, grassroots influences."[23]

Further, FM began to grow, adding more stations to more communities. FM was considered elitist and very local in programming, serving the special needs of the community with discussions, public affairs and local issues, drama, classical music, and other formats not often found on the traditional and considerably more popular general entertainment AM channels. When FM did carry pop music, it was highly targeted to the given community, unlike AM music shows, which were designed to appeal to the largest possible audience. Further, FM sets were comparatively expensive at the time—about forty dollars, compared to a few dollars for an AM radio—and few people invested in them. It would be two decades before the better quality of FM radios and the mandating of both AM and FM bands in new radios resulted in popular music formats moving to FM, with AM taking on the programming previously found on FM (with the exception of educational or public broadcasting radio stations, which by and large retained their local quality-oriented programming).

The 1940s accommodated both the growth of radio networks and the protection of local, independent radio stations and local programming. As noted in chapter 1, radio was the one free source of virtually every mode of entertainment and access to the stars of stage, screen, and radio. For most people, prime time on radio meant family gatherings in front of the living-room radio set to hear orchestras, bands, comedians, variety shows, drama, sitcoms, and documentaries, among other formats. Hollywood stars became stars of radio. Stars of the stage became prestige performers on radio, reaching in live time into every city and hamlet in the country. At the same time, local radio stations provided special services to their communities, in both programming and station participation in the affairs of the community. Owners were mostly local residents, as were staff members, who understood local needs and interests and programmed to meet them. It was the heyday of radio. For the industry and the public alike, it was a time when both were served by radio to a greater extent than in any other period.

In mid-century, another media development changed radio. The advent of television and, especially, the establishment of live-time national network programming in 1951, moved the stars and programming to television, eviscerated national radio networks as we had known them, and made radio even more local. The economics and program requirements forced upon radio by television had a far greater impact on intensifying localism than all the FCC regulations could possibly have had.

4 Changing the Broadcast Landscape

Radio Reinvents, Television Dominates, and an Act Reforms

At the advent of national television in 1951, radio networks were well established and powerful enough to have manipulated not only the growth of FM radio but the development of television, in timing and structure, that gave them control over the new medium. Notwithstanding the radio networks' reach and power, federal regulation had guaranteed a continuing diversity of local broadcasting. David A. Moss and Michael R. Fein, writing in *The Journal of Policy History*, state that "the three bland networks that the FCC long tolerated—and even fostered—may not have created the sort of vibrant diversity that Congress originally intended; but neither did they exercise tyrannous control over political speech." Moss and Fein believe that "the bulk of the evidence strongly suggests that the fear of concentrated control over mass communication mattered a great deal in the making of American radio regulation. The record also suggests that this concern about concentrated political power provided lawmakers with a perfectly reasonable basis upon which to conclude that a property-rights solution would *not* have been socially optimal."[1]

Radio may not have known it at the time, but the diversity-of-ownership concept was to be strengthened by radio reinventing itself because it could not compete on the same national playing field with television. By becoming more and more local, radio, deliberately or not, also became more and more sensitive to local needs and local practitioners. In *Signals in the Air: Native American Broadcasting in America*, Michael Keith, one of the coauthors, observes that "one of the major problems Native [American] stations had in operating was the lack of trained local Native personnel. Too often it was necessary for licensees to bring in non-Natives to operate their stations. Outsiders, not knowing the local culture, were not able to adequately respond to local needs and this caused discord at some stations."[2]

In microcosm, this problem at Native American stations reflects the crux of the absentee conglomerate versus the local operator serving local needs, then and now. In the 1940s, the FCC had limited one entity's ownership of radio stations to seven AM and seven FM. In 1985, it became twelve AM and twelve FM, in 1992 eighteen and eighteen, in 1994 twenty and twenty, and in 1996 the national cap was entirely eliminated. Television caps followed a similar pattern: from three in the 1940s to five in 1953, then for some years joining radio in the "rule of sevens" (7-7-7), twelve in 1984 with a maximum national reach of 25 percent of the population, and to no limit on the number of stations owned in 1996 with a maximum reach of 35 percent of the population. In 2003, the FCC extended the maximum coverage to 45 percent.

While many critics expected radio to die in the years following the establishment of national television networks and the increasing domination of that medium, just the opposite occurred. By going local, it wasn't the stations that suffered; it was the networks. Sterling and Kittross state that the oft-told story that radio lost money in the 1950s is a myth: although network national advertising declined, radio income as a whole increased. The networks' share of advertising revenues went from 25 percent in 1952 to 6 percent in 1960. Local stations' share of advertising went from 52 percent in 1952 to 62 percent in 1960. Radio overall revenues increased from $624 million to $692 million during that period.[3]

As network radio declined in the early 1950s, local stations became more and more involved in programming that originated locally. These shows included local music groups, panel and quiz shows with local people, talks and public affairs programs with local personalities, and documentaries, docudramas, and dramas relating to local history and issues and featuring local performers. Not only were radio stations addressing more and more programming to the specific needs of the community, but by producing more and more programs locally, they were involving more and more local people in the station's operations.

Radio's New Template

By the late 1950s, network radio had almost entirely disappeared, except for specialized subnetworks providing particular formats for a limited number of hours per day or week to interested stations. The prime-time evening entertainment fare retained only vestiges of its past: some variety shows and an increasing number of talk shows. A few network radio programs were popular for a while, including an NBC weekend magazine, *Monitor,* which provided a variety of formats from news and documentaries to comedy to music, and a highly creative NBC science fiction program, *X-Minus-One.* A few radio network personalities, such as Arthur Godfrey on CBS, continued to draw large audiences. Godfrey also starred on television at that time. Soap operas remained on radio longer than other popular formats, but they, too, gradually segued entirely into television.

Radio took what appeared to be lemons and made lemonade by combining what was left to it: local emphasis and local programming, especially music. Local radio stations returned to much of the programming that marked their beginnings three decades earlier: live announcers and other on-air personnel providing programs specifically oriented to local tastes, with music chosen by disc jockeys at the forefront. For a while, competing local stations went head-to-head with the same kinds of programming and tried to do on the local level what networks had done on the national scene: reach the largest number of potential listeners with a variety of formats and/or with a variety of music. This middle-of-the-road music morphed into what seemed like a more competitive format: playing the best-selling records or, as it became known, the Top 40 format. With the selection of music pretty much the same, then, on most stations, how did listeners choose which station to listen to? The stations themselves solved that problem by making the individual disc jockeys the stars of the programs. It was at that time that rock music took hold of the nation. Local deejays were identified with the type of music they played. Sterling and Kittross note that "for most of the 1950s, the important thing was combining records and radio to create instant events in the minds of the listeners—the task of the disc jockey."[4] Listeners began to tune in stations based on which disc jockey(s) they preferred.

Local stations began to consider the special music tastes of their communities and of affinity groups in their signal areas. Specialized formats began to grow and replace Top 40 and other generalized formats. Country and western music, for example, was adopted as the principal or sole format by a number of stations. Stations that were falling behind in the ratings because they didn't have the music resources or promotional budgets or popular disc jockeys to compete with the stations that had, decided to become even more local. Instead of looking for the largest slice of the audience pie—and frequently having to settle for crumbs—they decided to take a smaller slice of the pie that they could count on being there for them. This strategy came to be called "narrowcasting" (as differentiated from *broad*casting). For example, instead of being a "rock" station, a station became "acid rock" or "folk rock" or "country rock" or "urban rock," aimed at a segment of the listening community that could draw sufficient advertising dollars and that would also remain loyal to the particular station format that was unique in the area. A narrowcast audience may have been a smaller piece of the pie than the station ideally wanted, but it was steady and a sufficient piece to satisfy a small station's budget appetite. Even within a given format, a station often aimed at a limited demographic segment. For example, an urban rock station might logically target urban, usually black, populations in a city. However, some urban rock stations found they could get consistently better ratings by selecting so-called urban rock music that appealed not to urban listeners but to suburban white teenagers.

Susan Douglas, in *Listening In,* describes it this way.

> Between 1946 and 1948 advertising on radio by local businesses quadrupled. Stations also became more specialized, developing distinct personalities and catering to specific market segments by playing "beautiful music," airing talk shows, or repeating the Top 40 over and over. What would eventually be called narrowcasting began as stations targeted teens, or Christians, or country and western fans, or African-Americans with particular music and focused advertising, all presented by distinctive announcers. And radio listening, especially in the home, became a less communal and a more individualized activity.[5]

Douglas notes that evening family listening hours were gone and that, like in the early days of radio, listening became more personal, one individual with a radio in their bedroom or automobile or even bathroom. She further notes that despite the all-consuming competition from television, Americans actually bought more radios, in part due to the industry's "radio in every room" campaign. Unlike radio previously and television at that time, there was no longer a need for group listening or watching the same show: different members of a family now could and did listen to different radio programs at the same time. "By 1954," Douglas states, "70 percent of American households had two or more radios, and 33 percent had three or more. Listeners developed personal bonds with the personification of postwar radio, the disc jockey. And what they turned to radio for most was music and news. Things had come almost full circle."[6]

The rise of FM radio prompted another approach to localism. In the early 1960s, the cost of FM receivers continued to put AM radio as the most popular service. Resolved to push the higher-quality FM sound and to encourage the filling of FM frequency space, the FCC put a freeze on most applications for new stations in what was considered a crowded AM band for much of the 1960s and 1970s. Further, the FCC banned duplicate programming on co-owned AM and FM stations—which the AMs had been doing to save money on programming their revenue-losing FMs. FM receivers dropped in price from forty dollars and more to only a few dollars. The development of transistors and small portable radios further expanded FM growth as youngsters increasingly carried their music with them. Entrepreneurs knew where their audiences were, and popular music moved from AM to the higher-sound-quality FM stations. FM expanded and so did its audiences, and AM struggled to find new audience-attracting formats. More local specialized formats were the answer, formats that did not depend on the sound quality that made FM the service of choice for music. News and sports, with some AMs introducing all-news formats, all-talk formats, religious formats (especially in conservative "Bible Belt" sections of the country), and formats oriented to ethnic and racial minorities not served by mainstream media were developed by AM stations for the specific demographics of their local communities.

Marc Fisher, writing in the *American Journalism Review*, notes that in the 1950s, the "nets' heyday was over. Resources increasingly were diverted to provide more programming for the nation's new love, television. Radio became largely a jukebox, and news was cut back to a five minute summary at the top of the hour . . . Since then the only new trend in radio has been a powerful push toward narrowcasting, the kind of specialization that is now changing the way Americans watch TV. Top 40 radio that broadcast music that everyone might listen to gave way to formats designed for demographic slivers of society—oldies, country, rock, alternative, black music, Latin music."[7]

Fair and Balanced Medium

In the 1960s, the FCC took a remarkable pro-consumer (and in the minds of some, anti-industry) turn following John F. Kennedy's inauguration as president in 1961. His nominee for chair of the FCC, Newton Minow, interpreted and immediately implemented some of the White House's new philosophies for government. Among them were the establishment of an FCC Office of Network Study to determine whether television networks had obtained too much control over their affiliates and the industry in general, impinging on local stations' commitments to localism as radio networks had done in an earlier era. Minow also established an Educational Public Broadcasting Branch, to facilitate the growth of noncommercial radio and television stations, which were all local and which were serving their communities of license more specifically than most commercial stations were. Although Minow left the FCC after two years, and Kennedy was assassinated shortly afterward, the JFK legacy continued in the form of FCC commissioners who continued these policies and national public attitudes that supported counterculture action of a pro-public, anti-corporate nature. Many of the FCC actions greatly strengthened localism in both radio and television.

Perhaps the most controversial of these issues was the Fairness Doctrine. Note that it was called a "doctrine," not a "law." There never was a Fairness *Law*. The doctrine developed through a series of FCC and Supreme Court decisions. Going to back to 1941, the FCC stated, in what it called the Mayflower Decision, that a licensee may not editorialize or in any other way be an advocate. In 1949, the FCC partially reversed itself, stating that although individual stations alone have the responsibility for determining the content of their programming, they also have a responsibility to "devote a reasonable percentage of their broadcasting time to the discussion of public issues *of interest in the community served by their stations* and that such programs be designed so that the public has a reasonable opportunity to hear different opposing positions on the public issues *of interest and importance in the community*" (emphasis added).[8]

The key judicial decision upholding the Fairness Doctrine occurred in 1969 when the Supreme Court, in *Red Lion Broadcasting Company v. FCC*, upheld the FCC's determination that a station that airs a personal attack on an individual must give that individual airtime to reply. The Court's decision included the statement that "it is the purpose of the First Amendment to preserve an uninhibited marketplace of ideas in which truth will ultimately prevail, rather than to countenance *monopolization* of that market, whether it be by the Government itself or a private licensee" (emphasis added).[9] The Fairness Doctrine did not require stations to air the views of any particular group, individual, or ideology; but if they aired any view, they were then obligated to air opposing views. In practice, the doctrine did not open the broadcast media to a wide range of viewpoints: (1) if a station aired one side of a issue that was controversial in the particular community that the station served, and (2) if an entity complained and asked the station for time to present an opposing view or views and the station declined, and (3) if the entity filed a complaint with the FCC, and (4) the FCC determined that the Fairness Doctrine was violated, only then might the FCC require the stations to present comparable time for the opposing view(s). Note that it was not "equal" time, which applies only to the purchase of political ads by bona fide candidates for a given political office.

Fairness Asunder

In subsequent years, broadcasters and some civil liberty organizations sought the elimination of the Fairness Doctrine on the grounds that it violated broadcasters' First Amendment rights. It essentially became an industry versus consumer argument, with organizations that represented other than the generally conservative views of most broadcasters, plus minority ethnic, religious, racial, social, and political groups who traditionally had no voice in the media fighting to retain the doctrine on one side and industry and those in favor of marketplace deregulation and abolishing the doctrine on the other. One of the key communication aims of the Reagan administration when it took office in 1981 was to eliminate the Fairness Doctrine. Although the FCC eliminated many regulations, including a number that bolstered local radio service, in the first few years of the Reagan presidency, it wasn't until 1986 that it got a clear legal opportunity to dissolve the Fairness Doctrine. A federal court dismissed an FCC ruling that a station had violated the Fairness Doctrine, stating that because there was not a fairness law, the FCC was not obligated to enforce the doctrine if it did not want to. And the FCC no longer wanted to.

Congress, which felt that the Fairness Doctrine served as a bulwark against conglomerate control and provided greater opportunity for more people for free speech on the local level, passed by large bipartisan majorities a Fairness Law. President Reagan vetoed it. Although the House of Representatives easily had enough votes to override the veto, the Senate appeared to fall a few votes short and the Fairness Doctrine was no more. Broadcasters and, as time went by, the fewer and fewer conglomerates that controlled more and more radio stations, could state whatever opinions they wished, carry interviews, public affairs, features, and news that presented whatever viewpoints they wished, with no obligation to present alternative, opposing, or even fair information or views.

In *Free Radio,* Lawrence Soley suggests that the demise of the Fairness Doctrine contributed importantly to a conformity of opinion in America, a stifling of dissent, and the disappearance of a diversity of viewpoints. The vast majority of commercial stations are owned by wealthy individuals or corporations who impose their global or national views on the public at the expense of alternative, sometimes local views and concerns. More-over, Soley writes, "Not only are representatives of labor and community groups rarely used as sources in news stories, but they are oftentimes not even permitted to buy advertising time from the commercial media to express their views. Because the Fairness Doctrine has been rescinded, broadcasting stations, like newspapers, can refuse to sell advertising time to groups or individuals holding views with which the corporate media do not agree."[10]

Further Changes and Expectations

Another controversial requirement emanated from a late 1960s–early 1970s FCC that still contained commissioners appointed by President Kennedy and his successor, Lyndon Johnson, such as Nicholas Johnson and Kenneth Cox, plus some key staff members who consistently put the public interest and consumer needs above corporate profit and growth. Ascertaining community needs required all stations to determine each year the ten most significant issues in their community of service and at the end of the year file a report with the FCC detailing the extent to which their programming dealt with these issues. The FCC made certain that the stations implemented this requirement seriously and not on a pro forma basis. Executives at the managerial level of the station were required to make personal contact with representatives of various groups in the community to determine firsthand what concerns and needs of these groups were. This resulted in many instances in a first-time opportunity for local organizations representing minority racial and ethnic groups, religions, labor, women, children's advocates, artists, and others previously underrepresented and underreported, if covered at all, in the media, to have their needs and issues publicly presented.

With few exceptions, broadcasters and their associates railed against this rule. They claimed that the requirement instituted an unnecessary staff and paperwork burden and was an incursion on their First Amendment rights. Instituted in 1971, ascertainment applied to radio and television both. In 1976, the FCC affirmed the ascertainment requirement by making it a yearly continuing responsibility. Like many other requirements designed to strengthen stations' local service, it was eliminated, with the radio requirements the first to disappear in 1981 and those for television three years later. The shift to corporate from consumer interests was well under way.

Another requirement abolished in the 1980s that helped promote localism was one promoted by FCC commissioners Cox and Johnson that required stations, depending on their market size, to devote from 6 percent (for FM stations) to 8 percent (for AM stations) of their entire programming schedule each week to news and public affairs. During the period it was in effect, local communities got more local news and public affairs than they had before or would afterward.

Prompted by a suit by the Office of Communications of United Church of Christ (UCC) in 1966 against the FCC for refusing to allow the UCC to participate in renewal hearings for TV station WLBT of Jackson, Mississippi, and ordered by a federal court to allow such participation, the FCC was forced to open up its renewal process to the public. WLBT had been accused of racism in employment and programming, but the FCC renewed WLBT's license without hearing the UCC's concerns and evidence. In a dissent from the FCC's decision, its chair, E. William Henry, made a key point that would affect the FCC's licensing process for years to come: that the pubic had a right to participate in that process. Not only did the court order the FCC to revoke WLBT's license, but it reinforced Henry's point about public participation in the license renewal process. From then on, various national and local public interest groups ranging from the National Black Media Coalition to the National Organization for Women to the GI Forum (representing Hispanic or Latino interests) to a wide variety of local organizations in the community of license were able to convince broadcast stations to devote more time to minority needs and local concerns in programming and employment. It was easier and economically advisable for stations to negotiate better service for these local groups than face their objections in what could become lengthy renewal hearings.

Deregulating the Public Interest

That salutary impact of public license renewal hearings on localism also disappeared in the 1980s during the Reagan administration's period of deregulation. The requirements of proof of service in the public interest, convenience, or necessity, usually by submission of lengthy documents including sample program logs, were scrapped, and stations, as they do today, merely had to submit basic information on the equivalent of a large-sized postcard. Barring egregious violation of the rules, principally those relating to engineering operations, renewal became virtually automatic. Without obligation to show operation in the public interest and extended license terms, stations felt little compunction to provide local service that might in any way reduce commercial income in those time slots.

The impact of FM radio as, first, a special local service can be seen by its growth compared to AM. At the end of the 1950s, there were five times as many AM stations on the air as FMs. At the end of the 1960s, the ratio had been reduced to about two to one. While both AM and FM stations on the air increased during the next few decades, FM growth was greater, and in 1994, for the first time, there were more FMs than AMs on the air.[11] In 2004, the FCC figures show 6,218 commercial FM and 4,771 commercial AM stations in operation. In the meantime, educational, later called public— or, to be more accurate for the class, noncommercial—FM stations proliferated, with 2,497 holding licenses in 2004. Noncommercial stations, in part because many of them operate on low power, appear to provide more dedicated local service than do commercial radio stations.

A once-popular noncommercial class of radio stations, ten-watters or class "D," were, because of their limited range and local operations, the epitome of broadcasting localism. Most of these stations were licensed to colleges and universities or to community groups, and staffed by volunteers: students and/or local townspeople. Gregory Newton notes in the *Encyclopedia of Radio* that "by their very nature, these operations were strongly committed to their community and would appear to personify the localism ideal, often featuring material not available through full-power [noncommercial] stations."[12]

In the late 1970s, the Corporation for Public Broadcasting (CPB) and public radio as represented by National Public Radio (NPR) had grown increasingly powerful since their establishment a decade before as result of the Public Broadcasting Act of 1967, and they sought the same kinds of controls over their media as RCA and NBC had forty years earlier. Despite the opposition of local groups, the ten-watt licensees, and even the chief of the FCC's own public broadcasting branch, the commission—under pressure from the CPB and NPR—required the ten-watt stations to either upgrade to higher power or become a secondary service forced to yield their licenses if any station went on the air with higher power that resulted in interference. The fact that these stations were contributing more importantly to specific local needs than the higher-power noncommercial stations made little difference to the FCC. Also of little import to the FCC, CPB, and NPR was the fact that many of these small stations belonged to the have-nots: the community group without resources to go to higher power, or the underfunded college, such as many of the predominantly African American colleges in the South that could not afford to upgrade their facilities. The ten-watters gradually disappeared from the airwaves. The noncommercial national and regional big players solidified their power, while the small, local players were decimated.

This beginning of deregulation, under Democrat president Carter's FCC chair Charles Ferris, went against the conventional wisdom that Democrats favored the consumer and Republicans favored industry. Consumer advocate Ralph Nader denounced the FCC under Ferris as one of the worst agencies in Washington. In another rule concerning the deregulation of radio programming guidelines, in 1979, the FCC declared that "communities of common interests need not have geographic bounds. . . . The economics of radio . . . allowed that medium to be far more sensitive to the diversity within a community and the attendant specialized community needs. Increased competition in large urban markets has forced stations to choose programming strategies very carefully."[13]

Economy of Size

The economics of radio in the real world, however, worked against localism, not for it as claimed by the FCC. For example, during the economic recession of the late 1980s and early 1990s, Newton points out, radio station owners "cut back or eliminated local air staffs and news operations." With the relaxation of multiple ownership rules and an increasing number of stations on the air, it was not surprising that conglomerates increasingly used satellite-delivered formats, other syndicated programming, and automation "to create a significant economic incentive for many licensees to reduce localism to commercials and weather forecasts." Newton aptly sums up what happened to localism during that period: "Though frequently lauding localism in policy pronouncements, the FCC has seldom promulgated, and even more infrequently enforced, local program guidelines or requirements. Nearly all of those that ever existed, such as the fairness doctrine, the ascertainment primer, commercial guidelines, and news and public-affairs guidelines, disappeared by the mid-1980s. . . . It is practically impossible to set firm local content guidelines under the current regulatory philosophy, which moves much of the control from government policy to marketplace competition."[14]

In 1980, as accelerated deregulation was about to begin, law professor Tom Collins published an article that foresaw the increasing decline of localism. He cited two principal elements of localism: station licenses should be distributed geographically in a such a manner that every community and every person should be served by a station, and stations should be obligated to determine the local community's needs and orient their programming to meet those needs.[15]

During the 1980s, deregulation gave greater and greater autonomy to the industry and required fewer and fewer commitments that reflected localism in radio broadcasting. Elliott Parker has noted how during the 1980s the FCC put less stress on public interest regulations and more on permissive marketplace forces. He writes, "Beginning with the deregulation of radio in 1981, the Commission has eliminated the non-entertainment program guidelines, ascertainment rules, commercial guidelines and program logging requirements. During the period of deregulation, the FCC relaxed some of the licensing and license renewal rules that attempted to insure a degree of localism in the daily operation of radio stations. The Commission has relaxed local ownership rules and various requirements related to the daily operation of radio stations."[16]

Parker further notes additional areas of deregulation during the 1980s that weakened radio's local voice. These include removing local ownership requirements, no longer requiring owner participation in the affairs of the station's community, the reduction of required on-premises personnel during the business hours, locating the main studio as far as twenty-five miles from the community in which the station is licensed, and the lack of designated types of programs that might be considered as meeting local needs. Combined with voice tracking and satellite delivery of programs, the concept of localism has considerably changed.[17] Radio began losing local owners and gaining absentee owners, a situation solidified with the passage of the 1996 Telecommunications Act.

Muzzled Voices

In a memorandum backing a 1998 suit against the federal government seeking to overturn the FCC's licensing policies, attorneys for Free Speech and Steal This Radio, organizations supporting local community microstations, made the point that the increasing mergers in the radio industry since the 1980s had the effect of forcing a further decline in the amount of minority ownership of stations, which concomitantly decreased diversity and local service in programming. The memorandum notes that since the early 1980s there has been a resurgence of network programming in radio, most of which is delivered via satellite, further deteriorating local programming. In addition, the memorandum states that the FCC's elimination of ten-watt noncommercial stations to accommodate NPR's desire for more frequency space for more high-powered noncommercial stations of at least 100 watts resulted in a marked decrease in community radio stations that had operated as ten-watters and the loss of the local programming they had featured. The memorandum stresses the two major objectives of the FCC's 1965 Policy Statement on Comparative Broadcast Hearings—to provide "the best practicable service to the public" and to secure the "maximum diffusion of control of the media of mass communications"—and cites key factors in the statement, including "integration of ownership with management" and "localism."[18] The suit claimed, among other things, that the FCC has not properly enforced these factors.

Even before 1996, the gradual dissolution of a cap on station ownership presaged the Telecommunications Act's almost total elimination of antimonopoly regulations in broadcasting. In 1984, the seven AM–seven FM cap on ownership was changed to twelve and twelve. In 1992, the limit was raised again, to eighteen and eighteen. It was not too surprising, therefore, when in 1996 national ownership limits were entirely eliminated. While local organizations, minorities, and consumer organizations saw this mandate for consolidation as an out-and-out industry power grab, others saw it as a logical outcome of the technological and economic changes in the medium. Professor Philip Napoli asks whether the definition of localism should extend beyond that of geography. He thinks cultural and political rationales should also be used as bases for a definition of localism and, more specifically, for program content. "Local origination alone," he says, "may not be sufficient, given that a program that originates locally could conceivably not address or appeal to the cultural values or beliefs of the local community. Similarly, from a political standpoint; locally originated programming need not necessarily address local political issues and concerns. . . . Programming that caters to the cultural or political interest or concerns of a particular community could very well be produced outside the geographic boundaries of the community."[19]

Contrarily, former FCC commissioner Nicholas Johnson has pointed out that there is a need to separate "content and conduit." Johnston contends

If you are going to permit the conduit owner and operator to also own some of the content flowing over that conduit, then you've created an economic conflict of interest for that operator who may gain by keeping competitor's material off, or in some other way disadvantaging the competitor. . . . If you listen up and down the [radio] dial throughout most of the geographic area of the United States, you will find very little diversity. Why is that? Because radio stations tend to be operated by members of the Republican Party and the local Rotary Club, who are operating them as a business for which revenue is generated through the sale of advertising, and for which they want to purchase programming at the cheapest possible rate.

Johnson further notes that "one of the many consequences of this concentration of power is the loss of localism."[20]

Did Congress deliberately and knowingly abandon its long-held concept of localism when it enacted the Telecommunications Act of 1996, or did it believe that consolidation and conglomeration did not necessarily affect local services, as Napoli states above? Let's examine the 1996 act, its provisions, and its impact on the field of communications, most specifically on radio.

5 In Whose Best Interest?

Diversity, Localism, and Consolidation

The Telecommunications Act of 1996 arguably changed the communications playing field in America to a greater degree than even the Radio Act of 1927 or the Communications Act of 1934. While the 1927 and 1934 acts were logical outgrowths of the development of the media in the United States, most particularly broadcast services, the 1996 act not only expanded the areas of government jurisdiction but was a radical change in the structures of and relationships among all the media—including broadcasting—principally through the nub of the act: deregulation.

In *The Broadcast Century and Beyond,* the authors describe the act as follows.

> The Telecommunications Act of 1996 legislated the most sweeping changes in telecommunications in the United States in more than 60 years, and reversed laws, rules, and regulations that had been built up over decades. The anti-monopoly rules were virtually totally eliminated, specifying no caps on the number of radio stations owned by one entity, and expanded dual ownership in individual markets, depending on the market size. The 12-station limit on one entity's TV ownership was also eliminated, with the FCC charged with developing new, broader standards. Reversing the 1941 network duopoly rule, the act permitted ownership of two networks, provided one was not purchased by another. *Broadcasting & Cable* [the industry magazine] headlined a story on the lifting of ownership limits for radio thusly: "Radio Supergroups: They're off."

The Act allowed common ownership of broadcast networks and cable systems. It allowed cable-MMDS [Multichannel Multipoint Distribution Systems] cross-ownership under certain conditions. Broadcast license terms, for both TV and radio, were extended to 8 years. VDT [Video Display Terminal] rules were repealed and TELCOS [telephone companies] were permitted to deliver video signals. Conversely, cable systems were permitted to enter the area of telephone service. Atlantic Bell and NYNEX merged, providing a huge conglomerate offering cable as well as local and long-distance telephone service.

The new Act required cable systems to scramble any programs the subscriber deemed unsuitable for children. All new sets old were required to have a V-chip and the industry was required to develop a ratings system within a year as a guide for parental use of the V-chip, or the FCC would itself set up a rating system. Congress seemed to be obsessed with indecency. Fines for broadcast or cable obscene programs were raised from $10,000 to $100,000. Congress also managed to pass a Communications Decency Act, in which anyone using the Internet for alleged indecent material could be fined up to $25,000 and jailed for two years, although it was not clear what exactly would be considered indecent. Anyone even under suspicion of sending or receiving indecent material on the Internet could have their phone lines tapped by the FCC. The moment the bill was signed by the President, a number of citizen organizations, such as the ACLU, filed suit, and the federal courts stayed implementation of the cyberspace indecency provisions pending First Amendment Review by the Supreme Court [which subsequently found the Communications Decency Act to be unconstitutional].

Renewal of licenses was made virtually automatic, and competitive applications would not be allowed. Cable rates were deregulated, beginning in 1999. The Act also limited the granting of advanced TV [also called HDTV, high definition television] licenses to incumbent broadcasters. [Rupert] Murdoch was one of the first on the bandwagon, stating he would convert the Fox-owned stations immediately, although there was still a need for integrated production and operation components linked to high-speed computer networks.[1]

Consumer representatives and independent stations were very concerned about the impact of the elimination of multiple ownership limits, but they were also worried about the lifting of the duopoly rules. Now one entity could own up to half of the radio stations in any given market, with a restriction of eight in markets with forty-five or more radio stations, with a scaling down to five in a market with fourteen stations. With that kind of consolidation control in their market, independent stations wondered how they could survive economically. Rather than face possible bankruptcy, they began selling out to the conglomerates. Within a few years, relatively few locally controlled and programmed independent stations remained.

In *Stay Tuned*, Sterling and Kittross quote from the key provisions of the Telecommunications Act of the 1996 that relate to the broadcast media.

PURPOSE OF THE ACT:

To promote competition and reduce regulation in order to secure lower prices and higher quality services for American telecommunications consumers and encourage the rapid deployment of new telecommunications technologies.

LICENSE PERIOD:

Each license granted for the operation of a broadcasting Station shall be for a term not to exceed 8 years.

LICENSE RENEWALS:

The Commission shall not consider whether the public interest, convenience, and necessity might be served by the grant of a license to a person other than the renewal applicant . . . [unless the applicant has failed to meet each of the following three standards:]

(a) the station has served the public interest, convenience, and necessity;
(b) there have been no serious violations by the licensee of this Act or the rules and regulation of the Commission; and
(c) there have been no other violations by the licensee of this Act or the rules and regulations of the Commission which, taken together, would constitute a pattern of abuse

OWNERSHIP OF RADIO STATIONS:

. . . eliminate . . . any provisions limiting the number of AM or FM broadcast stations which may be owned or controlled by one entity nationally [and] eliminate . . . the restrictions on the number of television stations that a person or entity may directly or indirectly own, operate, or control, or have a cognizable interest in, nationwide and . . . by increasing the national audience reach limitation for television stations to 35 percent . . .

. . . permit a person or entity to own or control a network of broadcast stations and a cable system . . .[2]

Assessing the Act

What was the impact of all this on radio? Did it affect the practice as well as the concept of diversity and localism? Reactions and actions were highly passionate. Let's examine some of the actual results of the act and some of the judgments and interpretations of broadcasters, listeners, and representative groups.

A Benton Foundation Internet publication, the *Digital Beat,* evaluated the impact on radio of the Telecommunications Act of 1996 in terms of communication in a democracy. An article, "Radio for the Next Millennium," argues that communities in the United States have largely depended on radio to provide an open forum for the widest range of local viewpoints and an outlet for local music. They note that radio is an exceedingly inexpensive form of communication reception and that the transistor has made such reception constantly and immediately available. It suggests that the Telecommunications Act of 1996 changed radio more dramatically than any other service: "Unprecedented consolidation has led to the creation of corporate radio giants that are enjoying record advertising revenues, while nearly crushing the diversity and localism that have long been hallmarks of American radio." The article goes on to state that diversity has disappeared from the radio dial, citing as one example the large decrease in minority ownership of radio stations following the passage of the act. The article quotes former FCC commissioner Susan Ness: "In a country that receives such a benefit from having a melting pot . . . we lose that richness when the media are largely owned by one segment of the population."[3]

This view is reiterated in a National Lawyer's Guild (NLG) paper on "Broadcasting, the Constitution, and Democracy." Reiterating that radio was the medium most affected by the act, the NLG notes that the act permitted one company to own as many as eight stations in a single market and that in less than two years following the passage of the act, 4,000 of the country's 11,000 radio stations were sold and 1,000 mergers took place. "Small chains have been acquired by middle-sized chains, and the middle-sized chains have been gobbled up by the massive giant companies who have come to dominate the industry" and who run their stations' programming from a national headquarters.[4]

Hardly a foe of corporate America, the *Wall Street Journal* agreed with such criticism, stating that "relative to television and other media, radio is inexpensive for both broadcasters and consumers. It is ideally suited for local control and community service. Yet radio has become nothing but a profit engine for a handful of firms so that they can convert radio broadcasting into the most efficient conduit possible for advertising. Across the nation, these giant chains use their market power to slash costs, providing the same handful of formats with barely a token nod to the communities in which the stations broadcast. On Wall Street corporate consolidation of radio may be praised as a smash success, but by any other standard this brave new world is an abject failure."[5]

Journalist Yon Lambert, writing in the Columbia, South Carolina, *Business News* in 1997, examines the impact of consolidation on a number of communities. Noting the unprecedented number of radio mergers since the passage of the Telecommunications Act of 1996, he thinks that the deregulation that "left just a few leviathan companies in control of the airwaves in most cities" raises some significant questions about the future of radio: "how programming methods will change, what will happen to advertising rates, which jobs will remain and whether there is enough competition." While some of the radio managers he interviewed believed their programming would improve under the "supergroups," "some industry insiders found the speed with which it happened alarming." He cites on insider, a radio consultant, who said, "We have gone from a well-diversified ownership base to one which is extremely consolidated and dominated by a few giants on Wall Street." Lambert notes that local radio "is a very different place than it was in early 1996" and that "in Columbia, three corporations will soon own 13 of the city's top 15 commercial stations."[6]

Andy Sullivan covered for Reuters a study by the Future of Music Coalition (which is discussed in more detail in a later chapter). "Airwaves in many cities are dominated by a few media behemoths that offer little in the way of local content," Sullivan reported. "While deregulation has allowed companies like Clear Channel Communications Inc. to buy up struggling radio stations across the country, the new owners have often pursued profitability by slashing costs, rather than seeking to lure listeners with unique content. As a result, local airwaves are often dominated by a handful of companies that offer a portfolio of similar-sounding radio stations." The story quoted Future of Music Coalition research director Kristin Thomson: "Much of radio on a local level has become bland and formulaic and not locally programmed."[7]

In a 1999 study, Daniel Rapela found the following effects of consolidation under the 1996 act:

> Local, independent broadcasters are becoming a thing of the past, unable to compete with the larger, more powerful firms. . . . The sudden rush of media mergers and acquisitions has also led critics to voice concerns about the localism of the radio medium. . . . The number of owners continues to decline, as conglomerates become larger and larger. . . . Critics maintain that consolidation has led to shrinking playlists and less local content, while radio owners say that there is more of a variety than ever before. . . . Ethical concerns about downsizing come into play as larger companies buy up locally owned radio stations. . . . There is less of a need for employees and talent. . . . Downsizing helps conglomerates cut costs, but some people inevitably lose their jobs.[8]

While media corporations praised the Telecommunications Act of 1996 as forwarding the principles of free speech and establishing a new marketplace for greater economic efficiencies and higher-quality programming and service to the radio public, consumer groups wondered how a bill that they considered so inimical to the public interest could get through Congress. *In These Times* presented its analysis just as Congress enacted the legislation. It claimed that "the law was not created with consumers in mind. In effect, the bill was bought and paid for by the very telecommunications conglomerates it is supposed to bring under the discipline of the market. Far from mandating competition among telecommunication companies, the act encourages already-mammoth corporations to pursue further media and allows businesses to form alliances with their supposed rivals in other sectors, greatly reducing the risk that new technologies will provide consumers with meaningful choice." The reporter quotes Kevin Taglang of the Benton Foundation: "A lot of the public interest sector felt totally shut out. No one saw the final draft of the bill before it was passed. The industry found a Congress it could work with; a Congress that doesn't allow the public into the debate was a perfect setting for getting the bill through."[9] The article details some of the fund-raising meetings for politicians, particularly some of the leaders in the Republican-controlled Congress who could shepherd the bill through.

> Looking at the industry's campaign contributions lobbying efforts and bill-writing is the only way to explain much of the Telecommunications Act. The law is filled with provisions that make no sense from a public interest point of view but make perfect sense for the industries involved.

. . . For decades, the FCC has regulated ownership of stations, saying that it was necessary to prevent concentrated ownership from monopolizing scarce spectrum space . . . but the Telecommunications Act looks at the spectrum not as a public resource to be shared but as a private preserve whose investment value must be protected.[10]

Downsizing Diversity

The most important consideration for most of the public is the impact of consolidation upon the programming that they listen to. Let's look briefly at how some programming was affected. As noted earlier, a later chapter will deal with the most popular aspect of radio programming, music, and any discussion of it at this point will be fleeting. After music, news and talk are significant program elements of contemporary radio.

Marc Fisher summed up his evaluation of what has happened to the programming in the *Washington Post*. Radio has been the test case for consolidation, he concludes:

Ever since the 1996 easing of restrictions on ownership, big media companies have faced off against musicians, activists and some of the few remaining mom and pop station owners. The media companies say the airwaves offer a more bountiful selection of artistic riches than ever before and that they have brought big-city talent to backwater communities, replacing farm reports, swap chops and amateurish deejays. But listeners hear the nation's broadcasters pressing the culture to its lowest common denominator in a cynical money grab. Rush Limbaugh, Howard Stern and Tom Joyner are piped into your hometown by satellite.[11]

Fisher notes that in Washington, DC, listeners have far fewer music choices than they previously had, although Clear Channel maintains that it has added many new formats in the markets where it has acquired new stations. Fisher points to a study that concludes that although the formats appear to be different, they have almost identical playlists. "If deregulation was supposed to let a thousand flowers bloom," Fisher writes, "most of the garden appears to be in Clear Channel's yard."[12]

Fisher quotes Radio One executive Alfred Liggins's defense of conglomeration: "We're now a healthier industry and you have more choices. Is it tougher for the little guy, the mom and pop owner? Yeah. But that little guy could not provide the same level of talent or service." Fisher responds that "there is a downside to diluting the localism that has given radio its distinctive edge since the dawn of the Top 40 era in the 1950s. Radio for decades played a crucial role in building community—from deejays visiting high schools to run record hops to news departments that provided essential coverage of storms, riots, elections and scholastic sports. Consolidation and cutbacks in local staffing have eliminated many of these functions."[13]

In a 1998 report on the impact of the consolidation, *USA Today* interviewed several key industry executives. Jacor CEO Randy Michaels was quoted as saying, "What we have for the very first time is the opportunity to think about our business the way any other retailer would think about their business, and that's regionally." Capstar CEO Steve Hicks said, "In smaller markets, you can have trouble attracting quality talent. But we can have one quality person do eight stations from one location, and it's all customized."[14]

USA Today's story also noted that consolidation appeared to be reducing the diversity of content for listeners in addition to reducing the diversity of ownership of stations. A *USA Today* study showed that less than two years after passage of the 1996 act, the number of radio station owners dropped 14 percent even as the number of stations on the air grew. (Within a few more years, the number of different owners would decrease by almost 50 percent.) The article stated that consolidation is "also turning a business with deep local roots into one that's more distant, where the evening weather forecast in Fayetteville, Ark., may have been recorded hours before, 500 miles away in Austin, Texas." The article quoted former FCC chair William Kennard: "I don't think anybody anticipated that the pace [of consolidation] would be so fast and so dramatic. The fundamental economic structure of the radio industry is changing from one of independently owned operators to something akin to a chain store." And Andrew Schwartzman, president of the Media Access Project, added that under consolidation "the local angle just gets lost completely."[15]

The Inside Radio Web site reported that the "average morning audience of 4 million people is listening to one of 25 syndicated personalities. In some cases these personalities are heard on a few stations in one region of the country. In other cases, the affiliate rosters number more than 100 stations and carry the program coast-to-coast. If you talk to most radio-industry execs and analysts, radio's localism is one of the medium's strongest, most important characteristics—the 'killer-app' to combat competition from satellite-delivered radio, or the encroachment of Internet-only webcasting. That kind of thinking may be a thing of the past."[16]

Unfortunately, one of the dinosaurs in the new economic model may be local audiences. Audiences want to connect with local stations beyond passive listening to program materials. They want to feel that the owners and managers have some connection to the local community. They want program content, such as news, weather, sports, political information, and other program elements that relate to and connect the stations to the local listeners.[17]

No News Is Bad News

What's the status of news under consolidation? Marc Fisher declares in the *American Journalism Review* that "a tidal wave of consolidation generated by the Telecommunications Act of 1996's loosening of ownership limits has put most big- and medium-market stations under the control of a handful of corporations, which have shown little interest in paying for local newsgathering and enormous interest in cutting out expensive budget items such as reporters and wire services." He notes that the decline of news on radio began in the deregulatory period of the 1980s when the FCC eliminated station requirements for news and public affairs programming. According to Fisher, in most markets one of the two national news services provide "not only traffic and weather reports, but also the newscasts on virtually all the stations in town." And the problem is similar at all levels of news coverage, with small towns and rural areas especially affected. Fisher quotes general manger of CNN Radio and a member of the board of the Radio-Television News Directors Association Robert Garcia: "The little 1,000 watt station that competes in newsgathering with the weekly newspaper is pretty much gone. Those news operations are becoming very rare because of a lack of ad revenue. Mom and Pop shops that spent their ad money locally are replaced by large chains like WalMart that spend their ad money nationally, at the expense of local news on the radio."[18]

Journalist Andrew Ferguson described one example of what happens when conglomeration eliminates local news coverage.

> In the early morning of January 18, 2002, a train derailment near Minot, North Dakota, sent a poisonous cloud through much of the town. Immediately, police tried to broadcast emergency instructions to the community via one of the local radio stations. Thanks to the 1996 deregulation, all six of Minot's stations are owned by Clear Channel Communications. And on January 18—in keeping with common practice at large radio companies—the stations were broadcasting programming fed by satellite from San Antonio-based Clear Channel. Which meant there was no one to answer the phone at any of the stations—or to break into programming to broadcast news of the emergency.

"The phone line was out," Minot resident Jennifer Johnson told the *Bismarck Tribune* a few days later. "The only thing on the radio was music. No one was telling us what happened or what to do. We were trapped."[19]

Ferguson says that only one person died, but things could have been a lot worse because the deregulation of ownership rules have ceded

> local control to distant, unresponsive owners with only the most tenuous ties to the communities they serve. . . . [Radio] retains an importance out of proportion to its commercial muscle. Being highly mobile and nearly ubiquitous, following us from living room to car to shopping center, radio is woven into people's lives in a way matched by no other electronic medium. And its appeal has traditionally been local. A home-grown radio station binds a community together as a good newspaper does. Its loss to a distant and out-of-touch proprietor can have unforeseen consequences.[20]

Bill McKibben, in an article in *Harper's Magazine* in late 2003, compared the local programming and services of one radio station in his area of Vermont with the trend in most other regions of the country, the localism of his station making it "a very strange station" in the atmosphere of consolidation. "Modern radio stations aim for a particular niche—say, thirty-five-year-old males who want sports around the clock. But it's a rare place in our society where Thelonius Monk and stock-car racing coexist. It's radio that actually reflects the reality of local life, and it seems very strange because it's all but disappeared everywhere else." He notes that on his local station, one can hear talk shows from the left as well as from the right, jazz, sports, stock-car racing, school reports, senior citizen information—"You hear, in other words, things that *other people* are interested in. Which is pretty much the definition of a community." He laments that "local sounds good, but most of American history has been spent transforming local into national and now global. . . .It's true you can hear anything from anywhere at any time, but, oddly, it's gotten a lot harder to hear much about your immediate vicinity. . . . That's one reason why people rose up last summer to fight the FCC when it moved to make the world even safer for the Clear Channels."[21]

The Ever Fading Voice

Many critics have been concerned about the impact of consolidation on America's democratic political process. Media manipulation by politicians has been going on since the advent of media—from the telling of the news of the state in ancient Greece's agora to Mussolini's use of radio in Italy in the 1920s (he was quoted as saying that if it weren't for radio, he wouldn't have the control he did over the Italian people) to Hitler and Goebbel's remarkably effective use of film as well as radio to present-day TV attack ads and sound bites that mark American political campaigns. "Whoever controls the media controls the politics of the country" has become not only an axiom, but a truism that is practiced by all political parties and by those who support one party or one candidate. In the United States, with few exceptions, we have found in the past several decades that the order of finish in a political race is commensurate with the amount of money the candidates have spent on television advertising. While there is an equal-time rule (Section 315 of the Communications Act of 1934), it does not guarantee equal time for all candidates for a given office; it guarantees only that if a station sells political air time to one candidate, it must offer to sell an equal amount of time to all other bona fide candidates—and other candidates may not be able to afford to buy equal time. Otherwise, the station can favor one candidate in its news broadcasts, public affairs programs, interviews, and in all other programming except those designated as entertainment. It can, indeed, laud one candidate and vilify the other. It can continually feature one candidate and completely black out the other. In effect, the media in the United States can determine which candidate wins—and have done so.

The Pew Research Center for the People and the Press reported a study that emphasized the importance of local TV stations (it did not report on radio) in election campaigns. A spokesperson for the Kerry-Edwards campaign in 2004 said the campaign "absolutely recognizes that local media matter a tremendous amount. . . . We try to do all we can to recruit as much local coverage as we can get."[22]

Consolidation has put conservative, mostly Republican-supporting companies, in control of most U.S. media. Patrick Burkart turns to the theories of cultural critics such as Jacques Ellul and Jean Baudrillard to explain how this limits discussion and helps form public opinion. Ellul wrote extensively about propaganda, arguing that it "can be misused in lying campaigns, exerting secret, nefarious, and manipulative effects on society." Baudrillard details "how the contemporary technologies of professional journalists and shock jocks, operating on radio and television, sustain levels of political support and symbols of cultural legitimacy by staging a never-ending spectacle in the popular media."[23]

Burkart uses these concepts as a base to describe how America's media are dominated by talk show hosts who reflect the right-wing views of the mainly Republican owners of the media. In the panoply of talk shows, right-wing Republicans such as Rush Limbaugh and G. Gordon Liddy are relatively moderate compared to the far-right extremists who make up the mix of talk shows on America's airwaves. There are dozens of right-wing talk shows being syndicated by multistation conglomerates to their stations throughout the country. At the same time, in early 2005, there was only one very limited network of liberal talk shows—Air America. Anchored by Al Franken, it had continuing difficulties throughout the year of its debut in April 2004, but by the end of the year appeared to be getting some encouraging ratings. In some instances, as soon as a mega-owner acquired a station with a liberal talk show, that show was canceled. What does this result of consolidation bode for the American political system? The impact of these talk show personalities and beliefs on the American electoral process has been clearly demonstrated. While our media are not controlled by a central governmental power using the media to maintain its power, do we face the same kind of control of information and ideas by favored elements of the private sector?

In Eugene, Oregon, in 2002, for example, an attorney, Edward Monks, wrote a newspaper report on radio talk shows. He found that "the spectrum of opinion on national political commercial talk radio shows ranges from extreme right wing to very extreme right wing—there is virtually nothing else." On two major Eugene radio stations, he found that "there are 80 hours per week, more than 4,000 per year, programmed for Republican and conservative talk shows, without a single second programmed for a Democratic or liberal perspective. . . . Political opinions expressed on talk radio are approaching the level of uniformity that would normally be achieved only in a totalitarian society." He notes, ironically, that right-wing talk show hosts spend much of their time complaining about "the liberal media."[24]

At a Midwest Forum on Media Ownership in early 2003, media historian Gretchen Soderlund submitted that free speech in America is an endangered species because "we have built-in checks to government control, but not corporate control." At the same forum, *Lumpen* magazine writer Ed Marszewski speculated whether President George W. Bush would be president without the domination of right-wing media in 2000. He suggested that without a diverse media system, "you can kiss your democracy goodbye."[25]

Frank A. Blethen, publisher and CEO of the *Seattle Times,* asks,

Can American democracy survive the loss of an independent press and a diversity of voices? The answer is a resounding no! . . . Our democracy is more fragile than we'd like to admit. And the concentration of our media in large, public companies is posing one of the greatest threats ever to its survival. . . . Justice Louis Brandeis, writing for the Supreme Court, once stated: "Publicity is justly commended as a remedy for social and industrial diseases. Sunlight is said to be the best of disinfectants; electric light the most efficient policeman."

Indeed, a diverse press is the watchdog that protects integrity of our Constitutional process. Frighteningly, today's ownership concentration and the blatant disinvestment in news which we are witnessing is, in and of itself, an untold story that may lead to our eventual undoing. . . . If democracy is to survive we must change the course of this terrible trend toward media concentration, and invigorate a diverse and independent press.[26]

Many critics have expressed concern that the public doesn't even know how media consolidation has affected their political beliefs and limited or ignored local political information because the media, acting as judge and jury, simply do not report how they manipulate news and information, or how laws and regulations, or lack of them, permit them to do so. Professor Steven Barnett put it this way: "Within the media sector, media owners have access to the one of the key drivers of opinion formation—the mass media themselves. As consolidation increases between newspapers, TV, online, and other areas of publishing [and, of course, radio], different parts of the media empire can be exploited not just to cross-promote other parts of the empire but to promote forceful arguments about how governments should be legislating in the very areas which might limit corporate expansion in that field."[27]

Former FCC commissioner Nicholas Johnson noted that "as one member of Congress said at the time [of the passage of the Communications Act of 1934], 'if we should ever allow such a potentially powerful medium to fall into the hands of the few, then woe be to those who would dare to disagree with them.' Of course, that is exactly what we are now doing: letting the power fall into fewer and fewer hands, and it is equally true today that 'woe be to those who would dare to disagree with them.'"[28]

David A. Moss and Michael R. Fein, professors at Harvard and Brandeis, respectively, have dealt with the political impact of consolidation. They note that "the early advocates of the FRC and the FCC rested their case on a combination of spectrum scarcity on the one hand and broadcasting's special political significance on the other."[29] They quote from an article by Senators Ernest Hollings and Byron Dorgan in the *Washington Post* in 2001: "For decades, our communications policy has imposed sensible restrictions on media ownership to promote and preserve multiple, independent voices. . . . If media consolidation is allowed to continue unfettered . . . local control, local coverage and a robust marketplace of ideas will suffer."[30]

Moss and Fein conclude that the current debate "revolves around the special political significance of broadcasting. And despite the fact that there are many powerful and influential interests involved, it still appears that current debate (like the historical one) can be understood fundamentally as a contest of ideas about how best to serve the public interest."[31]

Radio for Peace International (RFPI), an independent shortwave radio operation headquartered in Costa Rica, has for years broadcast alternative political ideas and information. In 2003, it was temporarily forced off the air by thugs who destroyed some of its facilities. It likened this action, on a global scale, to what is happening locally throughout much of the world through media consolidation. "The closure of alternative media voices . . . is all too common. . . . The North American model of mass media mergers is de rigueur and in the wake of such consolidation, many independent voices . . . are being silenced. . . . In a globalized era . . . there is an apparent growing dearth in the free interchange of truthful and accurate reportage put out by independent media sources. . . . In 1983, 50 corporations controlled half or more of the media industry. Today [2003], this number is less than a dozen and is ever-shrinking. The role of alternative media is more important than ever."[32]

Technocratic Imperialism

A key element facilitating conglomerate reduction of local programming and local management of radio stations is technological innovation. Voice tracking, customized satellite delivery, and automated studios are increasingly used by conglomerates to reduce costs. With voice tracking, a radio personality can record in twenty minutes the speaking linking four hours of programming, which means many stations can be supplied with full schedules, including overnights and weekends, with a minimum of personnel costs. The programming can be distributed in real time or used at a later time.

Satellite delivery permits quick and easy distribution on a mass scale. A given personality can be featured on any number of group-owned stations simultaneously or, depending on the time zone, at the same local time on the same day. Automation has been around for a long time, at first used by individual stations to preprogram segments of the day when appropriate on-air and technical personnel were not available and/or to reduce operating expenses. Combined with voice tracking and satellite delivery, automation allows group owners to operate a station with virtually no personnel and no local program costs, the group stations sharing the same programming.

Group owners, however, claim that they are not replacing local talent entirely with the new technology, including automated stations. Rather, "digital studios are making the jobs of on-air talent easier, without limiting their localism or creativity. Owners also point out that digital satellite technology can eliminate mediocre talent by bringing major-market voices to smaller cities, where stations may not be able to afford quality announcers."[33]

Daniel Rapela summarizes an article by Lydia Polgreen in the *Washington Monthly:* "New satellite and Internet technology allows a technician at a small station to literally cut and paste bits of local news, weather and banter into piped-in programming with a click of a mouse on a computer screen. Stations can even apply this technology to listener requests and live remotes, by simply clicking and dragging bits of dialogue into the appropriate places. The computer technology makes the broadcast seem local and, in many cases, it is hard for the listeners to know they are hearing something that originated from a different town."[34]

One of the techniques used by the group owner AMFM in the late 1990s was the Star System. The AMFM digital broadcasting center in Austin, Texas, employed ten top talent deejays who could be heard on stations in various parts of the country, including Hawaii. Here is how it works. The stations report to the center the kinds of music they want, plus information on local events. The music is stored in computerized data bases. The deejay prerecords a program, interspersing local information with the music, and the entire show is sent to the given station the next day. Voice tracking, automation, and satellite delivery make the listener think they are listening to a local personality do a show live. The station doesn't tell them differently. The radio companies believe they are not only achieving greater fiscal efficiency but are providing listeners with greater professionalism in the programming. Critics believe that this technological approach homogenizes radio, reduces diversity and localism, and deceives the audience as well.[35]

In 2002, the FCC authorized digital radio following strong lobbying by the NAB. It has been a boon to large group owners. But the technology, which gives larger stations the ability to broadcast both digital and analog signals, also can drown out low-power, community radio stations. Digital technology, as implemented via FCC regulations, adds to the demise of localism.[36]

Daniel Rapela quotes Clear Channel executive Pam Taylor: "At a small station in a small market, it costs a lot to have a live, local person on the air even 12 hours a day. If you limit on-air live time to morning and afternoon drive, you can get the rest of the day's programming from the hub."[37] (This book's authors, who worked at one time as on-air and control room personnel with small radio stations, recall that those stations operated with satisfactory to substantial profits prior to the availability of the new technology, despite having the requisite quota of personnel for all of the station's dayparts, and wonder whether the key purpose of the current application of technology is really about more profits.)

Rapela also quotes Gigi Sohn of the Media Access Project. "What turns some listeners off to corporate radio is that corporate radio ignores localism," Sohn states, adding that companies are able to do what is "cheapest and easiest" by virtue of satellite technology, but that corporate radio stations view themselves as "entertainers, and not as citizens with civic duties to serve their local communities."[38]

By the end of the year 2000, eight companies controlled most of the media in the United States, including radio, television, cable, films, videotapes and DVDs, audio recordings and CDs, and books. These were the Disney company, AOL–Time Warner, Rupert Murdoch's NewsCorp, Sony, General Electric, AT&T, Seagrams, and Bertelsmann. In the years since then, even more consolidation has resulted in greater media power. In 2004, six companies reputedly controlled 90 percent of the programming and 90 percent of the advertising revenues throughout the entire world.

Think Globally, Act Locally?

Former FCC commissioner Rachel Chong represented the attitudes of federal regulators who agreed with the industry's march to consolidation. In what she described as her farewell speech as a commissioner, to the National Association of Broadcasters radio convention in 1997, she noted that she opposed "overregulation" and supported "marketplace-friendly" approaches. She stated that she "consistently opposed unnecessary government encroachment on program content." She focused on the Telecommunications Act of 1996.

> Some argue that localism will be lost if there is industry consolidation. They claim big companies will turn their backs on serving local needs. But as you and I know, successful broadcasters would as soon abandon

localism as put hemlock in their coffee! . . . I've learned a few things in my tenure as a Commissioner, and one of those things is that terrestrial radio broadcasters, regardless of the size of their parent company, know that localism is what makes them successful. It's what differentiates you from your new competitors—competitors like cable-provided audio, DARS, Internet radio, and CD players. Another thing I have learned is that permitting one entity to own multiple stations in a market doesn't necessarily harm diversity. Quite the contrary, a single owner of multiple stations might be in a position to counter-program, using a format that could not be sustained on a stand-alone station. When that happens, listeners get more choice, not less. In short, I believe the radio industry—not government—should decide how to deal with the new competitive realities that you face.[39]

Another former FCC commissioner, Nicholas Johnson, who strongly opposed consolidation even before the passage of the 1996 act, discussed consolidation's potential effect on localism.

One of the many consequences of this concentration of power is the loss of localism. . . . We see that with the radio stations that are simply picking up a music service off of a satellite and rebroadcasting it with conventional radio transmitter technology out to their listeners. We see it with these direct satellite-to-home services, and we see it with the nationally distributed cable services, and the network services that go out to the local conventional radio and television station. The result is that we're not getting a local service. The nationally-distributed media are not dealing with local issues. Folks who say, "Think globally, act locally," are going to have a tough time either thinking or acting locally if they don't have the foggiest notion of what's going on in their own community, and they are not going to get it by watching nationally-distributed news and information and entertainment services. . . . We simply must have viable, strong, vibrant, thorough, fair, investigative, local media. If we are not going to have federal regulation and federal control, then we need to have more active local participation, and that requires that people be informed, and that requires that their local media inform them, and that those local media have a capacity for finding out what's going on in the local community.[40]

Given the perceived impact of the Telecommunications Act of 1996 and subsequent consolidation on local radio, what are or should be a radio station's principal contributions to the community it serves? We asked that question of our group of practitioners and experts (see chapter 1). Their views stressed commitment on the part of station owners, and programming and services that not only serve but involve the community.

Ed Shane believes that

> radio's unique contribution is the social connection and sense of community that shared information creates. The news, weather, and surveillance information (like traffic reports, agri-business reports, etc.) unify us without our being conscious of it. Commercials, too, are important elements of local culture. . . . [R]emotes really do work for the advertiser. . . . Park the station van in front of the grocery store or on the curb by the strip mall, invite people in the audience to participate, and damned if they don't drop by. . . . The retailer of course, gets the benefit of increased traffic . . . The station gets the benefit of one-to-one relationship with its listeners.

Michael Brown also advocates community participation: "The principal contribution is to provide a voice for the local community that can be heard by many, and to potentially lead and organize discussions about community issues (information and editorials). It can provide entertainment specific to the community. . . . Its principal contribution is that it can be a vital, living part of the community."

Jay Allison, Christopher Maxwell, and Christopher Sterling emphasize the idealistic principles that determine the station's services to its community. Allison advocates "intelligent public discourse, promoting civility, building empathy and understanding among people who share a place, informing citizens so they might better contribute to positive change." Maxwell describes the station's ideal contribution as "interaction, reflection, responsiveness." Sterling takes the same approach, citing former FCC commissioner Lee Loevinger's "reflective-projective" theory of broadcasting. Sterling says that stations must do both: "reflecting and projecting local community interests, concerns, special factors, etc."

Lynn Christian describes the need for tolerance and partnership between the owner and the listener, particularly in light of the new services that major communication companies will provide in the future. He says, "The local radio station's voice and personality need to be recognized by local citizens and community leaders as a good friend, not an adversary, who shares with them the concerns of current problems or needs of their region and is willing to actively participate in local affairs in order to make their community a better place to live . . . and then take the issues to the station and put them on the air."

Valerie Geller also stresses the connection between the station and the community, especially through its programming. She states, "In addition to just letting people know what is going on, covering local issues, public service, politics, safety issues and local events going on around town, [stations need to understand that] human beings are tribal. We love stories. We like to be connected to the tribe. As people get busier and tend to live further away from city centers, or move from family, local radio can help provide a feeling of connection to 'tribe' or local community. Particularly local talk shows where audience participation is a part of the show."

Donna Halper stresses "responsiveness and accountability": "Not all communities are alike and radio should still have a duty to serve those who are in the local community, giving them the music they want, the information they want, the opportunity to hear about the issues that affect their lives, etc. When I was growing up, radio was like a best friend. I believe it still should be doing that—befriending the local audience and being a reliable resource for both entertainment and information."

Within a few years after the FCC's implementation of the no-limit ownership rules of the Telecommunications Act of 1996, it was deluged with complaints from consumer groups, ordinary citizens, civic leaders, and members of Congress who had become increasingly concerned with the burgeoning control of America's information by a select few and the disappearing contributions of radio to the health, welfare, and culture of local communities. They called on the FCC to do something about what they felt was an undemocratic concentration of power. The FCC said it would look into reregulation that could prevent further erosion of diversity and localism. In 2003, it issued new regulations—that extended even further the consolidation of American media. While not as dramatic as the 1996 act, the 2003 regulations generated much praise from the media industry, much condemnation from consumer and citizen groups, and much debate in the months before the June 2, 2003, FCC decision and in the months after it.

6 Lights Through the Smoke Screen

Ownership Deregulation and Local Opposition

By the beginning of 2003, the FCC was under great pressure to do something about consolidation. On one hand, it was pressured by the public sector and by some members of Congress who felt that its implementation of the Telecommunications Act of 1996 had resulted in a disintegration of diversity and localism. On the other hand, it was pressured by the media industry, particularly through its lobbying arm, the NAB, and by some members of Congress who felt that its implementation of the 1996 act did not go far enough in opening a deregulated marketplace for media owners. The FCC had been working on the issue for some time and the previous October had released a number of studies mandated by the 1996 act's requirement that the FCC review ownership rules every two years.

When the FCC chair, Michael Powell, announced that the FCC was going to study the issue and propose new ownership rules, both sides immediately gathered their forces to make their concerns and desires known. The regulations the FCC intended to consider further relaxing were some of the antimonopoly restrictions not completely eliminated in 1996, mainly those dealing with duopoly—the number of stations any one entity could own in one market—and cross-ownership, the control of multiple media, such as newspapers, radio, and television stations in the same market.

In January, *USA Today* reported on the issue, emphasizing the importance of the what the FCC might do in its lead paragraph: "An earthquake may soon jolt the media landscape in many communities as a result of a major debate raging at the Federal Communications Commission." The story quoted FCC commissioner Michael Copps: "The rules go to the heart and soul of what our media system is all about. How much localism and regional creativity will we be able to get? And it goes to the nature of political dialogue and the multiplicity of voices. I don't think there's anything as important that the FCC will consider this year."[1]

Those who didn't want any further deregulation of the existing limits were afraid that the changes would result in even less localism and diversity and eliminate local news that might be controversial: "School board and road-building decisions won't get covered. And if election coverage isn't balanced, fewer people will vote. This is about citizens and civic discourse, not consumers and profits." Industry advocates countered that only by allowing newspapers and stations to merge would they be financially strong enough to compete with the growing competition of cable and the Internet. Jeff Baumann, an NAB vice president, said, "Consolidation has been essential in preserving radio, which was cratering before the '96 Act. It preserved a lot of outlets."[2]

Diversity—or the lack of it—appeared to be the key argument for or against the FCC's proposed changes. Even *Business Week,* hardly a foe of big business, expressed concern over the lack of diversity that would result if the FCC approved greater consolidation. In an editorial entitled "Beware Media Consolidation" published just a week before the FCC was to vote on new ownership rules, the magazine warned that "more consolidation of the media is likely to lead to less access to diverse sources of information. Many news outlets already recycle news from network broadcasts and newspapers. In radio, the lifting of ownership caps has clearly cut the diversity of music played."[3]

Ethnic, racial, religious, gender, and other "minority" groups urged action by their members against further relaxation of ownership rules. Protests were held in front of the FCC's headquarters. One of the protest groups was the National Organization for Women, which criticized the FCC for lending a hand to the "giant corporations [that] are squeezing out what little diversity remains in the marketplace" and for facilitating "the media merger free-for-all that is threatening to rob us all of the independent voices, news and ideas that nourish a pluralistic, democratic society."[4] A year later, after the fact, protests concerning the negative impact of the FCC's action on ethnic and racial diversity continued. For example, in January 2004, the Radio-Television News Directors Association (RTNDA) and Unity: Journalists of Color (a consortium of the Asian American Journalists Association, the National Association of Black Journalists, the Native American Journalists Association, and the National Association of Hispanic Journalists) met to deal with the precipitous decline of ethnic and racial diversity and representation in the broadcast newsrooms of local stations throughout the country. Representatives of corporate media responded that they were committed to diversity.[5] Some months later, as this is being written, they were still "studying" the situation. Some months earlier, a similar meeting was held with representatives of women's organizations also included. The meetings seem to go on; diversity seems to decrease.

Weighing In on the Issue

Clear Channel took issue with the FCC's critics. Its chair and CEO, Lowry Mays, testified before a Senate committee in early 2003 that "dedication to local listeners is . . . necessary in order for radio stations to survive because listeners can easily switch to a competitor. . . . Radio has always been focused on local audiences, and successful radio operators remain true to that fundamental rule. That means music play lists are determined based on local audience demands, not by corporate headquarters." He said that radio is the least consolidated segment of the media industries, that Clear Channel's 1,200 stations constitute only 9 percent of all U.S. radio stations.[6]

The NAB urged the FCC to repeal the cross-ownership rule for radio and television. The NAB stated that the rule "is no longer needed to ensure diversity in local markets, but in its current form primarily serves to limit radio station ownership arbitrarily." The NAB added that its studies show that consolidation has enhanced program diversity in local radio markets.[7]

Some opponents of further deregulation pointed to the protests against and negative impact of greater media monopolization in other countries. Clear Channel and associated groups control 80 to 90 percent of New Zealand's radio, which has become highly commercialized and offers "a staple diet of wall-to-wall pop hits from the UK and USA. Lots of alternatives, but very little in the way of choice . . . New Zealand serves as a useful early warning system [to the United States]."[8] In Australia, the United Kingdom, and other countries, similar battles were taking place. Foreign ownership was a key issue in these countries, with American media companies the leading suitors. In the UK, for example, a proposal to waive the rules to permit foreign and multiple ownership was labeled "the Murdoch clause."[9]

While owners supported further deregulation, broadcast employees generally did not. One estimate indicated that since the passage of the 1996 act, consolidation had resulted in the loss of more than 10,000 jobs in radio. Two of the severest critics of big media, Robert W. McChesney and John Nichols, write in their 2002 book *Our Media, Not Theirs* that "the system works to advance the interests of the wealthy few, rather than the many." They believe that "the existing media system in the United States operates in a manner that is highly detrimental to the requirements of a democratic and self-governing society." As a corollary to this, they assert that "the current media system is the direct result of explicit government policies, and that these policies have been made in a corrupt manner with minimal public participation."[10]

It is this latter observation that was the subject of great contentiousness as the FCC moved toward its 2003 decision. FCC chair Powell had the initial review of the ownership rules done behind closed doors. He did not invite any public comment. The two Democrats on the commission, Michael Copps and Jonathan Adelstein, insisted that the potential impact of any FCC action required as much public input as possible. The three Republicans on the five-person commission refused to allow any. Members of Congress asked the FCC to share it findings and deliberations with Congress prior to taking any action; the majority on the commission refused. In the meantime, tens of thousands of letters, e-mails, and phone calls were coming in to the FCC, some 90 percent of which were against further relaxation of ownership rules. Absent public hearings on the issue by the FCC, as called for by Copps and Adelstein, citizen groups throughout the country began holding unofficial meetings on the subject at various universities. The FCC commissioners were invited to attend so they could hear the public's views before the FCC vote in June 2003. Of the thirteen major meetings, either Copps or Adelstein attended every one; Commissioners Powell and Martin attended only the first two and Commissioner Abernathy only one.[11]

At one of the "unofficial" hearings, at Duke University, Commissioner Adelstein stated that

consolidation can have good effects. In radio, as in any other sectors, economies of scale can lead to services that would not otherwise be possible. But consolidation also carries risks. One risk of consolidation to the public interest is the loss of localism, the degree to which news and information is relevant to, and programming is appropriate for, a particular community. Programming that serves the unique needs of local communities by definition varies from community to community. Consolidation, on the other hand, often leads to the homogenization of programming. Another risk of consolidation is the loss of a diverse array of voices and viewpoints over our airwaves. Diverse views fuel our public debate and strengthen our democracy.[12]

Comments from the public were predominantly against further deregulation of ownership limits. Many pointed out that radio already had suffered from much less local content and devotes much less of its resources to local journalism. Many complained that consolidation has given too few entities too much control over our political system. Others pointed out that the principles of localism, competition, and diversity were already too heavily eroded. Some noted that in early 2003, two corporate owners, Clear Channel and Viacom, controlled 42 percent of the listeners and 45 percent of the revenues, with four owners controlling about 70 percent of the market share in almost every local market.[13] Industry supporters, including media representatives, and some FCC commissioners, replied that greater local service would occur by loosening the remaining ownership restrictions because it would enable the multistation owners to bring higher-quality programming to local stations at less cost.[14]

Government Hearings

Pressures mounted on the FCC to hold its own public hearings, with Powell clearly appearing to want to push through the changes in secret and without having to justify actions clearly opposed by the overwhelming majority of Americans. Finally, with public prodding by Copps since September 2002, Powell agreed to have the FCC hold a public hearing. It was in Richmond, Virginia, and was described in *Mediaweek* as "the Michael Copps Show, in honor of the persistent Democrat who forced the meeting upon a reluctant Republican chairman."[15] It was the only official FCC public hearing on the rule changes Powell would allow.

When Copps pressed for more FCC official public meetings because "today we know far too little to make an informed decision," Powell indicated that the thousands of comments from the public and the comments at the Richmond meeting were more than enough for FCC consideration of the public's opinions in making its decision.[16]

Although the FCC may implement congressional law and case law (decisions regarding media promulgated by federal courts, definitively by the Supreme Court), Congress still retains authority over communications and can pass new laws at any time. Prior to the FCC June 2 decision on new ownership rules, some members of Congress were already considering legislation to prevent the FCC from permitting further consolidation or even to make the FCC pull back on some of its earlier deregulatory actions. Some members of Congress who were involved with communications committees and legislation, such as Senator Ernest Hollings and Representative John Conyers, called for congressional action. Representative Bernie Sanders introduced a bill that would prevent the FCC from changing the owner-ship rules and would authorize congressional hearings designed to produce new legislation on the matter. Sanders argued that "these media companies have been so greedy and so irresponsible that people across the country are saying: We've got to do something about them. The good news is that Congress can do something. We have the authority to develop regulations to limit monopolies."[17] (See appendix 6.1 for the full statement of Representative Sanders regarding "The Growing Concentration of Media Ownership.")

But Congress did nothing official, although about 150 members of Congress, liberals and conservatives from both parties, directed the FCC not to make any changes in the ownership rules. A broad coalition of organizations, including disparate and sometimes opposing groups such as the Leadership Conference on Civil Rights, the U.S. Conference of Catholic Bishops, the National Rifle Association, and the National Organization for Women, lobbied against a change. Various estimates place the number of e-mails and other communications received by the FCC and members of Congress protesting any further relaxation in ownership rules in the millions. Despite the strong national outcry, however, on June 2, 2003, the FCC issued new ownership rules. The vote was three to two, on strict Republican-Democrat party lines. Both radio and television were affected by the new rules.

Because there already were no limits on the number of radio stations a single entity could own nationwide, such ownership couldn't be expanded. The FCC retained the previous limit on ownership of radio stations in one market: (1) in a market with forty-five or more stations, a single entity could own eight stations, no more than five of which could be AM or, alternatively, FM; (2) in a market with thirty to forty-four stations, one owner could have seven stations, four of which could be in one service, AM or FM; (3) where there are fifteen to twenty-nine stations, one company may own six, with a limit of four in one service; in markets of fourteen or fewer stations, one owner may have five, with only three either AM or FM. A number of companies had already exceeded these limits in some markets; these were grandfathered in for an indefinite time. In addition, the FCC defined "market" in a way that enabled owners to exceed the eight-station limit. A study by the Center for Public Integrity, released in October 2003, showed thirty-four markets in which the eight-station limit was surpassed, with station ownership ranging from nine to fifteen. In all but six of those markets, Clear Channel was the conglomerate owner. Its regions of top market ownership, were Washington, DC-MD-VA-WV, fifteen;

Pittsburgh, PA, fourteen; Detroit, MI, thirteen; twelve in each of the following markets—Cleveland-Lorain-Elyria, OH; Greeley, CO; Newark, NJ; Newburgh, NY-PA; Riverside–San Bernardino, CA; and it owned eleven in Boston, MA-NH; Chattanooga, TN-GA; Cincinnati, OH-KY-IN; Grand Rapids, Muskegon-Holland, MI; Lexington, KY; Los Angeles–Long Beach, CA; Mansfield, OH; Santa Barbara–Santa Maria–Lompoc, CA; and Scranton–Wilkes-Barre–Hazelton, PA. The CPI study also found that the highest concentration of ownership by one company was in the smaller markets.[18]

The major changes for radio related to cross-ownership, where local stations could become part of local conglomerates of various media services, in most cases controlled by national conglomerates. The FCC maintained restrictions on cross-ownership in small markets of three or fewer television stations. In mid-sized markets, with between four and eight television stations, a single entity was now permitted to choose one of the three following options: (1) own one or more daily newspapers, one television station, and up to half the number of radio stations permitted in the local ownership rules noted above; or (2) own one or more daily newspapers and up to the limit of radio stations permitted in the given market, but no ownership of any television stations; or (3) own as many radio stations as permissible in the given market and, in markets of five or more television stations, own up to two TV stations. All limits were lifted on single ownership of newspapers, television stations, and radio stations in markets with nine or more TV stations.

The new rules drastically revised the limitations on national and local ownership of television stations. The previous limit on the percentage of the national population one owner could reach with an unlimited number of television stations was 35 percent; the FCC raised it to 45 percent. The duopoly prohibition limiting one entity to one television station in a market (ownership of two in certain overlapping circumstances was allowed) was relaxed. One company could now own two television stations in markets with five or more TV stations, and three television stations markets with eighteen or more, as long as only one of the stations was in the top four in the ratings. At the time, five companies already owned over 90 percent of the television stations in the United States—AOL–Time Warner, Murdoch's NewsCorp, General Electric, the Disney Corporation, and Viacom.

Reaction and Distraction

The response to the FCC's action was immediate. Industry representatives praised it, citizen groups condemned it, and many newspapers, particularly in local markets, editorialized against it. Many members of Congress, Republicans and Democrats, were critical. One report put it this way: "The heat is mounting against conglomerated radio. Some powerful senators, including Sen. John McCain, are beginning to wonder if Clear Channel and other deeply consolidated radio companies such as Citadel Communications are becoming too powerful. The senators' claims stem from what many consider to be a lack of diversity in radio programming. These senators say this fails to create a diverse dialogue in each community and could ultimately be viewed as a form of censorship."[19]

Ralph Nader expressed the feelings of consumer organizations generally, concluding that the ruling would not only permit giant media moguls to add to their radio, TV, and newspaper ownership throughout the country, but would "close more doors and ideas, speakers, writers, artists and small businesses either because doing so makes them more profits or the moguls disagree with their various viewpoints." Nader quoted Clear Channel CEO Lowry Mays as saying "We're not in the business of providing news and information. We're not in the business of providing well-researched music. We're simply in the business of selling our customers products." Nader also noted that the multitude who protested the FCC's ruling "want to hear other voices beyond the canned entertainment and political party lines that they are receiving" and that the people must continue to fight for mass media competition, diversity, and localism.[20]

John Hogan, the CEO of Clear Channel's radio operations, looked at the FCC's decision quite differently. He said that prior to the 1996 act a significant number of radio stations were losing money and in danger of going off the air. He said that deregulation and consolidation saved the radio industry. In his opinion, radio became more diverse, not less, because a single owner of multiple stations in a market will program different formats on the stations whereas a number of different owners will compete with each other with the same format. He did not think that Clear Channel's ownership of 1,229 stations at the time constituted "a consolidated industry" because it amounted to less than 12 percent of all radio stations in the country. He also avowed that he and Clear Channel placed "absolute" importance on localism and employed 900 program directors who are based in "local markets, their home markets" and who place an "incredible emphasis on providing local news, weather, traffic, sports information, school closings, blood drives, all of the things people want to know about their local communities."[21]

Local reports consistently took issue with Hogan's claim that Clear Channel was dedicated to localism. For example, later in 2003, the Internet publication BusinessNorth, covering Duluth, northern Minnesota, and northern Wisconsin, reported, "The world's largest radio company wants to be your local radio friend. So then, why has Clear Channel Communications dumped local talk radio shows on its newly acquired stations and replaced them with . . . a sports talk program originating 150 miles away . . . ?" The report also noted that the "entertainment conglomerate owns 1,225 U.S. radio stations and another 250 overseas. 36 U.S. TV stations; an outdoor advertising subsidiary; and an entertainment group that books live concerts, Broadway productions and sports events and manages 130 concert venues."[22]

A month before Hogan's comments, Univision, owner of fifty-three television stations at the time, announced that it was adding, with FCC approval, more than sixty radio stations to its holdings by merging with the Hispanic Broadcasting Corporation. Hispanic Broadcasting's biggest shareholder was Clear Channel Communications.[23]

As expected, the commission put a spin on its actions that made it appear that removing further the limits on duopolies and cross-ownership would, in fact, promote localism rather than further stifle it. In releasing its new ownership rules, the FCC made the following statement in a press release (for the full text of the press release and a summary of the new ownership rules, see appendix 6.2):

new limits on broadcast ownership are carefully balanced to protect diversity, localism and competition in the American media system . . . [that] will foster a vibrant marketplace of ideas, promote vigorous competition, and ensure that broadcasters continue to serve the needs and interests of their local communities. . . . The Report and Order adopted today is based on a thorough assessment of the impact of ownership rules on promoting competition, diversity, and localism. . . . The FCC strongly reaffirmed its goal of promoting localism through limits on ownership of broadcast outlets. Localism remains a bedrock principle that continues to benefit Americans in important ways. The FCC has sought to promote localism to the greatest extent possible through its broadcast ownership limits that are aligned with stations' incentives to serve the needs and interests of their local communities. . . . [The FCC] found that the current radio ownership limits continue to be needed to promote competition among local radio stations. Competitive radio markets ensure that local stations are responsive to local listener needs and tastes. By guaranteeing a substantial number of independent radio voices, this rule will also promote viewpoint diversity among local radio owners."[24]

Most critics couldn't match the rhetoric to the actions. Some compared it to an *Alice in Wonderland* fantasy, where up is down and black is white and words and actions go in opposite directions. DePaul University College of Law dean emeritus John C. Roberts, an expert on communications law and former Washington communications attorney, was one of the critics. He said, "Perhaps the most disturbing thing about these sweeping changes is the blatantly disingenuous, if not dishonest, explanations being given by FCC Chairman Michael Powell and his supporters for their actions." Roberts expressed concern that the

> Bush administration is pursuing radically conservative, business-oriented policies despite the fact that a majority of the American people apparently disagree with that course. . . . Comments from ordinary citizens, as well as many from consumer and communication watchdog groups . . . virtually all opposed easing the rules. Yet, then media conglomerates, supported only by the media conglomerates themselves, adopted new rules anyway. . . . In face of overwhelming opposition to its proposed changes, Powell would now like us to believe that he actually supports rules against concentration of the media, but was forced to take these deregulatory actions by the Congress and the courts. These justifications, to put it kindly, are highly questionable.[25]

Commissioners Copps and Adelstein strongly dissented not only on the content of the new rules, but on what they believed was a faulty process leading to the FCC's decision. They maintained that the new rules would result in an even greater and excessive concentration of control of the media by fewer and fewer corporations, and a further erosion of diversity and localism. Copps holds that the change in the rules "empowers America's new media elite with unacceptable levels of influence over the media on which our society and our democracy so heavily depend" and that the FCC's decision will result in "centralization, not localism . . . uniformity, not diversity . . . monopoly and oligopoly, not competition"[26] (for the text of Copps's dissent, see appendix 6.3). Adelstein predicted that "when this full document is finally made public, I expect it will be torn apart by media experts, academics, consumer groups, activists and, most of all, the American people. They will find it riddled with contradictions, inconsistencies, false assumptions and outcome-driven thinking."[27] He called the ruling "the most sweeping and destructive rollback of consumer protection rules in the history of American broadcasting" and said, "It violates every tenet of a free democratic society to let a handful of powerful companies control our media. The public has a right to be informed by a diversity of viewpoints so they can make up their own minds. Without a diverse, independent media, citizen access to information crumbles, along with political and social participation. For the sake of our democracy, we should encourage the widest possible dissemination of free expression through the public airwaves."[28]

By contrast, Commissioner Kathleen Abernathy, who supported Powell in further deregulation, said, "For me, given the rules we adopt today, the breakneck pace of technological development, and the ever-increasing number of pipelines into consumers' homes, it is simply not possible to monopolize the flow of information in today's world."[29]

Public Opposition and Government Initiatives

By the time the rule-making process was completed, the FCC had received over two million communications opposing its further loosening of the ownership rules and asking it to preserve localism. In the months following the June 2 decision, "localism" became the battle cry for both consumers and conglomerates, the former insisting that it was being consistently eroded and the latter insisting that it was being strengthened.

Consumer organizations appealed the June 2 rulings to the U.S. Circuit Court of Appeals (in Philadelphia), which, in September, issued an order staying the implementation of the new rules until it could decide the case. The plaintiffs argued that the new regulations would even further limit the diversity of information and other programming available to the public, such diversity and localism mandated by the Communications Act of 1934. The FCC, on the other hand, argued that it had the right and obligation to eliminate rules and regulations that it deemed to be outdated. In a filing on August 6, the FCC claimed the stay prevented the commission "from implementing other rule changes that this court upheld," and specifically asked the court to reconsider its stay of the new radio ownership rules.[30] While the court considered the case, the battle continued to rage.

Powell was under increasingly harsh criticism from the public and from a majority of the Congress; the media corporations appeared to be the principal supporters of both his rhetoric and actions. Finally, in what was perceived as a thinly veiled attempt to defuse the growing criticism of his leadership of the FCC, Powell announced that he was setting up a task force to study localism in response to the concerns expressed by the public. "We heard the voice of public concern loud and clear that localism remains a core concern of our public," Powell said. "And thus, I think it's time the Commission addresses it head on."[31]

The Localism Task Force was announced on August 20, 2003. Composed of staff members of the FCC, its stated purpose was to study what needed to be done to make sure that radio and television stations adequately served their local communities. This task force was formed along with one charged with studying how to increase the participation of racial and ethnic minorities, women, and small owners in the media. Powell also said he wanted the commission to speed up the issuance of licenses for low-power radio stations, which, because of their small broadcasting range, are operated locally and serve local needs. Powell said that the localism task force would seek "more direct ways to promote localism" and would look into laws and regulations relating to "public interest obligations, license renewals, and protecting the rights of local stations to make programming decisions for their communities."[32] The task force was scheduled to hold public hearings on localism in six cities in various parts of the country. Powell announced the task force and hearings after Commissioner Copps announced that, absent any FCC action on the localism, he would personally set up and hold hearings throughout the country.

Powell emphasized that these studies did not suggest that the FCC would back away from the June 2 loosening of ownership rules. And, inexplicably to many, he said that the study of localism in no way relates to the ownership rules.

Public reaction was swift and sharp. Powell did receive support from the industry for this initiative, the NAB, for example, stating that it (the NAB) "welcomes as review of the public services performed day in and day out by free, over-the-air broadcasters."[33] The rest of the United States, by and large, saw Powell's actions a ploy. Commissioner Copps said the study should have been done before the June 2 decisions. "You cannot use a blanket of study to quell the fire of public outrage about increasing the control of the public's airwaves by fewer and fewer conglomerates," he said. "What if we complete these studies and find out that localism is not served by consolidation? It will be too late."[34] Copps added, "We should have vetted these issues before we voted. Instead, we voted; now we are going to vet. This is a policy of ready, fire, aim." Copps concluded, "This proposal is a day late and a dollar short. We should have heeded the calls from over two million Americans and so many members of Congress expressing concern about the impact of media concentration on localism and diversity before we rushed to a vote."[35]

Among those members of Congress who were skeptical of Powell's motives in the localism study initiative was Senator Byron Dorgan, who commented, "It is a very curious strategy for the chairman to change the rules in a way that will dramatically damage localism and then, nearly three months later, propose a process to examine how those rules might affect localism."[36]

Other criticism was more harsh. Mark Cooper of the Consumer Federation of America declared that "talking about new rules to protect media localism, particularly when those rules creep into the area of content regulation, is merely an effort to divert attention from badly reasoned and badly written ownership rules."[37] Cooper added, "The only purpose of Mr. Powell's announcement was to try to defuse the political firestorm that erupted after their horrible decision of June 2."[38]

Jeff Chester of the Center for Digital Democracy said of Powell's announcement that it "is absurd on the face of it. This is a man who spent 18 months looking at the issue. Only now, after there's a unanimous uproar, does he decide to reexamine the issue. He is trying to shore up his support in Congress."[39] *Variety* magazine, noting that "critics of the new ownership rules cite serious lack of local programming and news as one of the main reasons why the regs need to be tightened, not relaxed," quoted Jonathan Rintels of the Center for the Creative Community, who called the localism study a "tacit admission that its media ownership rulemaking was fatally flawed." Rintels added that "unless the FCC stays the effective date of its new rules until these studies are completed, what the chairman proposes is akin to handing Fox (and other nets) the key to the media henhouse and then studying how many chickens they eat."[40]

In October, FCC commissioner Kathleen Abernathy, who had voted with Powell, came to his defense. She noted the "crescendo of concern voiced by members of Congress and the public."

> An important aspect of this concern relevant to the radio industry is the perceived loss of local control, local input, and locally-based programming that is seen as an unintended consequence of allowing licensees to own large numbers of stations nationally. . . . The fact that one company owns a hundred stations, or many more, isn't necessarily a bad thing, given that there are currently over 13,000 radio stations on the air. But, when one company can own 7 of the 8 stations in the local market, we have a problem. . . . Now, to the extent that increased ownership may be having unintended adverse effects on the amount or type of local programming, I do not believe that structural limits on ownership are the best way to address these concerns. . . . I therefore support Chairman Powell's recent announcement of a Localism Task Force, by which the Commission will take a close look at precisely how broad-

casters are serving their local communities. We can then determine what, if anything, must be done to promote this goal.[41]

At one of the task force's public hearings, the sentiments of the attendees were not so supportive. In San Antonio in February 2004, many in the overflow crowd vented their anger not only at the FCC but, as well, at their hometown-based conglomerate, Clear Channel Communications. In the crowd were only a smattering of supporters of the FCC's 2003 loosening of the ownership rules. One report of the San Antonio meeting said that musicians from around the state who came to the meeting "are blaming federal deregulation of broadcast media for shoving local talent off the nation's airwaves" and that "scores of walk-up witnesses" expressed outrage about "local radio news coverage—citizens wagged their fingers and even crooned about the impact of media consolidation among TV, radio and newspaper outlets."[42]

FCC chair Powell conceded that the Localism Task Force was prompted by complaints about the June 2, 2003, decisions, but stated that the FCC, whatever the task force discovered, would not go back on its ownership deregulation. Critics responded that localism and media ownership cannot be separated.[43]

A Reversal under Pressure

In June 2004, the Third U.S. Circuit Court of Appeals in Philadelphia issued its decision on the suit filed in September 2003 by consumer groups, including the Media Access Project and Consumers Union, against the FCC's June 2003 further deregulation of the ownership rules. The court "reversed the rules changes that would have allowed companies to own more radio and television stations in the same market . . . but also found that the FCC was within its rights to repeal a blanket prohibition on companies owning both a newspaper and a television station in the same city."[44] The court did ask the FCC to reconsider its cross-ownership action, especially in terms of the diversity principles the FCC used in abolishing the cross-ownership ban. In specific relation to radio, the court affirmed the FCC's use of Arbitron's (the radio rating system) definition of markets. But the court instructed the FCC to review its duopoly ownership caps by considering audience shares and other competitive factors.[45]

The Media Access Project head, Andrew Jay Schwartzman, stated that "the court recognized that debate and democratic values are more important than letting big media corporations grow bigger." The Consumer Union's Gene Kimmelman said that the court's ruling is "a complete repudiation of rules that would allow one or two media giants to dominate the most important sources of local news and information in almost every community in America." FCC Commissioner Copps, who strongly opposed the 2003 rules, stated,

We have now heard from the American people, Congress, and the courts. The rush to media consolidation approved by the FCC last June was wrong as a matter of law and policy. The Commission has a second chance to do the right thing. We must immediately move forward and redesign our media policy. This time we must include the American people in the process instead of shutting them out. We must rediscover our respect for core values of localism, diversity, and competition. We must protect and work to expand the multiplicity of voices and choices that support our marketplace of ideas and that sustain American democracy and creativity. To do all this we must engage the American people directly and gather a far more complete record of the impact of media consolidation on local communities. Therefore, the FCC should immediately take three steps. First, we should issue a notice confirming that until new rules are adopted, we will continue to apply the limits that were in effect prior to the June 2, 2003, decision. Second, I call upon the Commission to schedule a series of hearings across the country designed to give citizens true access to the decision makers at the Agency, and seek to gain a better understanding of the impact of media concentration on our communities. These hearings should begin immediately, and certainly no later than 30 days from now. Third, we need independent research studies on media concentration in a variety of markets so we can make a decision that has a more solid foundation.[46]

FCC commissioner Jonathan Adelstein, who had also strongly opposed the 2003 decision, stated his reactions to the court's findings as well.

This week, both Congress and the courts repudiated the FCC's reckless decision on media ownership. It no longer works to say "Congress and the courts made us do it," because the Commission has now been reversed by both. They got it right, and the FCC got it wrong. This is a vindication for the vast majority of the American public who opposed these rule changes. The court largely undid what could have been the most destructive rollback of media ownership protections in the history of American broadcasting. We now need to work together on a bipartisan basis to fix the rules so they comply with the court order and respond to Congressional and public concerns. We need a more inclusive discussion than we had last time in ways to move forward. This time the Commission should truly act in the interest of the American public rather than the corporate interests of media giants who want to get even bigger.[47]

Mark Cooper of the Consumer Federation of America thinks, "Public outcry was essential in bringing this issue to the forefront," and he urged consumers to continue to make their concerns known to the FCC and to the White House. He concluded that the FCC's actions "were never supported by public opinion."[48]

Newspaper and media conglomerate sources, while unhappy with the reversal of the FCC's duopoly expansion, were pleased with the cross-ownership decision and said they would continue to press for its inclusion in the new rules. The court continued its order blocking implementation of any of the FCC's rule changes pending an appeal to the Supreme Court.[49]

Shortly after the court's ruling, the FCC issued a Notice of Inquiry (NOI) on localism in broadcasting. Whether it was an intended follow-up on the Localism Task Force's work or a preemptive action to ward off increasing criticism by Congress as well as by citizen groups of the FCC's stance was arguable. In any event, the NOI suggested that the FCC appeared to be inclined to take some action regarding localism. FCC chair Powell maintained,

> Fostering localism is one of this Commission's core missions and one of three policy goals, along with diversity and competition, which have driven much of our radio and television broadcast regulation during the last 70 years. Today's Notice of Inquiry is another step in that long legacy and will serve as a primary information gathering source for the work of the Commission's Localism Task Force. Along with several public hearings, three of which have been conducted, to date, the Task Force will take the information filed in this NOI and the results of its own studies designed to measure localism in broadcasting and advise the Commission on steps it can take and, if warranted, will make legislative recommendations to Congress that would strengthen localism in broadcasting.[50]

Powell further asserted that the media had made great strides in serving local needs, especially with the addition of new media services including new broadcast stations, cable, satellite, and the Internet. He averred that the public was currently getting more local content than at any time in media history, but that broadcasters could provide even more.[51] The NAB immediately issued a statement of support for Powell's initiative, stating,

NAB looks forward to participating in the FCC's inquiry into broadcast localism, and we strongly believe that objective observers will conclude that America's local over-the-air stations have an unmatched record of community service. From telethons to tornado warnings, from Amber Alerts to school closing announcements, radio and television stations provide leading-edge local programming that has made the U.S. system of broadcasting the envy of the world.[52]

FCC commissioner Copps urged that the localism studies not be separated from the larger issue of media ownership and asked Powell to hold town meetings throughout the country to "get out of Washington and learn what ordinary citizens have to say."[53]

At the same time, the NAB sent a letter from its president to all member stations endorsing a letter from the FCC's Powell and the chair of the Senate Commerce Committee, John McCain, urging broadcasters to "ensure they are providing local communities with significant information on the political issues facing the community." NAB president Fritts added, "It is my personal belief that local broadcasters do an outstanding job" covering politics.[54]

Listening Locally

In mid-2004, the Localism Task Force began holding the six hearings around the country. The huge demand by citizens to make their concerns known prompted the FCC to set up a ticket-for-admission system on a first-come, first-served basis.[55] In May 2004, at one of the task force meetings in Rapid City, South Dakota, FCC chair Powell not only was criticized by participants because of his stand on ownership but was the subject of anger for flying back to Washington before the end of the three-day meeting, explicitly stating that he would not give the keynote address at the FCC's Indian Telecommunications Initiative workshop, nor would he participate in the Localism Task Force's hearings.[56] In July 2004, at the only Localism Task Force meeting on the West Coast, at Monterey, a raucous crowed of several hundred cheered Commissioners Copps and Adelstein for their strong stand on localism and booed representatives of the broadcast industry. Copps decried the increasing consolidation and said, "We need to start protecting the people's interest in the people's airwaves." Various presentations gave evidence that local stations throughout the country do not spend enough programming time on issues such as local politics, minority affairs, children's educational programs, and local musical performers. The prospect of automation precluding emergency information to the public was also noted. Broadcasters at the meeting insisted that they provided local service because it is good business to do so. "Politics are the lifeblood of local democracy," local station manager Joseph Heston said. "Localism is what sells tickets."[57] FCC chair Powell did not attend this meeting, either, although he did find time to attend meetings with industry leaders in the Monterey area. Questions accelerated concerning the sincerity of the FCC's leadership on localism.

At the end of 2004, the issue remained in the forefront. FCC commissioners Copps and Adelstein convened a forum on media concentration at Hamline University in Minnesota to provide further opportunity for citizen comment from a diversity of sources.[58] The NAB, joined by hundreds of radio and television stations, filed comments on the FCC's localism inquiry. The comments stressed the commitment of the broadcast industry to serve the needs and interests of its local communities and included examples of local programming ranging from coverage of community events to airtime for local musicians. "The NAB added that any rules related to localism requirements might well impinge on broadcasters' First Amendment rights."[59]

Music is the staple of radio broadcasting and, in addition to complaints about the lack of localism and diversity in news and public affairs, most listeners expressed increasing concern with the lack of localism and diversity in the choice of music. Let's look next at what has happened to localism in music as part of the increasingly quieted voice of local radio.

Appendix 6.1

The Growing Concentration of Media Ownership

The following conversation took place on the House floor during a session of Special Orders between Congressman Sanders and fellow members concerned with the upcoming June 2, 2003, Federal Communications Commission vote concerning media deregulation.

The SPEAKER pro tempore. Under the Speaker's announced policy of January 7, 2003, the gentleman from Vermont (Mr. Sanders) is recognized for 60 minutes as the designee of the minority leader.

MR. SANDERS. Mr. Speaker, in my view the issue that I and some of my colleagues are about to discuss, which is concentration of ownership in the media and the implications of more media deregulation as proposed by the Bush administration and FCC Chairman Michael Powell, is one of the very most important issues facing this country. One of the ways that we can know how important this issue is precisely by how relatively little media attention has been paid to it. The growing concentration of corporate ownership of media in the United States is in fact one of the least discussed major issues in this country because the media itself is in a major conflict of interest and chooses not to discuss it.

As bad as the situation is today, and when we examine this chart we will find out how bad it is, how few major multinational conglomerates like Viacom, AOL–Time Warner, Disney, Clear Channel, News Corporation and a few others, to what degree a few major corporations control what we see, hear and read, as bad as it is, it is likely to become much worse, much more dangerous for the future of democracy in this country if, as is proposed on June 2, the FCC votes for further media deregulation, regulations that have been on the books for years to protect localism, to protect diversity of opinion, to protect the clash of ideas.

Needless to say, there are many people and many organizations all across this country regardless of political orientation who are strongly opposed to changing these regulations and who do not want to see more media consolidation in this country. Millions of Americans do not want to see the handful of corporations who determine what we see, hear and read become three, become two, become one perhaps as a result of mergers and takeovers. These groups range across the political spectrum from

---

Source: Web site of U.S. representative Bernie Sanders, "The Growing Concentration of Media Ownership," May 15, 2003, http://bernie.house.gov/statements/20030520172034.asp.

progressive groups to conservative groups. According to the Associated Press yesterday, and I quote, "'The National Rifle Association joined the ranks of consumer groups, musicians, writers and academics who oppose easing the restrictions.

"The NRA asked its members to write Powell," that is the FCC Chairman, "and lawmakers in support of the existing rules, said Wayne LaPierre, the NRA's executive vice president." Quote from Mr. LaPierre: "These big media conglomerates are already pushing out diversity of political opinion."

Further, we have heard recently from organizations representing black broadcasters and Latino broadcasters. We have heard from musicians. We have heard from a wide spectrum of people who say what America is about is freedom, and we cannot have freedom if we do not have a clash of ideas. And it will be very dangerous for this country when a tiny number of multi-multibillion-dollar international conglomerates own virtually all of our newspapers, all of our radio stations, all of our television stations, all of our book publishing companies, all of the companies that produce the films that we observe.

At issue now is the FCC's review of rules that seek to protect localism so that back home they will have local news, that there will be a local radio station telling them what is going on in their community, that will preserve competition and diversity. These rules, among other things, currently limit a single corporation from dominating local TV markets. Do people want to live in a community where all of the local television stations are owned by one company? These rules that we have in place right now will prevent the merging of local television stations, radio stations, and a newspaper. Do people want to live in a community where one company owns their local TV station, owns the newspaper and owns radio stations? Do they think they are going to hear different points of view when that happens?

These regulations deal with the merging of two major television networks so that we will have just a few networks controlling all of the TV stations facing our country. Honest people might have differences of opinion on this issue, but one would think that there would be massive amounts of public discussion all over America. I can tell the Members that in my small State, the State of Vermont, which is one of the smallest States in this country, we recently had a town meeting on this issue, and 600 people came out to hear FCC Commissioner Michael Copps talk about that issue. We should be having town meetings like that all over America, and in my view and in the view of many of us in Congress, the FCC should delay making any decisions on June 2 and let the American people get involved in the process.

Mr. Speaker, it is my privilege now to yield to the gentlewoman from California (Ms. Woolsey) who has been very active on this issue. I thank the gentlewoman for being with us.

MS. WOOLSEY. Mr. Speaker, I thank the gentleman for yielding. Mr. Speaker, I am here today to join my colleagues and to thank the gentleman from Vermont (Mr. Sanders) for pulling this evening together so that we can speak out against a threat to America. It is not a threat to American lives, but a threat to American values. It is a threat to everything that this Nation stands for, every principle that this Nation was founded on, and every memory of every soldier that has fought and died or been harmed for the free exchange of ideas.

Today bureaucrats of the FCC and the overwhelming complacency of this Congress threaten that freedom. This past Monday I hosted a forum in my district, which is the two counties north of San Francisco across the Golden Gate Bridge. We had a forum with Federal Communications Commissioner Michael Copps about his agency's rules on media ownership. Nearly 400 of my constituents at 1 o'clock in afternoon, packed into an auditorium at Dominican University in San Rafael, were there to declare their opinions about what the FCC rules on media ownership will mean, and their opinion was that this is extremely important. This is an issue, however, that has been underreported by the very media that will be most affected.

In fact, as proof of that very underreporting, yesterday over a dozen concerned Democratic Members of Congress held a press conference right here on the Hill on the issue of media consolidation. I suppose no surprise, but not one member of the broadcast press showed up, and until a reporter from Roll Call, our newspaper here on the Hill, came to experience a press conference without press, we did not have anybody. So we disbanded and came back in honor of the person that was there from Roll Call.

It reminds me of the cliché about a tree falling in the forest. If Members of Congress speak out about media ownership, and the media does not cover the event, is democracy already dead?

No newspaper, radio station, or TV network is perfect. Allowing single corporations to monopolize the information that average Americans receive give big corporations like Rupert Murdoch and Ted Turner absolutely too much power.

On June 2 the Federal Communications Commission has scheduled a vote on new regulations that would break down the decades-long firewall between media ownership and single markets. Gone will be the prohibition against corporations owning newspapers and TV stations in the same town or cable TV networks and TV stations in the same town. Gone also will be the limits on number of TV stations and cable stations a corporation can own nationally.

The threat of a veto by President Clinton kept these rules from being changed in 1996, but now under the Bush Administration, FCC Chairman Michael Powell and a Republican majority on the Commission that is drunk on the ideology of the free market, these changes are very likely to be approved.

It is a sham and it is a shame that in a Nation of 280 million people, the FCC has held only one official hearing on this subject, just outside the Beltway in Virginia. If it was not for the FCC Commissioners, Commissioner Michael Copps and Commissioner Jonathan Adelstein, it is really doubtful that this discussion would have gone beyond a few lobbyists and public interest activists in the first place.

Since radio ownership regulations were relaxed under the Telecommunications Act in 1996, radio ownership diversity has decreased in our Nation by at least one-third. In the San Francisco market alone, seven stations are now owned by Clear Channel Communications, seven by Infinity Broadcasting, and three by ABC.

Across the Nation 10 companies broadcast to two-thirds of the Nation's radio audience and receive two thirds of the broadcast revenues. Hear me: Ten companies broadcast to two-thirds of the Nation's audience and receive two-thirds of the broadcast revenues. That is not okay, and it is going to get worse.

Has the quality of radio broadcasting improved because of these changes? Is there more local programming, more local news, a greater variety of programming? Is there free flow of information? Or is there censorship? Just ask the Dixie Chicks. They know what censorship is.

Power over ideas should not be subject to individuals with only ideas of profit on their mind. In America ideas are not just another commodity like butter or steel or cloth. Ideas are the lifeblood of our Nation. The FCC should be defending the free exchange of ideas, not giving corporate executives, not always too different from Enron's Ken Lay, not giving them the power to shut off the flow of ideas to American citizens.

Mr. Speaker, my colleagues and I are cosponsoring House Resolution 218 that calls on the FCC to examine and inform the public of the consequences of the new round of deregulation. It asks that the FCC allow for extensive public review and comment on any proposed changes to media ownership rules before issuing a final rule.

The least the FCC and Michael Powell can do is allow the people of America the opportunity to speak their mind about the elimination of freely exchanging ideas.

I thank the gentleman from Vermont for doing this Special Order.

MR. SANDERS. Mr. Speaker, I thank the gentlewoman.

Before I yield to the gentlewoman of Illinois (Ms. Schakowsky), I want to just emphasize a point that the gentlewoman from California (Ms. Woolsey) just made. I think sometimes when people turn on a television or they pick up a newspaper they say, well, a company owns this newspaper, and a lot of companies put out different newspapers, different types of television stations, and so forth and so on. What people are not aware of is the degree, the number of separate companies that one large corporation owns.

Let me start off with an example and go to Viacom. I suspect that most people have never even heard of Viacom. Who is Viacom? What is Viacom? So let me tell the Members a little bit about Viacom. Viacom is a huge multinational corporation that owns TV stations, radio stations, TV networks, and many other media outlets. For example, this is just Viacom, just Viacom. When we turn on CBS network, that is Viacom. We turn on the UPN network, Viacom. MTV, Nickelodeon, TV Land, CMT, TNN, VH1, Showtime, Movie Channel, Sundance Channel, Flick, Black Entertainment, Comedy Central. One would think they are watching different companies. They are not. That is Viacom.

They get off the TV now, drive into work, turn on the radio. There are 180 Infinity radio stations owned by Viacom.

What about local television stations? We have got the big CBS. What about the local television stations? They must be locally owned. Wrong. We have 34 stations that Viacom owns in Philadelphia, in Boston, in Dallas, in Detroit, Miami, Pittsburgh, among other places.

They are in radio. They are in television. But at least when I go from the movies I am getting away from this corporation, right? Not quite. When we watch Paramount Pictures, it is Viacom. MTV Films, Viacom. Nickelodeon, Contentville, the Free Press, MTV books, Nickelodeon books, Simon & Schuster.

I am into music now. That is not Viacom. Wrong. Famous music publishers: Pocket Books, Viacom. Star Trek franchise; Scribner's Publishers, Viacom. Touchstone, Spelling Entertainment, Big Ticket TV, Viacom Productions, King World Productions, all one company. One company. And they say it is not enough. We do not own enough media. We need to own more media. Break down the regulations so we can own more television stations, we can own more book publishing companies, and so forth. A very dangerous trend.

Now it gives me a great pleasure to yield to the gentlewoman from Illinois (Ms. Schakowsky), clearly one of the outstanding Members of the U.S. House of Representatives.

MS. SCHAKOWSKY. Mr. Speaker, I thank the gentleman from Vermont (Mr. Sanders) for giving me this opportunity because it is not every day that we get to come down to the floor of the House and defend the essentials of our democracy, to talk about defending the Constitution of the United States, the First Amendment, freedom of speech, freedom of the press.

It is the very core values of this country that we are talking about today. This is definitely the most important telecommunications issue of our time and, more than that, whether or not ordinary people are going to have access to divergent views. This is a value that our country has embraced from its beginning that we should have the opportunity to hear different voices, to get different opinions and make up our own mind.

So I am here today to call on Federal Communications Commission, its Chairman Mr. Powell, and President Bush to listen to the American people, to support media diversity and localism, and to not allow even more concentration of the media.

The Bush administration and the FCC have tuned out public voices and tuned in Rupert Murdoch. I suppose the gentleman will probably talk about him, and media barons, because people need to know who is controlling the messages that they hear when they want to get the news, when they want to know what is going on in the world and in our country.

People in my district and around the country are demanding that the FCC hear their voices. That is why just last week the Chicago City Council unanimously approved, by a vote of 50 to 0, a resolution that urges the FCC to strengthen existing media ownership rules, not to weaken them.

Today and yesterday I received 1,000 e-mails from my constituents. I am going to read one of them:

> Dear Congresswoman Schakowsky, Congress shall pass no law restricting the right to free speech. Letting one big business control all available news organs for any locality is a monopoly. Since when do corporations have a right to control our free speech? Since when do their rights trump the average citizen's? Is the Bush administration trying every means conceivable to control our means of debate and dissent?
>
> I urge you and your colleagues in Congress to promote a diverse balance and competitive media. Please stop the FCC rule change on June 2nd.

We allow media companies to use the airwaves in exchange for their assurance that they are serving the public interest, and it is the FCC's job to make sure that is so. Please hold the FCC to its mandate and oppose the rule change.

This is from one woman in my district. But imagine now two full reams of paper from individuals in my district with the very same message. They are sounding the alarm.

A free and open media is essential to our democracy. It promotes civic discussion, encourages public participation and policy debates, ensures representation of ideological, cultural and geographic diversity. I cannot overstate the importance of the FCC's review of media ownership rules in deciding whether the principles of the first amendment will be embraced in everyday reality, or only in theory.

Media ownership concentration is already a major threat to our democracy. In the last 25 years, the number of TV station owners has declined from 540 to 460, and the number of TV newsrooms has dropped almost 15 percent. Three-quarters of cable channels are owned by only six corporate entities, four of which are major TV networks. Seventy percent of all markets have four or fewer sources of original TV news production. In 1965, there were 860 owners of daily newspapers. Today there are less than 300.

The Supreme Court has maintained that the first amendment is designed to achieve the widest possible dissemination of information from diverse and antagonistic sources. Media ownership diversity is critical to ensuring that we protect the first amendment. Over the years, the courts have supported the belief of Congress that independent ownership of media outlets results in more diverse media voices, greater competition, and more local content.

Over the last few years, we have seen considerable ownership consolidation in the media, while, at the same time, we have seen important public interest protections eliminated. For the first 50 years after the enactment of the 1934 Communications Act, people had a right to petition the FCC if they found coverage to be one-sided. We called that the Fairness Doctrine. It required broadcasters to cover issues of public importance and to do so fairly, until, in 1987, under immense pressure from the media, it was eliminated.

Eliminating the law of the Fairness Doctrine, a major blow to consumers, was supposed to be alleviated by a blossoming of independent local outlets that would expand diversity by increasing competition. In other words, consumers would no longer be able to use the Fairness Doctrine to ensure that their views were represented on a specific media outlet, but the thought was we would be able to present those views through competing media in the same market.

Unfortunately, the public is now faced with increased concentration, not increased competition, and no longer has the Fairness Doctrine to fall back on. The FCC should reinstate the Fairness Doctrine. At the very least they should not even allow more ownership concentration that makes the loss of the Fairness Doctrine more onerous. Greater media ownership concentration limits the public's access to diverse viewpoints.

Radio provides an example of what can happen when media ownership rules are abolished. In 1996, Congress eliminated the national ownership caps for radio. The result? Greater consolidation in the radio industry. In almost half of the largest markets, the three largest corporations control 80 percent of the radio audience. This has made it harder for diverse opinions to be heard.

Just last month, Clear Channel refused to air an advertisement in which I was inviting people to an event that was organized for people who opposed the war in Iraq. It was a gathering, and I wanted a commercial to air on the radio to see if people wanted to come. Clear Channel refused to put that advertisement on the air.

MR. SANDERS. I am assuming you were prepared to pay for that ad?

MS. SCHAKOWSKY. Absolutely. This was a paid-for ad.

MR. SANDERS. What we have now, and I think people should be aware of this, is it a bad situation when the media does not provide adequate coverage for different points of view, and that is what we are seeing. What the gentlewoman is saying is that when individuals want to buy time at the going rates, they are not even allowed to do that. That is an outrage, that is unacceptable, and we are seeing more and more of that.

If I like your point of view, you can buy an ad on my radio station; if I do not, sorry, we do not want your money.

MS. SCHAKOWSKY. That is exactly right. This was not a public service announcement. This was not asking a favor of the radio station. This was we want to buy an ad that invites people to a public gathering on the issue of most importance in the country at the time, and we were not able to buy that ad. They would not sell it to us, even as its affiliates were organizing pro-war rallies around the country on the air.

Yesterday, as has been pointed out, 11 Members of the United States House of Representatives, the Democratic whip, the Democratic leader of our caucus, the gentleman from Vermont (Mr. Sanders), who has been organizing around this issue of media concentration, an expert on the subject, held a press conference, and nobody came. There was not one TV camera, not one radio station. Two small print outlets came, we are grateful to them; but clearly, a decision was made not to cover this. And I want to challenge those media giants who did not come to explain how that blackout was not motivated by a conflict of interest.

MR. SANDERS. If I could interrupt for a moment, we are a Nation which, as I think everybody knows, is pretty equally divided. The last election, Mr. Gore and Mr. Nader received somewhat more votes than Mr. Bush and Mr. Buchanan. Congress is almost equally divided. The Senate is almost equally divided. Polls show a certain number of people are Democrats, an equal number are Republicans, and you have a lot of independents out there. This is not an extreme right-wing country. It just is not.

I would ask people to think for a moment about the phenomenon of talk radio, in a Nation which is divided pretty equally politically, people on the left, people on the right, let me just mention the folks who are on talk radio: Rush Limbaugh, G. Gordon Liddy, Oliver North, Sean Hannity, Armstrong Williams, Blanquita Collum, Michael Savage, Neil Boorts, Bob Grant, Bob Dornan, Michael Medved, Michael Reagan, Matt Drudge, Laura Schlesinger, Don Imus, Michael Graham, Ken Hamblin, Laura Ingraham, and many, many others.

What do they have in common? They are all extreme right wing.

And now let me read you the names of the progressive voices.

That is it. There are not any. There are not any. Liberal voices, virtually none.

Now, how come in a Nation in which more people voted for Gore than for Bush, there are no national voices speaking for working families, speaking for the middle class, speaking for the environment, speaking for women's rights? No voices. I am not talking about a minority; I am talking no voices.

Is that an accident? Well, as the gentlewoman from Illinois (Ms. Schakowsky) was saying, I do not think it is an accident. I think one has to be very naive not to see the connection between the large corporations who own the media, their desire for lower taxes for the rich, their desire to take American jobs to China, where people are paid 20 cents an hour, their anti-unionism, their lack of respect for the environment, and the fact that talk radio is dominated by these right-wing forces.

MS. SCHAKOWSKY. If I could just add, here is the final request I have, and it is so simple, that the Federal Communications Commission, before it makes a decision on June 2 to allow even greater concentration, would travel around the country and hold more public forums, listen to the people, give an opportunity to the 1,000 people that wrote to me and the thousands and millions more who want to participate in this decision making, let their voices be heard.

Finally, I want to say, let us consider, and I hope pass, House Resolution 218, offered by the gentleman from New York (Mr. Hinchey), which calls on the FCC not to weaken current ownership rules that protect media diversity, and also calls on the FCC to better examine and inform the public about the consequences of further media concentration and allow the public to comment on any proposed changes. This is the least we can do to protect freedom of speech.

MR. SANDERS. Mr. Speaker, I thank the gentlewoman for all of her efforts on this issue. I think her appeal is exactly right. Why should the American people not be able to participate in this debate?

Mr. Speaker, it is my pleasure to yield to the gentleman from Washington (Mr. Inslee).

MR. INSLEE. Mr. Speaker, I thank the gentleman for letting me join him.

I think this is perhaps one of the most important and least talked about issues in American democracy during this Congress, and it is fascinating to me that an issue that has such large ramifications, has such a bearing on Americans' ability to know what is going on in their government and their world, is such a closely held secret from the American people. The reason it is a closely held secret is it is not reported in the media.

This is one of the most important, contentious issues. This should make great fodder for talk shows and radio talk shows and newspapers. It ought to sell a lot of newspapers because it is contentious. Yet there is a black-out on this subject for the American people, and that is why I want to thank the gentleman for doing this Special Order to talk about it.

The reason I came to the floor this afternoon is I think it strikes at the very heart of a basic American value. There are five values actually inscribed on the bar of the House right behind the gentleman from Vermont (Mr. Sanders). I can read them. They are Union, Justice, Tolerance, Liberty, and that is the one that is in question here, is the liberty interests of Americans, because you cannot have liberty or democracy if you do not have multiple sources of information.

Clearly, when the rules were amended years back to allow further consolidation in the industry, guess what you got? You got further consolidation in the industry. It is not exactly rocket science that will be required to predict the results if the FCC allows this further deregulation of the industry. If they do allow further consolidation in the industry, you will have further consolidation in the industry, and when you have further consolidation in the media industry, you have fewer real choices to get access to diverse opinions. Republican, Democrat, up or down, left or right, tall or short, you will have less real choice.

Let me say why that has been borne out in real practice. Some of the people who have advocated for this change, to allow further consolidation in the industry, to allow the bigger to get bigger and swallow the smaller stations, have suggested that because, for instance, there are a lot of radio stations out there, that in fact there is no damage to the value of liberty and diverse opinions.

But they forget one very central fact: when you want to know whether there is diverse opinion in the media, you have to follow a rule, and that rule is this: follow the money. You might have 10, 15, 100 radio stations; but if they are all owned by the same corporation or individual, you do not have 100 voices. You have the same person with 100 megaphones.

Does that help American democracy? Does that help diverse opinions? No. It centralizes it. It reduces the number of voices that America has, and that is exactly what the empirical evidence has shown.

Since the last effort to allow consolidation in the industry, we have 34 percent fewer owners of radio stations. Now, it is of academic interest how many stations we have; but we have fewer voices because we have fewer owners of radio stations, and we have fewer views on the spectrum of political thought and historic thought and spiritual thought than we should have, because we allowed more consolidation, and we got more consolidation; and we have less liberty interests as a result because there are fewer voices in the spectrum to be heard.

Now, I want to say just one more thing, and then I will yield to the gentleman from Vermont (Mr. Sanders).

To me, a taste of what is coming in the media we have in what we got from the FCC, which is a blackout. Because here we have this incredibly important rule to American democracy, and what did the FCC do? What did they do? They are supposed to be working for us. They held one hearing in Virginia.

MR. SANDERS. Mr. Speaker, after being begged to do that.

MR. INSLEE. After being begged by multiple people, they held one hearing 2,500 miles from my district.

Mr. Speaker, the Forest Service, by contrast, when they considered the roadless rule, which is another important rule, they held six hearings, multiple hearings in Washington. This is under the cover of darkness. This avoids sunlight, which is the best anecdote to any virus of political thought; and it is a rotten shame the FCC has to do this under the cover of darkness.

MR. SANDERS. Mr. Speaker, if I might, I would mention to my friend that the FCC has a Web site that people can currently e-mail to, and the overwhelming majority of people who are contacting the FCC are saying, do not go forward with more deregulation, which I find interesting. And the gentleman's point is well taken. I think that there would be tens of thousands of people from California to Maine coming out to these hearings if they had the courage to meet the people rather than just talk to the big corporate bosses.

MR. INSLEE. Mr. Speaker, if I may report from Seattle what happened, two courageous members of the FCC came out and were willing to listen to citizens on their own time a few months ago; and over 300 people, I think, turned out, once we got a little bit of the news out. We did not have much cooperation from the media, of course, who about 99.9 percent of them in the audience were very, very concerned about this further consolidation. And I think that voice is an overwhelming one across America.

MR. SANDERS. Mr. Speaker, before I yield to the gentlewoman from California (Ms. Watson), I want to touch on another aspect of this. People may say, well, this is outside the Beltway. Maybe Members of Congress are complaining, they did not get a good story, they are angry about their lack of courage. That is not the issue here.

The issue here is that in a democratic society, we do not know what goes on unless all issues of importance are discussed, it is not whether somebody gets a good story or whether they are on TV or not; it is whether whole segments of American life get the discussion that they need

Now, we know, we know that we have seen everything that we ever wanted to see about Michael Jackson, about all the other scandals that we have heard about. But here is an issue that gets very little discussion.

We have been told that with all of the explosion of technology, with the global economy, with the use of computers and e-mails and faxes, what we are told, which is true, is that the productivity of the average American worker has substantially increased. That is the good news. The bad news is that the tens of millions of Americans today, despite the increase in productivity, are working longer hours for lower wages. The reality is that in America we have lost several million jobs, decent-paying jobs in the last few years because of a disastrous trade policy where companies are throwing American workers out on the street and running to China. Have we seen much discussion about that on the TV? In the newspapers? I do not think so.

The reality is, the middle class in this country is shrinking. The rich are becoming richer. The richest 1 percent own more wealth than the bottom

95 percent. How does that touch into the media? What the media does, to a large degree, is deflect attention. Here is a scandal, we hope you get involved. Here is a ball game, maybe you are interested in that. But do not worry if your job goes to China; do not worry if the minimum wage has not been raised in years and you are making $5.15 an hour. You do not have to worry about that. Do not worry if a pharmaceutical company has contributed tens of millions of dollars to the Republican Party so you end up paying the highest prices in the world for prescription drugs. You are too dumb to worry about that. We have another scandal for you.

So the issue does relate to the lives and well-being of every American in our country. We have a right. We are not stupid people. We believe in democracy. We understand honest people have differences of opinion, but we want to be able to discuss the most important issues facing the middle class, facing working families. And we are not able to do that because of the enormous conflicts of interest that exist between these very, very large corporations.

MR. INSLEE. Mr. Speaker, if the gentleman will yield, just one more quick point. This is an issue that ought to unite Republicans and Democrats. It really should. I know the gentleman from Vermont (Mr. Sanders) has talked about talk radio. But I just believe, no matter whether you are vanilla or chocolate or Neapolitan here, you ought to stand up and say that it is not healthy when America has 20 or 30 percent less TV stations and half as few newspapers. This should be an all-American, bipartisan statement that America deserves diverse opinions so that they can make decisions and do not have to trust just one.

Mr. Speaker, I thank the gentleman for his efforts.

MR. SANDERS. And I thank the gentleman for his efforts.

Mr. Speaker, the gentlewoman from California (Ms. Watson) is courageous and active on this issue, and I thank her for being with us.

MS. WATSON. Mr. Speaker, on June 2, the FCC is scheduled to meet to discuss a proposal by Chairman Powell to relax regulations on media ownership. The proposal will allow large media companies to acquire a bigger share of the national market and more television stations in any given local media market. Other restrictions on cross-ownership, owning radio stations, TV stations, and newspapers in the same local market will also be lifted.

Many of us here in Congress are concerned that the rule changes proposed by Chairman Powell have not been properly vetted for public and congressional comment and that their impact on minority media ownership and content could be deleterious. Minority owners and their share of the radio and television market is at an all-time low due to media consolidation during the last two decades. Chairman Powell's proposed rule changes could provide the knock-out blow, not only to minority ownership, but to a diversity of opinions and viewpoints that are critical to the free flow of information in a democratic society.

I am very concerned during this period of time that there is a climate that says you cannot say this, you cannot say that, you cannot dissent. It is a threat to democracy.

Now, as a Member of the Congressional Black Caucus, we are getting to Chairman Powell our concerns, because the FCC, as a Federal regulatory agency for mass media communications, has long-established rules following the 1945 Supreme Court declaration that the widest possible dissemination of information from diverse and antagonistic sources is essential to the welfare of the public; that a free press is a condition of a free society.

Over the past two decades, however, many rules designed to enhance diversity, competition, and localism have been weakened, creating unprecedented consolidation of media sources. For example, since the passage of the 1996 Telecommunications Act, the number of radio station owners has decreased by at least 1,100, representing a 30 percent decline. Among the remaining radio station owners, only 175 minority broadcasters owned 426 stations in 2000, or about 4.0 percent of the Nation's 10,577 commercial AM and FM radio stations. Furthermore, most of these minority owners continue to own AM, rather than FM stations, thus facing limited listenership.

Minority owners' share of the commercial television market is even more distressing. As large conglomerates continued to consolidate ownership of television stations throughout the 1990s, only 23 full-power commercial television stations were owned by minorities at the end of the decade, representing only 1.9 percent of the country's 1,288 licensed stations. That level is the lowest since the tracking of such data. In addition, since most minority owners are primarily single-station operators, they face additional difficulty in competing against the larger group owners.

The consolidation of media ownership has also adversely impacted programming diversity. For example, Clear Channel Communications, which controls over a quarter of the Nation's commercial radio market, has instituted homogeneous play lists nationwide, eliminated play time for local musicians, and severely cut back most local news services. Black Entertainment Television, after its merger with media giant Viacom, canceled many of its popular public affairs programs, including "BET Tonight with Ed Gordon," "Lead Story," and "Teen Summit." These examples are object lessons on how media consolidation can limit creative voices, dissenting views, and consumer choice. Our airways need to have the widest range of viewpoints that are representative of American society.

So, Mr. Speaker, it is an outrage that we would be considering even more consolidation. Where are our voices going to be heard? I am very troubled with the atmosphere in which we live in America today, because we are being muzzled, we are being gagged by the big boys, and that is troubling for a democratic system.

MR. SANDERS. Mr. Speaker, I want to pick up on a point that the gentlewoman made. She mentioned Clear Channel; and some people say yes, well, Clear Channel is a radio network, but they are much more than a radio network. And the point that I am trying to make and that all of us have been trying to make today, getting back to this chart, is that a handful of giant media conglomerate corporations are owning more and more of what we see, hear, and read; and this is not what a democracy is about.

I would remind my colleagues in Congress and all Americans that in the last days of the Soviet Union, which was a totalitarian society, people thought, well, I guess they had one newspaper and one television network, and that was it. It was a totalitarian society. That is wrong. There were dozens and dozens and dozens of different newspapers, different magazines, different television stations, all over the totalitarian Soviet Union. The only problem was that all of those television stations, radio stations, newspapers, and magazines were only controlled by either the government of the Soviet Union or the Communist Party. Many, many different outlets, but limited ownership. What we are seeing here is many, many outlets and increasingly fewer owners.

Let me say a word about News Corporation; people probably do not know. What is News Corporation? Well, it is owned by a gentleman named Rupert Murdoch, who was born in Australia, part of a newspaper publishing family in Australia. News Corporation today owns much of the media in Australia. Big deal. Well, they also own much of the media in the United Kingdom. They own a lot of the media in Eastern Europe. They are increasingly owning more media in China. And guess what? They already own a whole lot of media and other companies in the United States, and they want more.

So what you are looking at is one man who happens to be a right-wing billionaire controlling huge amounts of media all over the entire world, which makes him, in fact, one of the most powerful people in the world.

In the United States, news corporations owned by Mr. Murdoch, 22 television stations, including stations in New York, Los Angeles, Chicago,

Dallas, Washington, Minnesota, Houston, Orlando and Phoenix. He owns the Fox Broadcasting Network. He owns Fox News. He owns Fox Kids, Fox Sports, the Health Network, the National Geographic. He owns TV Guide. He owns the TV Guide Channel. He owns Fox Sports, radio, the Golf Channel. He also isn't content with broadcast media. He happens to own the New York Post. And this is really a small number of what he owns. He owns the Times in London, one of the leading papers in the United Kingdom. He owns the Sun in the United Kingdom, one of the large circulation tabloids there; He owns the News of the World. He owns the TV Guide Magazine in the United States. He owns a conservative magazine called the Weekly Standard.

But that is not all that he owns. He owns Harper Collins, one of our major publishing houses. He owns Regan books. He owns Amistad Books. He owns William Morrow and Company. That means if you want to get a book published, you have got to go through these guys.

Not only that, he has tremendous impact on sports in America. People say, I do not care about books, but I really am interested in sports. Well, he happens to own or at least be part owner of the Los Angeles Dodgers, the Los Angeles Kings, the Los Angeles Lakers, the New York Knickerbockers, the New York Rangers.

Well, I am not interested in sports, but I am interested in music. He owns Festival Records. He owns Mushroom Records, and he owns much, much more.

Now, the point here is it is not just Mr. Murdoch and news corporations. I have talked about Viacom before. It is not just AOL–Time Warner. It is not just Disney. It is not just Clear Channel. It is a handful of corporations that control more than you think they do, and the end result of that is that entire issues of great concern to the American people are not discussed at all because these guys really are not interested in discussing it.

I read recently that Mr. Bush's proposal for $720 billion in tax breaks is gaining support in America. Well, I can see why: Because there has been relatively little opportunity in the media for those of us who disagree, who think that it is a bad idea that the richest 1/10 of 1 percent get as much in tax breaks as the bottom 89 percent. How many people know that? How many people know that as a result of that budget, there will likely be cutbacks in Medicaid, Medicare, veterans needs, education, environmental protection? Because if you give away all of that money, you will have less for the needs of working families and the middle class.

How many people know that if you do that huge tax break, you are going to end up with a $10 trillion national debt that we are leaving to our kids and our grandchildren? Not a whole lot of discussion about that because Mr. Murdoch and the guys who make tens of millions of dollars a year want tax breaks for the rich. They want the American taxpayer to subsidize them, to give them billions of dollars in corporate welfare.

Do you think General Electric, which owns NBC, is going to be talking about all the welfare that General Electric gets through its nuclear power efforts? Maybe, but I do not think so. Do you think that General Electric, which owns NBC, will be talking about all the jobs that GE destroyed in the United States, all the American workers they threw out on the street as they moved to Mexico and China? I do not think so.

So this issue is not some kind of inside-the-beltway abstract issue. It gets to the heart and the soul and the core of what America is about, and that is if we are to remain a democracy where honest people have honest differences of opinion, we have got to get all of the information. We cannot have a handful of conglomerates who have their own special interests determining what we see, hear and read. And that is why, just to recapitulate what all of my colleagues who have been up here have said, it is enormously important that on June 2 the FCC does not go forward and further deregulate the media so you will end up with even an even smaller number controlling what we see, hear and read.

At the very least, Mr. Powell has got to stop the process. He has got to have public hearings all over America. We need studies to understand what this will mean, what more deregulation will mean to the quality of American democracy, what it will mean to the ability of communities to get local news, what it will mean to small businesses and the ability of small businesses to function within the media area.

This is an enormously important issue. I would hope that anyone who needs more information about this can go to my Web site at Bernie.House.gov.

I hope that more people will get involved in this extremely important issue. I want to thank all of the Members of Congress who have been here today.

Appendix 6.2

FCC Sets Limits of Media Concentration

Unprecedented Public Record Results in Enforceable and Balanced Broadcast Ownership Rules

Washington, D.C.—The Federal Communications Commission (FCC) today adopted new broadcast ownership rules that are enforceable, based on empirical evidence and reflective of the current media marketplace. Today's action represents the most comprehensive review of media ownership regulation in the agency's history, spanning 20 months and encompassing a public record of more than 520,000 comments.

The FCC stated that its new limits on broadcast ownership are carefully balanced to protect diversity, localism, and competition in the American media system. The FCC concluded that these new broadcast ownership limits will foster a vibrant marketplace of ideas, promote vigorous competition, and ensure that broadcasters continue to serve the needs and interests of their local communities.

FCC Responds to Congressional and Court Directives

In the 1996 Telecommunications Act, Congress mandated that the FCC review its broadcast ownership rules every two years to determine "whether any of such rules are necessary in the public interest as a result of competition." The Act requires the FCC to repeal or modify any regulation it determines to be no longer in the public interest. The FCC's decision today found that all of the broadcast ownership rules continue to serve the public interest either in their current form or in a modified form.

Recent court decisions reversing FCC ownership rules emphasized that any limits must be based on a solid factual record and must reflect changes in the media marketplace. In the *Fox v. FCC* decision, for example, the court said the FCC had "provided no analysis of the state of competition in the television industry" or even an explanation as to why the rule in question was necessary to either safeguard competition or enhance competition.

The *Report and Order* adopted today is based on a thorough assessment of the impact of ownership rules on promoting competition, diversity, and localism. This careful calibration of each rule reflects the FCC's determination to establish limits on broadcast ownership that will withstand future judicial scrutiny.

FCC press release describing the commission's June 2, 2003, vote on media ownership limits. *Source:* Swing Music Net, http://www.swingmusic.net, June 2, 2004.

New Limits Protect Viewpoint Diversity

The FCC strongly affirmed its core value of limiting broadcast ownership to promote viewpoint diversity. The FCC stated that "the widest possible dissemination of information from diverse and antagonistic sources is essential to the welfare of the public." The FCC said multiple independent media owners are needed to ensure a robust exchange of news, information, and ideas among Americans.

The FCC developed a "Diversity Index" in order to permit a more sophisticated analysis of viewpoint diversity in this proceeding. The index is "consumer-centric" in that it is built on data about how Americans use different media to obtain news. Importantly, this data also enabled the FCC to establish local broadcast ownership rules that recognize significant differences in media availability in small versus large markets. The objective is to ensure that citizens in all areas of the country have a diverse array of media outlets available to them.

New Rules Promote Competition and Choice for Americans

The FCC affirmed its long-standing commitment to promoting competition by ensuring pro-competitive market structures. The FCC said it is clear that competition is a policy that is intimately tied to its public interest responsibilities and one that the FCC has a statutory obligation to pursue. The FCC said consumers receive greater choice and more innovative services in competitive markets than they do in markets where one or more firms exercise market power.

Although the primary concern of antitrust analysis is in ensuring economic efficiency through the operation of a competitive market structure, the FCC's public interest standard brings a closer focus to the American public. Thus, the FCC has a public interest responsibility to ensure that broadcasting markets remain competitive so that the benefits of competition, including lower prices, innovation and improved service are made available to Americans.

The FCC acknowledged that cable and satellite TV service compete with traditional over-the-air broadcasting; Today Americans enjoy a significant amount of choice for seeking news and information and thus the new rules limiting local and national TV ownership are designed to better reflect this additional competition. The FCC found that pro-competitive ownership limits must account for the fact that broadcast TV revenue relies exclusively on advertising; whereas cable and satellite TV service have both advertising and subscription revenue streams.

The FCC also explained that because viewpoint diversity is fostered when there are multiple independently owned media outlets, the FCC's competition-based limits on local radio and local TV ownership also advance the goal of promoting the widest dissemination of viewpoints.

Localism Affirmed as Important Policy Goal

The FCC strongly reaffirmed its goal of promoting localism through limits on ownership of broadcast outlets. Localism remains a bedrock principle that continues to benefit Americans in important ways. The FCC has sought to promote localism to the greatest extent possible through its broadcast ownership limits that are aligned with station incentives to serve the needs and interests of their local communities.

To analyze localism in broadcasting markets, the FCC relied on two measures: local stations' selection of programming that is responsive to local needs and interests, and local news quantity and quality. Program selection is an important function of broadcast television licensees and the record contains data on how different types of station owners perform. A second measure of localism is the quantity and quality of local news and public affairs programming by different types of television station owners. This data helped the FCC assess which ownership structures will ensure the strongest local focus by station owners to the needs of their communities.

FCC Reiterates Importance of Promoting Minority and Female Ownership

The FCC strongly reaffirmed its long-standing objective of encouraging greater ownership of broadcast stations by minorities and women. The FCC said this will benefit radio and television audiences by promoting greater diversity, innovation, and competition. The FCC furthered its objective of creating greater opportunities for new entrants in the broadcasting industry by carving out special transactional opportunities for small businesses, many of which are owned by minorities and women.

Limits on Concentration Serve the Public Interest

In sum, the modified ownership rules adopted today provide a new, comprehensive national and local regulatory framework that will serve the public interest by promoting competition, diversity and localism. Today's Report and Order adopts a set of cross-media limits to replace the newspaper/broadcast and radio/television cross-ownership rules; modifies the local television multiple ownership rule; strengthens the local radio ownership rule by modifying the local radio market definition; incrementally modifies the national television ownership rule; and retains the dual network rule. A summary of the broadcast ownership rules adopted today is attached.

The FCC also adopted a *Notice of Proposed Rulemaking* on non-Arbitron radio markets. Details are included in the attached summary.

A Summary of the Broadcast Ownership Rules Adopted on June 2, 2003
Dual Network Ownership Prohibition (originally adopted 1946):

The FCC retained its ban on mergers among any of the top four national broadcast networks.

Prohibition Promotes Competition and Localism

The FCC determined that its existing dual network prohibition continues to be necessary to promote competition in the national television advertising and program acquisition markets. The rule also promotes localism by preserving the balance of negotiating power between networks and affiliates. If the rule was eliminated and two of the top four networks were to merge, affiliates of those two networks would have fewer networks to turn to for affiliation.

Local TV Multiple Ownership Limit (originally adopted in 1964):

The new rule states:

- In markets with five or more TV stations, a company may own two stations, but only one of these stations can be among the top four in ratings.
- In markets with 18 or more TV stations, a company can own three TV stations, but only one of these stations can be among the top four in ratings.
- In deciding how many stations are in the market, both commercial and non-commercial TV stations are counted.
- The FCC adopted a waiver process for markets with 11 or fewer TV stations in which two top-four stations seek to merge. The FCC will evaluate on a case-by-case basis whether such stations would better serve their local communities together rather than separately.

TV Limit Enhances Competition and Preserves Viewpoint Diversity

The FCC determined that its prior local TV ownership rule could not be justified on diversity or competition grounds. The FCC found that Americans rely on a variety of media outlets, not just broadcast television, for news and information. In addition, the prior rule could not be justified as necessary to promote competition because it failed to reflect the significant competition now faced by local broadcasters from cable and satellite TV services. This is the first local TV ownership role to acknowledge that competition.

The new role permits local television combinations that are proven to enhance competition in local markets and to facilitate the transition to digital television through economic efficiencies. Finally, the new rule's continued ban on mergers among the top four stations will have the effect of preserving viewpoint diversity in local markets. The record showed that the top four stations each typically produce an independent local newscast.

Because viewpoint diversity is fostered when there are multiple independently owned media outlets, the FCC's competition-based limits on local TV ownership also advance the goal of promoting the widest dissemination of viewpoints.

National TV Ownership Limit (originally adopted in 1941):

The FCC incrementally increased the 35% limit to a 45% limit on national ownership.

- A company can own TV stations reaching no more than 45% share of U.S. TV households;
- The share of U.S. TV households is calculated by adding the number of TV households in each market that the company owns a station. Regardless of the station's ratings, it is counted for all of the potential viewers in the market. Therefore, a 45% share of U.S. TV households is not equal to a 45% share of TV stations in the U.S.
- On March 31, 2003, there were 1,340 commercial TV stations in the U.S. Of these 1,340 stations, Viacom owns 39 TV stations (2.9%), Fox owns 37 (2.8%), NBC owns 29 (2.2%) and ABC owns 10 (0.8%).

National Cap Protects Localism and Preserves Free Television

The FCC determined that a national TV ownership limit is needed to protect localism by allowing a body of network affiliates to negotiate collectively with the broadcast networks on network programming decisions.

The FCC also found that the current 35% level did not strike the right balance of promoting localism and preserving free over-the-air television for several reasons.

1. The record showed that the 35% cap did not have any meaningful effect on the negotiating power between individual networks and their affiliates with respect to program-by-program preemption levels.

2. The record showed the broadcast network owned-and-operated stations ("O&Os") served their local communities better with respect to local news

production. Network-owned stations aired more local news programming than did affiliates.

3. The record showed that the public interest is served by regulations that encourage the networks to keep expensive programming, such as sports, on free, over-the-air television.

Record Supports Maintaining UHF Discount

- The FCC decided to maintain the "UHF Discount" when calculating a company's national reach because it currently serves the public interest. The FCC said that more than 40 million Americans still have access only to free, over-the-air television.
- Evidence in the record demonstrates that UHF stations have smaller signal coverage areas than VHF stations, which has a very real impact on UHF stations' ability to compete.
- The UHF discount has promoted the entry of new broadcast networks into the market. These new networks have improved consumer choice and program diversity for all Americans, including those with and without cable and satellite TV service.
- For these reasons, the FCC maintained a 50% discount for calculating the national reach of UHF stations. However, the FCC determined that when the transition to digital television is complete, the UHF discount would be eliminated for the stations owned by the four largest broadcast networks. The FCC will determine, in a future biennial review, whether to include any other networks and station group owners in the UHF discount sunset. The FCC drew this distinction to ensure that its resolution of the UHF discount issue will properly account for its goal of encouraging the formation of new, over-the-air broadcast networks.

Local Radio Ownership Limit (originally adopted in 1941):

The FCC found that the current limits on local radio ownership continue to be necessary in the public interest, but that the previous methodology for defining a radio market did not serve the public interest. The radio caps remain at the following levels:

- In markets with 45 or more radio stations, a company may own 8 stations, only 5 of which may be in one class, AM or FM.
- In markets with 30–44 radio stations, a company may own 7 stations, only 4 of which may be in one class, AM or FM.
- In markets with 15–29 radio stations, a company may own 6 stations, only 4 of which may be in one class, AM or FM.

- In markets with 14 or fewer radio stations, a company may own 5 stations, only 3 of which may be in one class, AM or FM.

Radio Limit Promotes Competition and Viewpoint Diversity

Although Americans rely on a wide variety of outlets in addition to radio for news, the FCC found that the current radio ownership limits continue to be needed to promote competition among local radio stations. Competitive radio markets ensure that local stations are responsive to local listener needs and tastes. By guaranteeing a substantial number of independent radio voices, this role will also promote viewpoint diversity among local radio owners.

Geographic Arbitron Markets Implemented

The FCC replaced its signal contour method of defining local radio markets with a geographic market approach assigned by Arbitron. The FCC said that its signal contour method created anomalies in ownership of local radio stations that Congress could not have intended when it established the local radio ownership limits in 1996. The FCC released that loophole by applying a more rational market definition than radio signal contours. The FCC said applying Arbitron's geographic markets method will better reflect the true markets in which radio stations compete.

- All radio stations licensed to communities in an Arbitron market are counted in the market as well as stations licensed to other markets but considered "home" to the market.
- Both commercial and noncommercial stations are counted in the market. The FCC determined that the current rule improperly ignores the impact that noncommercial stations can have on competition for listeners in radio markets.
- For non-Arbitron markets, the FCC will conduct a short-term rulemaking to define markets comparable to Arbitron markets. These new markets will be specifically designed to prevent any unreasonable aggregation of station ownership by any one company.
- As an interim procedure for non-Arbitron markets, the FCC will apply a modified contour method for counting the number of stations in the market. This modified contour approach minimizes file potential for additional anomalies to occur during this transition period, while providing the public a clear rule for determining the relevant radio markets.
- In using the contour-overlap market definition on an interim basis, the FCC made certain adjustments to minimize the more notorious anomalies of that system. Specifically, the FCC will exclude from the market any

radio station whose transmitter site is more than 92 kilometers (58 miles) from the perimeter of the mutual overlap area. This will alleviate some of the gross distortions in market size that can occur when a large signal contour that is part of a proposed combination overlaps the contours of distant radio stations and thereby brings them into the market.

Cross-Media Limits

This rule replaces the broadcast-newspaper and the radio-television cross-ownership rules. The new rule states:

- In markets with three or fewer TV stations, no cross-ownership is permitted among TV, radio and newspapers. A company may obtain a waiver of that ban if it can show that the television station does not serve the area served by the cross-owned property (i.e., the radio station or the newspaper).
- In markets with between 4 and 8 TV stations, combinations are limited to one of the following:

    (A) A daily newspaper; one TV station; and up to half of the radio station limit for that market (i.e., if the radio limit in the market is 6, the company can only own 3) OR

    (B) A daily newspaper; and up to the radio station limit for that market; (i.e., no TV stations) OR

    (C) Two TV stations (if permissible under local TV ownership rule); up to the radio station limit for that market (i.e., no daily newspapers).

In markets with nine or more TV stations, the FCC eliminated the newspaper-broadcast cross-ownership ban and the television-radio cross-ownership ban.

Promotes Diversity and Localism

The FCC concluded that neither the newspaper-broadcast prohibition nor the TV-radio cross-ownership prohibition could be justified for larger markets in light of the abundance of sources that citizens rely on for news. Nor were those rules found to promote competition because radio, TV and newspapers generally compete in different economic markets. Moreover, the FCC found that greater participation by newspaper publishers in the television and radio business would improve the quality and quantity of news available to the public.

Therefore, the FCC replaced those rules with a set of Cross-Media Limits (CML). These limits are designed to protect viewpoint diversity by ensuring that no company, or group of companies, can control an inordinate share of media outlets in a local market.

The FCC developed a Diversity Index to measure the availability of key media outlets in markets of various sizes. The FCC concluded that there were three tiers of markets in terms of "viewpoint diversity" concentration, each warranting different regulatory treatment.

- In the tier of smallest markets (3 or fewer TV stations), the FCC found that key outlets were sufficiently limited such that any cross-ownership among the three leading outlets for local news broadcast TV, radio, and newspapers would harm viewpoint diversity.
- In the medium-sized tier (4–8 TV stations), markets were found to be less concentrated today than in the smallest markets and that certain media outlet combinations could safely occur without harming viewpoint diversity. Certain other combinations would threaten viewpoint diversity and are thus prohibited.
- In the largest tier of markets (9 or more TV stations), the FCC concluded that the large number of media outlets, in combination with ownership limits for local TV and radio, were more than sufficient to protect viewpoint diversity.

Radio and TV Transferability Limited to Small Businesses

The FCC's new TV and radio ownership rules may result in a number of situations where current ownership arrangements exceed ownership limits. The FCC grand-fathered owners of those clusters, but generally prohibited the sale of such above-cap clusters. The FCC made a limited exception to permit sales of grand-fathered combinations to small businesses as defined in the *Order.*

In taking this action, the FCC sought to respect the reasonable expectations of parties that lawfully purchased groups of local radio stations that today, through redefined markets, now exceed the applicable caps. The FCC also attempted to promote competition by permitting station owners to retain any above-cap local radio clusters but not transfer them intact unless there is a compelling public policy justification to do so. The FCC found two such justifications: (1) avoiding undue hardships to cluster owners that are small businesses; and (2) promoting the entry into the broadcasting business by small businesses, many of which are minority- or female-owned.

Appendix 6.3

Statement of FCC Commissioner Michael J. Copps on Media Consolidation and Diversity

I dissent because today the FCC empowers America's new media elite with unacceptable levels of influence . . .

I dissent to this decision. I dissent on grounds of substance. I dissent on grounds of process. I dissent because today the Federal Communications Commission empowers America's new Media Elite with unacceptable levels of influence over the ideas and information upon which our society and our democracy so heavily depend.

This morning we are at a crossroads—for television, radio and newspapers and for the American people. The decision we five make today will recast our entire media landscape for years to come. At issue is whether a few corporations will be ceded enhanced gatekeeper control over the civil dialogue of our country; more content control over our music, entertainment and information; and veto power over the majority of what our families watch, hear and read.

Two very divergent paths beckon us.

Down one road is a reaffirmation of America's commitment to local control of our media diversity in news and editorial viewpoint, and the importance of competition. This path implores us not to abandon core values going to the heart of what the media mean in our country. On this path we reaffirm that FCC licensees have been given very special privileges and that they have very special responsibilities to serve the public interest.

Down the other road is more media control by ever fewer corporate giants. This path surrenders to a handful of corporations awesome powers over our news, information and entertainment. On this path we endanger time-honored safeguards and time-proven values that have strengthened the country as well as the media.

So the stakes are high—higher than they have been for any decision the five people sitting here today have ever made at this Commission. How do we decide which path to choose?

We should begin by examining the law. What does the law tell us? The Communications Act tells us to use our rules to promote localism, diver-

Source: Common Dreams News Center, June 2, 2003, http://www.commondreams.org/views03/0602-14.htm.

sity and competition. It reminds us that the airwaves belong to the American people, and that no broadcast station, no company, no single individual owns an airwave in America. The airwaves belong to all the people. And the Supreme Court has upheld media protections, stating that "it is the purpose of the First Amendment to preserve an uninhibited marketplace of ideas in which truth will ultimately prevail, rather than to countenance monopolization of that market, whether it be by the Government itself or a private licensee."

We should then look at the world of experience. What practical, real world experience do we have to guide us? Radio deregulation gives us powerful and relevant lessons. When Congress and the Commission removed radio concentration protections, we experienced massive, and largely unforeseen, consolidation. We saw a 34 percent reduction in the number of radio station owners. Diversity of programming suffered. Homogenized music and standardized programming crowded out local and regional talent. Creative local artists found it ever more difficult to obtain play time. Editorial opinion polarized. Competition in many towns became non-existent as a few companies bought up virtually every station in the market. This experience should terrify us as we consider visiting upon television and newspapers what we have inflicted upon radio. "Clear Channelization" of the rest of the American media will harm our country.

We should, finally, seek out the counsel and wisdom of the American people: Commissioner Adelstein and I have attended public hearings across the country with conservatives and liberals, broadcasters and creative artists, concerned parents and civil rights activists, church leaders and educators. Our Commission has seen close to three quarters of a million people register their views—more than for any proceeding in Commission history. And in a nation that can be deeply divided on important issues, these citizens are uniquely unanimous on the question of whether this Commission should allow further media concentration. They are screaming that we should protect local broadcasting, diversity of programming and opinion, and the ability to compete with the huge companies. We should heed their conservatism—their urgent call to refrain from abandoning time-honored protections when so much is at stake and so much is unknown about the consequences of what we are doing here today.

The majority instead chooses radical deregulation—perhaps not quite so radical as originally intended a year ago before Americans found out what was going on and began to speak out—but radical nevertheless. This decision allows a corporation to control three television stations in a single city. Why does any company need to control three television stations anywhere? The decision allows the giant media companies to buy up the remaining local newspaper and exert massive influence over a community by wielding three TV stations, eight radio stations, the cable operator, plus the already monopolistic newspaper. The decision further allows the already massive television networks to buy up even more local TV stations, so that they could control up to an unbelievable 90 percent of the national television audience. Where are the blessings of localism, diversity and competition here? I see centralization, not localism; I see uniformity, not diversity; I see monopoly and oligopoly, not competition.

Will the vaunted 500-channel universe of cable TV save us? Well, 90 percent of the top cable channels are owned by the same giants that own the TV networks and the cable systems. More channels are great. But when they're all owned by the same people, cable doesn't advance localism, editorial diversity or competition. And those who believe the Internet alone will save us from this fate should realize that the dominating Internet news sources are controlled by the same media giants who control radio, TV, newspapers and cable.

Don't tell me that those of us who feel strongly about this are being too emotional. Some would have us believe that this is merely an ordinary examination of our rules that we conduct every two years. Let's not kid ourselves. This is the granddaddy of all reviews. It sets the direction for how the next review will get done and for how the media will look for many years to come. As for the emotion, I have seen the concern, the deep feeling and outright alarm on the faces of people who have come out to talk to Commissioner Adelstein and me all across this country. Are they emotional? You bet. And I think they are going to stay that way until we get this right.

Why did the Commission get this so wrong? Good, sustainable rules are the result of an open administrative process and a serious attempt to gather all the relevant facts. Bad rules and legal vulnerability result from an opaque regulatory process and inadequate data. Unfortunately, today's rules fall into the latter camp. This proceeding has been run as a classic inside-the-Beltway process with too little outreach from the Commission and too little attention paid to the public. This is the way the Commission usually does business, we are told. Well, I submit this is too important to be treated on a business-as-usual basis. So Commissioner Adelstein and I traveled across the country to attend as many hearings and forums as we could.

I am also troubled that the Commission has refused to publicly disclose the rules we are voting on today. What possible harm can come from transparency? How can telling Congress and the public what we plan to do possibly be bad? Isn't the animating spirit of our "notice and comment" procedure to make sure our people know as much as possible about the specifics of what is being proposed?

And so, we arrive at today. Citizens across this country will hear for the first time the proposals that we are adopting. Some of the details of the rule changes have leaked to the press. Even with this incomplete information, the public reaction against the proposed changes has been unlike anything the FCC has ever experienced. Of the nearly three quarters of a million comments we have received, nearly all oppose increased media consolidation—over 99.9 percent.

We've heard bipartisan concern from more than 150 Members of Congress, including the Congressional Black Caucus, the Congressional Hispanic Caucus and the Congressional Asian Pacific American Caucus, asking us to slow down and put these proposals out for public comment before we vote. Some of those Members of Congress are here today and I thank them for coming.

Dozens of organizations—from the National Rifle Association to the National Organization for Women—have weighed in with their concerns about media concentration and the process by which we are dealing with it. City councils across this country in such places as Chicago, Seattle, Philadelphia, San Francisco, Atlanta, and Buffalo, as well as a whole state—Vermont—have gone on record against media concentration.

As Brent Bozell of the Parents Television Council so aptly put it, "When all of us are united on an issue, then one of two things has happened. Either the Earth has spun off its axis and we have all lost our minds or there is universal support for a concept." Well, it's the concept—a transcending, nationwide concept.

The FCC is not, of course, a public opinion survey agency. Nor should we make our decisions by weighing the letters, cards and e-mails "for" and the letters, cards and e-mails "against" and awarding the victory to the side that tips the scale. But even this independent agency is part of our democratic system of government. And when there is such an overwhelming response on the part of the American people and their representatives in Congress assembled, we ought to take notice. Here the right call is to take these proposals, put them out for comment and then—only then— call the vote. The spirit underlying the "notice and comment" procedure of independent agencies is that important proposed changes need to be seen and vetted before they are voted. We haven't been true to that spirit. Today we vote before we vet.

And what are we voting on? The majority decides to allow TV networks to control up to 45 percent of the audience—up to 90 percent once the strange decision to keep the UHF Discount is considered. Merrill Lynch predicts this decision will result in a "Gold Rush" where the national networks buy up the remaining local broadcasters. This decision is made without an adequate explanation for why 45 percent is not just an arbitrary number pulled out of a hat, and despite exhaustive and largely uncontested evidence supporting the existing cap by local broadcasters. I frankly doubt the courts will be impressed.

Some have argued that free over-the-air television is doomed unless we allow more concentration. The facts tell a different story. The networks not only reach consumers over the air through their own highly profitable stations and through affiliates, but they are also guaranteed carriage to cable subscribers. Indeed, they own much of cable. The networks command an enormous advertising premium, recently receiving a record $9.4 billion in up-front prime-time advertising for the next season. They have ownership in most of their profitable programs, and these are subsequently put into syndication or "repurposed"—the fancy new term for a re-run. This argument that the only way for the poor among us to continue receiving free, over-the-air television is to allow already powerful networks to grow more powerful would have been better left unsaid.

The majority, inexplicably, maintains the UHF Discount. Under the UHF Discount, UHF TV stations are considered to reach only 50 percent of the households that VHF TV stations reach for purposes of determining whether a company has exceeded the national cap. Once upon a time, that was warranted. The Commission found that over-the-air UHF stations reached fewer viewers than VHF stations because their signals were different. But UHF and VHF stations reach an identical number of viewers when delivered over cable TV facilities. Today, over 85 percent of consumers receive their signal from cable and DBS. Program carriage requirements ensure that cable consumers receive the UHF signal, and DBS operators are required to carry all UHF stations in any market where they carry any local channel.

With 85 percent of Americans experiencing no difference between UHF and VHF stations, the discount no longer makes sense. Eliminating the entire discount may be unwarranted, but at a minimum it requires replacement with a number that reflects the reality of today's technology and marketplace.

The more you dig into this Order, the worse things get. The Order finds:

- That further concentration in already highly-concentrated markets is acceptable.
- That in a town with only four TV stations, it is acceptable for the top-rated television station to buy the only daily newspaper.
- That consolidation going forward will enhance news programming, despite considerable record evidence showing that increased concentration more often than not reduces quality news.

There are other things this order could have done. Commenters addressed the need to require more independent programming on our airwaves so that a few conglomerates do not act anti-competitively to control all of the creative entertainment that we see. These proposals should have received the serious attention they deserve in this decision. Over the past decade, we have witnessed a substantial increase in the amount of programming owned by the networks. In addition to the obvious loss of diversity, this has also entailed the loss of thousands of jobs, including creative artists, technicians and many, many others. Years ago, we had protections against this kind of program ownership. Now that the majority is loosening outlet ownership rules, we ought to be looking at the consequences of having no limits on who owns the programming.

The Order could have addressed having a legitimate license renewal process to partially protect against the risks of further consolidation. The system has degenerated into one of basically post-card license renewal. Unless there is a major complaint pending against a station, its license is almost automatically renewed. A real, honest-to goodness license renewal process, predicated on advancing the public interest, might do more for broadcasting than all these other rules put together.

The Order could have analyzed the impact of media concentration on indecent and excessively violent programming. Some have suggested that there may be a link between increasing consolidation and increasing indecency on our airwaves. The Commission fails to address this issue in its analysis. It seems plausible that there is such a connection. I don't know the answer to this question. I do know this: we have no business voting until we take a serious look at the matter and amass at least a credible body of evidence.

The Order could have addressed the impact of media concentration on women and minority groups. We know that there are substantially fewer radio station owners today than there were before the rules were changed in 1996. People of color now make up less than four percent of radio and television owners. The National Association of Black Owned Broadcasters tells us that the number of minority owners of broadcast facilities has dropped by 14 percent since 1997.

We have not even attempted to understand what further consolidation means in terms of providing Hispanic Americans and African Americans and Asian-Pacific Americans and Native Americans and women and other groups the kinds of programs and access and viewpoint diversity and career opportunities and even advertising information about products and services that they need. America's strength is, after all, its diversity. And our media need to reflect this diversity to nourish it.

Today's Order puts most such questions off into the future, with the exception of a curious plan to allow a small business, perhaps a minority firm, to buy a consolidated block of outlets from an incumbent who exceeds the limits. That would require deeper pockets than most such firms could afford. I would prefer to look for real opportunities for small entrepreneurs instead of encouraging them to buy large consolidated properties.

All this means that I am deeply saddened by the Commission's actions today. Some have characterized the fight against this seemingly pre-ordained decision as Quixotic and destined to defeat. But I think, instead, that we'll look back at this 3-2 vote as a Pyrrhic victory.

This Commission's drive to loosen the rules and its reluctance to share its proposals with the people before we voted awoke a sleeping giant. American citizens are standing up in never-before-seen numbers to reclaim their airwaves and to call on those who are entrusted to use them to serve the public interest. In these times when many issues divide us, groups from right to left, Republicans and Democrats, concerned parents and creative artists, religious leaders, civil rights activists, and labor organizations have united to fight together on this issue. Senators and Congressmen from both parties and from all parts of the country have called on the Commission to reconsider. The media concentration debate will never be the same. The obscurity of this issue that many have relied upon in the past, where only a few dozen inside-the-Beltway lobbyists understood the issue, is gone forever.

I believe, after traveling almost the length and breadth of this land, that our citizens want, deserve, and are demanding a renewed discussion of how their airwaves are being used and how to ensure they are serving the public interest. I urge my colleagues to heed the call. I want to thank the hundreds of thousands of people who have attended hearings, filed comments, written letters to the editor, and contacted the Commission. You have made a difference. And if you stay the course now, the chances have improved that we can yet settle this issue of who will control our media and for what purposes and to resolve it in favor of airwaves of, by and for the people of this great country.

Thank you.

7 Disharmony in the Air

Downsizing Music Playlists

Complaints about the impact of the 1996 Telecommunications Act's deregulation of radio ownership came thick and fast the moment music selections began to change. Reports indicated that radio stations were "beginning to sound the same coast to coast" and that disc jockeys at corporate stations "were given little discretion in what songs they could play."[1] Despite industry promises that the 1996 deregulation would result in more diversity on radio, in 1998 Marc Fisher wrote in the *Washington Post,* "In recent months, I have asked executives at several big radio companies to cite examples of the new diversity of programming they had promised. Not a one came up with anything but slight variations on the standard, bland 'adult contemporary' music formats that dominate the dial." He noted that listeners all over the country were coming together to protest in organizations such as Americans for Radio Diversity, "to revive the local feel of radio in an era of distant owners and nationally syndicated programming."[2]

Clear Channel CEO Lowry Mays insisted that there was, indeed, more diversity, that "there is absolutely no question whatsoever that there is a significant amount of diversity that did not exist prior to consolidation," citing the rock format as an example. He stated that at one time there was just one basic rock format, similar from station to station, but since consolidation there are many variations of rock formats in major markets. The *Washington Business Journal* agreed: "Rather than producing blandness or sameness, consolidation is providing more diversity, not less, as

140

larger broadcast companies attempt to have signals in as many sectors as possible."[3]

However, a survey by Paragon Research in 1998 found that 84 percent of radio listeners wanted stations to stop playing the same songs over and over, 75 percent believed that stations should play more than one or two songs from a CD or album, 80 percent wanted stations to play more than just the popular songs from an album or CD, 77 percent wanted unfamiliar songs from an album or CD and 54 percent wanted more unfamiliar new music.[4] Clearly, the overwhelming majority of listeners were not happy with the industry's interpretation of diversity. Jeremy Wilker of Americans for Radio Diversity said, "Everybody's really fed up with the state of radio, the repetitiveness. . . . I wish we had a community station." Gigi Sohn of the Media Access Project agreed, decrying the "homogenization of radio, with everything sounding the same from city to city—the same 10 songs, the same formats, etc."[5]

Erika Shernoff wrote, "Large conglomerates like Clear Channel and Infinity Broadcasting own thousands of radio stations. Clear Channel designates one programming director for a particular format in an area, giving sometimes a hundred radio stations the same play list. These stations then have local DJs insert voiceovers into the programs, forming, basically, a nationally syndicated radio show."[6]

Journalist and media critic Marc Fisher acknowledges that Clear Channel has added new formats such as hip-hop and alternative rock to a number of its stations in many cities. He also notes other views. that even when new formats are added by the conglomerate companies, the music they play "is the same old stuff." Studies have found that the "different" formats have essentially the same playlists, with as many as three-fourths of the songs overlapping. Fisher explains that the huge cost of station acquisitions in the 1990s has forced Clear Channel to cut costs and raise ad rates, squeezing more profit from individual stations by firing local disc jockeys and announcers and replacing them with deejays who are in stations thousands of miles away and who toss in "a few local references for verisimilitude. . . . News operations have been eliminated or outsourced. . . . Programming that once mirrored local standards now takes on the coarseness of New York and Los Angeles." Fisher argues further states that "if deregulation was supposed to let a thousand flowers bloom, most of the garden appears to be in Clear Channel's yard." Even among some Clear Channel executives there is private criticism of their system that requires record companies to pay to have their songs aired, a situation that musicians have been loudly protesting. Singer Tom Petty sums up the situation in his song "The Last DJ," which contains the lines "There goes your freedom of choice . . . there goes the last human voice . . . there goes the last DJ."[7]

Ann Chaitovitz, national director for sound recordings for the American Federation of Television and Radio Artists (AFTRA), is concerned that "consolidation of radio ownership has erected barriers making it nearly impossible for local artists to receive airplay on their local stations. . . . Creativity often develops locally, and with consolidated radio ownership, this creativity is prevented from both receiving airplay where it is locally popular and from breaking out to broader markets."[8] Noted jazz musician and professor Ellis Marsalis Jr. supports Chaitovitz's contention, stating that he himself has learned the hard way "how difficult it is to get my music onto ever-tighter radio play lists." He adds that "many of our artists barely survive because they cannot garner radio air play in major markets."[9] Clear Channel is regularly accused of limiting playlists, favoring artists who tour through the company's concert wing. It denies such favoritism.

Censoring the Song

The political use of music also became an issue after consolidation. Writing in the *New York Times,* Brent Staples observed that during the Vietnam War popular music played a crucial role, with radio stations throughout the country playing political songs that became popular hits. As an example, he cites Crosby, Stills, and Nash's "Ohio," about the killing of antiwar demonstrators at Kent State University by the Ohio National Guard. The song became a key antiwar message, played on stations nationally. Staples contends that today, under consolidation,

> a comparable song about George W. Bush's rush to war in Iraq would
> have no chance at all. . . . There are plenty of angry people, many with
> prime music-buying demographics. But independent radio stations that
> once would have played edgy, political music have been gobbled up by
> corporations that control hundreds of stations and have no wish to rock
> the boat. Corporate ownership has changed what gets played—and who
> plays it. With a few exceptions, the disc jockeys, who once existed to
> discover provocative new music, have long since been put out to pas-
> ture. The new generation operates from play lists dictated by Corpo-
> rate Central—lists that some D.J.s describe as "wallpaper music."[10]

The aftermath of the September 11, 2001, attack on the World Trade Center and the Pentagon and the war on Iraq in 2003 generated restrictions by corporate owners on the content of music played. Tom Morello, former guitarist of Rage Against the Machine, said that he saw a list of 150 restricted songs sent to Clear Channel stations after 9/11, including John Lennon's "Imagine" and Nena's antinuclear "99 Luft Balloons." Morello said it was "an overt act of censorship directly tied to media consolidation." Many musicians testified that they were afraid to express their personal views on political issues, especially on the U.S. actions in Iraq, for fear that their recordings would be banned. When a member of the Dixie Chicks band criticized President Bush's actions regarding Iraq, the group's songs were banned by Cumulus and on other conglomerates' stations. The Dixie Chicks' manager, Simon Renshaw, testified at a Senate hearing that "what happened to my clients is perhaps the most compelling evidence that radio ownership consolidation has a direct negative impact on diversity of programming and political discourse over the public airwaves." Many musicians who wanted to speak out against Bush's war policy did not because they were afraid that "radio will ban my songs."[11] They had good reason for feeling this way.

Despite the myth about "liberal media," the media are overwhelmingly conservative in ownership and control, and during the war on Iraq they used their power to favor pro-Bush performers and rhetoric and discriminate against alternative or dissident ideas. For example, Clear Channel, which had made a leasing agreement with a group called Project Billboard for a billboard in New York City's downtown area during the Republican convention in August 2004, backed out when they learned that the billboard advertisement was critical of the White House's war policy (the ad showed a bomb and the words "Democracy is best taught by example, not by war"). Project Billboard, according to the *New York Times*, alleged that the Clear Channel turnabout reflected its close ties to President Bush and the Republican party.[12]

Brent Staples wrote in the *New York Times*, "Corporate radio's treatment of the Dixie Chicks argues against those who wish to remove all remaining federal limits on corporate ownership—not just of radio, but television as well. The dangers posed by concentrated ownership go beyond news and censorship issues, to the heart of popular culture itself. By standardizing music and voices around the country, radio is slowly killing off local musical cultures, along with the diverse bodies of music that enriched the national popular culture."[13]

More musicians have been speaking out against consolidation, however, since the initial impact of the 1996 act became evident. They have contended "that consolidation of recording labels and radio stations has homogenized music across the country and stifled free expression." They say "that it is becoming more difficult for new artists to break into the mainstream and that the quality of music is suffering."[14] Many musicians have testified before Congress, and hundreds have signed petitions to the FCC protesting any further relaxation of the ownership rules.

Same Old Tune

In May 2002, the Future of Music Coalition (FMC), an organization composed of representatives and individuals in the fields of music, technology, and intellectual property, conducted a survey in partnership with the Rockefeller Foundation and the Media Access Project to determine people's attitudes toward radio. The survey found that listeners opposed federal deregulation that permitted more consolidation of radio stations, that listeners want local deejays to have more control over their stations' programming, and that they wanted "more new music, less repetition and more songs from local bands and artists." Pam Taylor of Clear Channel insisted, however, that her company's own surveys shows that listeners are getting the music they want.[15]

In November 2002, the FMC published a report of its extensive study of the effects of radio ownership consolidation after the Telecommunications Act of 1996, "Radio Deregulation: Has It Served Citizens and Musicians?", arguably the most comprehensive and forceful document on the impact of conglomeration on radio music programming. The report stressed that the consolidation of radio stemming from the Telecommunications Act of 1996 has resulted in less competition and diversity in radio and a serious erosion of localism. It concluded that ownership deregulation has harmed the public, the music played, and musicians. Statistical studies showed that almost every music format is controlled by an oligopoly and that four companies controlled more than half of the music played on radio stations throughout the country and the outlets for two-thirds of the listening public.

Among the report's other findings: a conglomerate's economic power in any given market forces small independent stations to the edge of bankruptcy, enabling the conglomerate to acquire additional stations cheaply and thereby further eliminating local station programming and services. In many of these markets the conglomerate owners operate several stations that sound similar to save operational costs, eliminating diversity in programming; conglomerates have increased the diversity of formats in many markets, but within these formats there is a homogeneity of bland, similar songs, and little if any new or alternative music. Fewer songs are being played, with many titles retained on playlists for extended periods of time; the similarity of music on radio has turned many listeners away from radio stations to other sources for their music, such as the Internet, where a greater variety of music is available.

Both support and criticism of the study were quick to follow. Consumer groups and media watchdog organizations praised and supported the report and coalition. Senator Russell Feingold reflected the views of a number of concerned members of Congress, stating that the report reflected complaints he had received from many of his constituents and that he would do what he could in Congress to advance legislation limiting anticompetitive practices in the media industry.[16]

The National Association of Broadcasters reflected the views of industry in attacking the report. The NAB stated that the FMC's study was flawed and had little credibility, and that radio format diversity had, in fact, increased by 7 percent since the 1996 act. The NAB maintained that radio is one of the least consolidated industries in the United States, with 4,000 separate companies owning the more than 13,000 radio stations in the country. The NAB argued that the top ten radio station owners account for less than half (49 percent) of radio revenues, in contrast to the FMC's findings that these top ten account for 67 percent. The NAB called the charge that listeners are dissatisfied with radio a "myth," citing an NAB study that found that 75 percent of Americans tune in to radio every day, that "radio does a good job of playing the kinds of music they like," and that 95 percent listen to the radio every week.[17]

Report to Congress

Shortly after the issuance of its report, the Future of Music Coalition's director, Jenny Toomey, testified in Congress that "consolidation has resulted in a small number of dominant companies, not competition; it has resulted in extensive local oligopolies, not localism; it has resulted in format homogeneity, not diversity in programming; and it has resulted in a smaller number of gatekeepers for music and news, not a diversity of viewpoints." Toomey asserted that deregulation has failed and that radio needs a new direction, a return to

the traditional priorities of localism, diversity and competition. Can local artists have a legitimate chance to get on commercial radio in their hometowns? Is there not only diversity of format, but also diversity of ownership and, dare we say, diversity of programming target populations who may not fall into the most attractive marketing demographics? And is there a competitive environment that allows for the kinds of small, independent stations that tend to focus on local content and genres of music that are rarely seen from the conglomerates?[18]

(See appendix 7.1 for the full text of the FMC's testimony.)

In September 2003, the Future of Music Coalition filed a petition with the FCC asking it to reconsider its June 2 action further deregulating ownership rules. It expressed particular concern with the FCC's use of a concept of competition in justifying its new regulations that allegedly ignored the importance of localism and diversity. The petition further objected to the FCC's inclusion of noncommercial radio stations in its judgments that certain markets had satisfactory local radio service, and it objected to the FCC precluding consideration of tightening ownership rules, as opposed to only relaxing them, in its Report and Order.[19] (See appendix 7.2 for the Executive Summary of the Future of Music Coalition's petition.)

One of the key defenses of the industry to the charges made that programming in general and music in particular had become homogenized was that syndicated programming was of a higher quality than the program and music a given station could produce on its own. *Radio Ink,* in July 2004, summarized the attitudes of conglomerate and individual station representatives on this subject at a Programmer's Roundtable discussion.[20] Kerry Wolfe, on-air personality at a Clear Channel station in Milwaukee, claimed that his local program "blows away" some nationally produced programs. Clay Hunnicut, program director of a Nashville station, said that sometimes national programming is better and sometimes local programming is, arguing that "a lot of times they [national sources] get artists and guests that a local station would not have access to." Don Kelley of Greater Media conceded that "in an age when branding a station at every opportunity is crucial, syndicated shows tend to be too generic." Barry Kent of a Terre Haute station maintained that syndicated programs can provide artists that a medium or small market doesn't have access to, and that a syndicated live show is much better than what the individual station can do. Gregg Swedberg of Clear Channel reiterated that the corporate resources of a conglomerate enable it to "put almost anything on the air . . . [and] we can localize it, so it would be very difficult for anyone to put something better on the air." Darryl Parks of Cincinnati's WLW affirmed his interest in "entertaining, compelling, quality" syndicated programming but noted that "there's also a lot of mediocre programming out there, and most of it is just poor Limbaugh imitators doing the 'Bush-Good, Kerry-Bad' talk shows." Phil Boyce of WABC, New York, felt that local stations are capable of producing higher quality programs and said that his network has syndicated some of his locally produced shows. Mike Hammond, from the Citadel-Knoxville market, said, "I feel we have local talent that can produce network quality programs with even better production values."

To the extent that these comments reflect the attitudes of affiliated local stations as whole, it would appear that local programming of a high quality is possible, if not always available. The larger question is whether locally produced programming, especially that which feeds a network, is oriented to local needs and concerns to a greater extent than the syndicated programs the given station receives. To what degree are the local stations represented above—and in the country as a whole—providing a satisfactory local service that maintains the principle of localism in radio?

While consolidation bore the brunt of the attack for the disappearance of localism in music programming and in other radio services, other factors were also at play that challenged the voice and very existence of local radio. In the next chapter, we discuss the effect of some of these factors, particularly the Internet and satellite radio.

Future of Music Coalition

1615 L Street NW, Suite 520, Washington, DC 20036 • 202.518.4117

Radio Deregulation: Has It Served Citizens and Musicians?

EXECUTIVE SUMMARY

This report is an historical, structural, statistical, and public survey analysis of the effects of the 1996 Telecommunications Act on musicians and citizens.

Each week, radio reaches nearly 95 percent of the U.S. population over the age of 12.

But more importantly, radio uses a frequency spectrum owned, ultimately, by the American public. Because the federal government manages this spectrum on citizens' behalf, the Federal Communications Commission (FCC) has a clear mandate to enact policies that balance the rights of citizens with the legitimate interests of broadcasters.

Radio has changed drastically since the 1996 Telecommunications Act eliminated a cap on nationwide station ownership and increased the number of stations one entity could own in a single market. This legislation sparked an unprecedented period of ownership consolidation in the industry with significant and adverse effects on musicians and citizens.

What Did the Telecommunications Act of 1996 Aim to Accomplish?

The FCC is mandated by Congress to pursue the "core public interest concerns of promoting diversity and competition." [1] According to a 1996 speech by Reed Hundt, the FCC Chair who led the Commission during the Act's passage, the public had much to gain from the legislation:

> "We are fostering **innovation** and **competition** in radio.
> …The Commission's goal in this proceeding is to further
> competition, just as we seek to promote competition in other
> communications industries we regulate. But in our broadcast
> ownership rules we also seek to promote **diversity in**
> **programming** and **diversity in the viewpoints** expressed on
> this powerful medium that so shapes our culture." [2]
> [emphasis added]

---

[1] FCC Notice of Proposed Rulemaking, November 8th, 2001.

[2] "The Hard Road Ahead," Speech delivered by FCCChairman Reed Hundt, December 26, 1996. Appendix I of Patricia Aufderheide's, *Communications Policy and the Public Interest*, Guilford Press, 1999, p. 289.

This report supplies a comprehensive analysis of statistical radio industry data and a survey of public views on radio, raising serious concerns about the state of commercial radio. Deregulation has not met the aspirations and stated goals of Congress and the FCC.

Methodology for Statistical Analysis

Using data from BIA Financial Networks, we analyzed changes in the radio industry's structure from 1996 to 2002. We recorded the number of station acquisitions and the number of parent companies over time, and then focused on the holdings of the large parents. We estimated market shares nationwide using revenue estimates from BIA and Arbitron listenership estimates contained in the BIA database.

We also estimated market share by geographic market and programming format.[3] We used three classifications to categorize formats: two based on BIA data and one based on information from an established trade journal, *Radio and Records*. We employed two measures of choice in the radio programming available to consumers: "format variety," which refers to changes in the number of formats available per market, and "format redundancy," which refers to the phenomenon of one parent owning two or more stations with the same format, in the same market.

As one of the relevant labor forces in the radio industry, we studied the effects of deregulation on musicians. Using chart data from 1994, 1998, and 2002 published in *Radio and Records* and another industry publication, *Billboard Airplay Monitor*, we measured overlap in the songs played by different music formats. Also, using a classification method for record labels that we developed, we calculated the percentage of songs on the radio charts released by the recording industry's six (now five) major label conglomerates.

Methodology for Public Opinion Survey

The Future of Music Coalition commissioned a public opinion survey to measure citizens' satisfaction with commercial radio. From May 13, 2002 to May 20, 2002, Behavior Research Center, a private research firm, conducted in-depth telephone interviews with a random sample of 500 respondents throughout the U.S., aged 14 years or older. The survey asked respondents fifteen questions about radio designed to measure listening habits and opinions on available programming and their views on issues such as radio station ownership and "pay-for-play" practices.

Based on data from the total sample, one can say with 95 percent confidence that the range of error attributable to sampling and other random effects is 4.5 percentage points.

---

[3] Formats – such as Top 40, Country, News, or Talk – describe the type of music, discussion, or information offered by radio stations.

Major Findings

EVIDENCE OF CONSOLIDATION

1. Ten parent companies dominate the radio spectrum, radio listenership and radio revenues. Deregulation has allowed a few large radio companies to swallow many of the small ones. Together these ten parent companies control two-thirds of both listeners and revenue nationwide. Two parent companies in particular, Clear Channel and Viacom, control 42 percent of listeners and 45 percent of industry revenues.

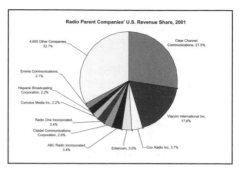

2. Consolidation is particularly extreme in the case of Clear Channel. Since passage of the 1996 Telecommunications Act, Clear Channel has grown from 40 stations to 1,240 stations -- 30 times more than congressional regulation previously allowed. No potential competitor owns even one-quarter the number of Clear Channel stations. With over 100 million listeners, Clear Channel reaches over one-third of the U.S. population.

3. Oligopolies control almost every geographic market. Virtually every geographic market is dominated by four firms controlling 70 percent of market share or greater. In smaller markets, consolidation is more extreme. The largest four firms in most small markets control 90 percent of market share or more. These companies are sometimes regional or national station groups and not locally owned.

4. Virtually every music format is controlled by an oligopoly. In 28 of the 30 major music formats, nationwide, four companies or fewer control over 50 percent of listeners.

EFFECTS OF CONSOLIDATION

5. A small number of companies control the news Americans hear on the radio. Four parent companies control two-thirds of the nation's News format listeners. Two such firms, Viacom and Disney's ABC Radio, also control major television networks.

6. Format consolidation leads to fewer gatekeepers. A small number of companies control what music is played on specific formats. Coupled with a broad trend toward shorter playlists, this creates few opportunities for musicians to get on the radio. Further, overwhelming consolidation of these formats deprives citizens the opportunity to hear a wide range of music.

7. Increased format variety does not ensure increased programming diversity. From 1996 to 2000, format variety – the average number of formats available in each geographic market – increased in both large and small markets.

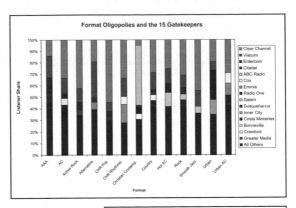

Yet format variety is not equivalent to true diversity in programming. Formats with different names have similar playlists. Analyzing data from charts in *Radio and Records* and *Billboard Airplay Monitor*, revealed considerable format homogeneity – playlist overlap between supposedly distinct formats: as much as 76 percent.

Furthermore, radio companies regularly operate two or more stations with the same format in the same geographic market. Such format redundancy undermines a common economic assumption that station owners with multiple stations in a market would program differently, in order to avoid competing against themselves. We found 561 instances of format redundancy nationwide, amounting to massive missed opportunities for format variety, which might in turn enhance programming diversity.

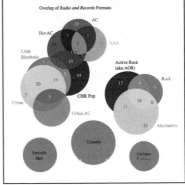

8. **A "twin bottleneck" limits musicians' access to radio.** Radio's oligopolies interact with a five-company recording industry oligopoly, hurting musicians and citizens. Eighty to 100 percent of radio charts are dominated by songs released by the five (previously six) major label conglomerates. This "twin bottleneck" makes access to the airwaves even more difficult for musicians – and reduces choice for citizens.

CITIZENS' VIEWS ON RADIO AND CONSOLIDATION

9. **Radio reaches a large portion of adults on a weekly basis, but time spent listening is at a 27-year low.** In September 2002, Duncan's American Radio reported that the "average persons rating" – the percentage of the U.S. population listening to the radio in any average quarter hour – has experienced a near-17 percent drop in listening over the last 13 years.

10. **Citizens favor preservation of independent and locally owned stations.** Eighty percent of survey respondents support action to prevent further consolidation. Thirty-eight percent would go

a step further, supporting congressional action that encourages more local ownership of radio stations.

11. **Radio listeners want less advertising**. Industry wide, the amount of advertising per hour has grown significantly over the last several years. A 2000 study found that advertising "clutter" had increased six percent nationwide in 1999, though by 2000 the amount of ads had leveled off. [4] When asked about the quantity of ads, 60 percent of survey respondents said that radio has too much advertising.

12. **Radio listeners want to hear a wider range of music that includes local musicians**. Twenty-five percent of survey respondents said they hear too little of the music they like; 38 percent said that local artists are underexposed on the radio.

13. **Radio listeners want longer playlists with more variety**. Seventy-eight percent of those surveyed would rather hear programming from a longer playlist – one with more songs – than from a shorter one. Fifty-two percent of those surveyed said that less repetition, more new music, or more local acts would most make radio more appealing.

14. **Citizens support action to stop "indie" promotion**. Sixty-eight percent of those surveyed support congressional involvement to curb the use of payola-like systems that use third parties to let record companies pay radio stations for airplay.

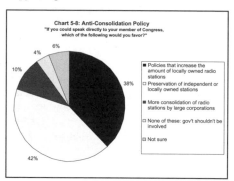

15. **Citizens support efforts to grow low power FM radio**. Seventy-five percent of survey respondents said they would welcome low power radio stations into their communities.

Conclusions

The radical deregulation of the radio industry allowed by the Telecommunications Act of 1996 has not benefited the public or musicians. Instead, it has led to less competition, fewer viewpoints, and less diversity in programming. Deregulation has damaged radio as a public resource.

This research makes an overwhelming case that market consolidation intended by the act does not serve the diverse needs of Americans citizens. Substantial ethnic, regional and economic

---

[4] "Study Finds Fewer Ads on Radio," *Billboard Magazine*, May 5, 2001 and Kathryn Kranhold, "Advertising on Radio Increases 6%; San Francisco area sees 20% Rise", *Asian Wall Street Journal*, April 13, 2000.

[5] Comments at the Conference of the National Association of Broadcasters, September 13th, 2002.

populations are not provided the service to which they are entitled. The public is not satisfied and possible economic efficiencies of industry consolidation are not being passed on to the public in the form of improved local service.

In September 2002, the FCC announced a period of open review of the current ownership rules, suggesting it may consider further deregulation of the radio industry. FCC Chairman Michael Powell described this as "the most comprehensive undertaking in the area of media ownership in the commission's history." We welcome this review period and offer these findings to the debate as cautionary data. "Open review" should not imply open season for increased corporate media control. Facilitating continued consolidation will speed the unfolding tragedy of our rapidly closing public airwaves. The FMC sincerely believes that deregulation should not receive a further endorsement from Congress or the FCC.

About the Future of Music Coalition

The Future of Music Coalition is a Washington, DC-based not-for-profit collaboration between members of the music, technology, public policy and intellectual property law communities. The FMC seeks to educate media organizations, policymakers and the public about music/technology issues while bringing together diverse voices to develop creative solutions to challenges in this space. The FMC also aims to identify and promote innovative business models that will help musicians and citizens benefit from new technologies.

About the Primary Authors

Kristin Thomson is a community organizer, social policy researcher, entrepreneur and musician. After graduating with a BA in Sociology from Colorado College in 1989, Kristin moved to Washington, DC where she worked for two years as a national action organizer for the National Organization for Women. She left NOW in 1992 to make a full-time commitment to Simple Machines, an independent record label she co-ran with Jenny Toomey. In 2001, Kristin graduated with a Masters in Urban Affairs and Public Policy from the University of Delaware. Currently, she manages research projects for the FMC and works for the DC-based public relations firm Bracy Tucker Brown.

Peter DiCola is a graduate student pursuing a law degree and a PhD in economics at the University of Michigan in Ann Arbor. His research interests include labor economics, public finance, industrial organization, and intellectual property law. Peter's interest in the radio and music industries began at college, where he spent a year booking independent rock, jazz and electronic music at the Terrace Club in Princeton, NJ. He also worked as a DJ at WPRB-Princeton for three years. Before entering graduate school, Peter was a consultant with Mercer Management Consulting in Chicago. His projects there involved organizational design and statistical survey research. Peter joined the FMC in 2000 to study the effects of technological change on the musicians' labor market. He currently serves as Director of Economic Analysis for the FMC in addition to his graduate studies.

Future of Music Coalition

1615 L Street NW, Suite 520, Washington, DC 20036 • 202.429.8855

Radio Deregulation:
Has It Served Citizens and Musicians?

**Testimony of the Future of Music Coalition
on
"Media Ownership: Radio"**

**Submitted to the Senate Committee on
Commerce, Science, and Transportation**

January 30, 2003

Jenny Toomey, Executive Director
Michael Bracy, Director of Government Relations
Peter DiCola, Director of Economic Analysis
Walter McDonough, General Counsel
Kristin Thomson, Research Director
Brian Zisk, Technologies Director

www.futureofmusic.org

Good morning. On behalf of the Future of Music Coalition, it is my honor to testify this morning on the critical issue of how radio consolidation is affecting musicians and citizens. This is a timely hearing, and we applaud you for holding it. We also applaud the participation of the other witnesses, as we firmly believe that the public deserves an open, honest discussion about these issues, especially in an environment where further deregulation is under consideration at the FCC.

First, I will provide a quick background about myself and the Future of Music Coalition. Second, I will outline some of the conclusions of our recently released study on the impact of radio consolidation on musicians and citizens. Finally, I will talk about the importance of radio as a medium, and what we can do to make it better.

About Jenny Toomey and the Future of Music Coalition

My name is Jenny Toomey. I am a musician, entrepreneur and activist. I have released seven albums and toured extensively across the United States and Europe. For eight years, I co-ran an independent record label called Simple Machines. I know first hand both the difficulties that independent artists face in getting their music played on commercial radio and the opportunities that are presented by non-commercial radio stations that -- thankfully -- have been very supportive over the years.

I speak to you today both as a working artist and as Executive Director of the Future of Music Coalition, a not-for-profit think tank I co-founded three years ago with Michael Bracy, Walter McDonough and Brian Zisk. The Future of Music Coalition examines issues at the intersection of music, technology, law, economics and policy, in search of policies, technologies and business models that can benefit musicians and music fans. The FMC is built on the idea that the music industry is broken at a very basic level, as the very artists who create the works that are the hallmark of our culture struggle against structural impediments that make it difficult to achieve economic survival. It is our hope that increased awareness and engagement among artists, combined with thoughtful implementation of new technologies, will lead to new structures in a digital future that won't replicate the failures of our terrestrial present.

The Importance of Understanding the Effects of Radio Deregulation

As our organization began working on a wide range of issues – major label contract reform, healthcare for artists, webcasting royalties, peer-to-peer file trading – one issue continued to rise to the top: commercial radio. Everywhere we turned, there seemed to be another article, another letter to the editor, another emerging artist complaining about what was happening with radio in his or her specific community.

Radio is, of course, a critical hub of communications, entertainment and information in our society. The technology is ubiquitous – nearly all Americans own a radio. Historically, radio has been the most effective means of making new music available to local audiences, as program directors and disc jockeys kept the pulse of the industry in search of the next new act or the next new sound. When you read interviews with great musicians, they often reflect on the inspiration they found in their youth as radio connected them with sounds and words from across the world.

For many others, radio is primarily a business, where corporations seek to maximize profits by offering targeted programming intended to reach specific audience demographics preferred by advertisers. In this model, the argument goes, the public is served because broadcasters research what their targeted audience wants to hear, then deliver programming designed to maximize listener share.

We argue, however, that this is not the reason that radio has become such an important part of American culture. Rather, radio has worked over time because of the fundamental regulatory priorities of localism, diversity and competition. Certainly, we believe the strongest demonstrations of localism and diversity are found in non-commercial radio, where a wide range of musical genres and public affairs programs flourish. We encourage the Congress to pursue strategies that maximize the potential of noncommercial radio regardless of this discussion of consolidation of ownership.

In November 2002, the Future of Music Coalition released a study entitled "Radio Deregulation: Has it Served Citizens and Musicians?" The lead authors of the study, FMC board members Kristin Thomson and Peter DiCola, are both here today. We would like to enter the study into the record along with our testimony. The study is also available on our website at http://www.futureofmusic.org, and was entered as a public comment in the FCC's media ownership proceeding.

Background: The Goals of Deregulation

Radio is a public resource managed on citizens' behalf by the federal government. This was established back in 1934 when Congress passed the Communications Act. This Act both created the Federal Communications Commission (FCC) and laid the ground rules for the regulation of radio. The Act also determined that the spectrum would be managed according to a "trusteeship" model. Broadcasters received fixed-term, renewable licenses that gave them exclusive use of a slice of the spectrum for free. In exchange, broadcasters were required to serve the "public interest, convenience and necessity." Though they laid their trust in the mechanics of the marketplace, legislators did not turn the entire spectrum over to commercial broadcasters. The 1934 Act included some key provisions that were designed to foster localism and encourage diversity in programming.

Although changes were made to limits on ownership and FCC regulatory control in years hence, the Communications Act of 1934 remained essentially intact until it was thoroughly overhauled in1996 with the signing of the Telecommunications Act. But even before President Clinton signed the Telecommunications Act into law in February 1996, numerous predictions were made regarding its effect on the radio industry:

Fewer Owners

First, industry analysts predicted that the number of individual radio station owners would decrease. Those in the industry with enough capital would begin to snatch up valuable but under-performing stations in many markets – big and small.

Greater Financial Benefits for Radio

Second, station owners – given the ability to purchase more stations both locally and nationally – would benefit from economies of scale. Radio runs on many fixed costs; equipment, operations and staffing costs are the same whether broadcasting to one person or 1 million. Owners knew that if they could control more than one station in a market, they could consolidate operations and reduce fixed expenses. Lower costs would mean increased profit potential. This would, in turn, make for more financially sound radio stations which would be able to compete more effectively against new media competitors: cable TV and the Internet.

More Diversity

Third, there was a prediction based on a theory posited by a 1950s economist named Peter Steiner that increased ownership consolidation on the local level would lead to a subsequent increase in the number of radio format choices available to the listening public. According to Steiner's theory, a single owner with multiple stations in a local market wouldn't want to compete against himself. Instead, he would program each station differently to meet the tastes of a variety of listeners.

The Results of the Telecommunications Act

These were the predictions made prior to the passage of the Telecommunications Act, and clearly part of the argument made by broadcasters and their representatives on the importance of deregulation to the health of their industry. But what really happened? Enough time has lapsed to evaluate early predictions and note actual outcomes for the radio industry, musicians and citizens. Let's revisit these assumptions:

More Stations, Fewer Owners

Well, one prediction certainly came true: the 1996 Act opened the floodgates for ownership consolidation to occur. Deregulation has allowed a few large radio companies to swallow many of the small ones. Ten parent companies now dominate the radio spectrum, radio listenership and radio revenues, controlling two-thirds of both listeners and revenue nationwide.

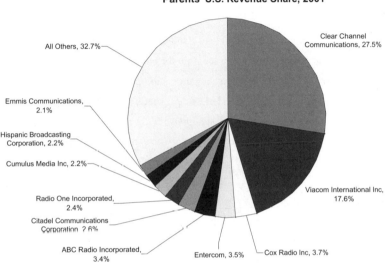

Parents' U.S. Revenue Share, 2001

- Clear Channel Communications, 27.5%
- Viacom International Inc, 17.6%
- Cox Radio Inc, 3.7%
- Entercom, 3.5%
- ABC Radio Incorporated, 3.4%
- Citadel Communications Corporation, 2.6%
- Radio One Incorporated, 2.4%
- Cumulus Media Inc, 2.2%
- Hispanic Broadcasting Corporation, 2.2%
- Emmis Communications, 2.1%
- All Others, 32.7%

You can see from the revenue pie chart[1] that ten firms control 67 percent of industry revenue. The rest of the industry – a total of 4,600 owners – controls just 33 percent.

One gets much the same picture from the numbers on listenership. The same Top 10 firms control 65 percent of radio listeners:

---

[1] Source data: Media Access Pro, BIA Financial Networks, data as of May 16, 2002.

Listener Rank	Parent Company	Arbitron Listeners (in Millions)	Nationwide Share of Listeners
1	Clear Channel	103.4	27.0%
2	Viacom	59.1	15.4%
3	Cox	13.2	3.5%
4	Entercom	13.1	3.4%
5	ABC Radio	12.6	3.3%
6	Radio One	11.3	2.9%
7	Emmis	10.6	2.8%
8	Citadel	10.5	2.7%
9	Hispanic Brdcstg.	8.7	2.3%
10	Cumulus	7.2	1.9%

An industry is an oligopoly in our terminology if the four largest companies control more than 50 percent market share. As you can see from the charts, the top four companies in radio control 52 percent of the revenue, making the radio industry an oligopoly. This means that we have *less* competition than before deregulation, not more. Oligopolistic control and socially beneficial competition are *opposites*. In general oligopolies can raise prices above competitive levels, restrict quantities of goods offered to the public, and – as we'll see in the radio industry – reduce the *quality* of what's offered to the public.

Two parent companies in particular – Clear Channel and Viacom – together control 42 percent of listeners and 45 percent of industry revenues. Clear Channel has grown from 40 stations to 1,240 stations -- 30 times more than congressional regulation previously allowed. No potential competitor owns even one-quarter the number of Clear Channel stations. With over 100 million listeners, Clear Channel reaches over one-third of the U.S. population. These two firms tower over the radio industry, and even over the other consolidators. Both own businesses in other media and advertising-based industries, such as network television, cable television, concert venues, and billboards.

---

[2] Source data: Media Access Pro, BIA Financial Networks, data as of May 16, 2002. The statistic for listeners is known in the radio industry as "Metro Cume Listeners." Generally speaking, the BIA database has metro cume listener figures only for stations in the Top 289 Arbitron-rated markets. Many stations with religious formats do not appear to report listenership or revenue figures to BIA.

Radio at the Local Level

Even bleaker is the picture at the local level, where oligopolies control almost every geographic market. In smaller markets, consolidation is more extreme where the largest four firms in most small markets control 90 percent of market share or more. These companies are sometimes regional or national station groups and not locally owned.

This next chart[3] shows the extent of consolidation in these market size categories. Each market size category is broken down by the extent of consolidation in its markets. Let's take an example. Among the markets ranked 101-289, 40 percent of the markets have four companies controlling 100 percent of the market share. 24 percent of the markets have four companies controlling 95 to 100 percent. 18 percent of the markets have four companies controlling 90 to 95 percent, and so on. Clearly consolidation is most extensive in the smallest markets.

Concentration by Market Size Category

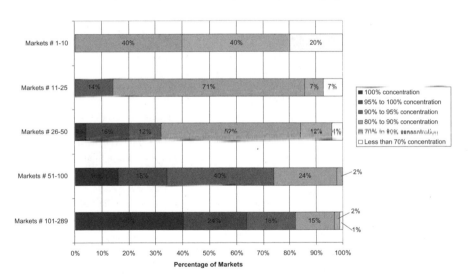

---

[3] Source data: Media Access Pro, BIA Financial Networks, data as of May 16, 2002.

But the larger point is that consolidation is extensive in *all* sizes of local markets. In 98 percent of all local markets, the top four companies control a 70 percent market share or greater. Such large shares for the biggest companies indicate that very strong oligopolies exist locally.

Benefits From Economies of Scale Aren't for Everyone
What about those benefits of economies of scale? They've certainly borne out for some, but not for everyone. Only the few radio station owners with enough capital to buy additional stations have benefited from deregulation. Station owners have consolidated their operations on a local level, frequently running a number of stations out of a single building, sharing a single advertising staff, technicians and on-air talent. In some cases, radio station groups have further reduced costs by eliminating the local component almost entirely. These group owners are benefiting from economies of scale, but what are the drawbacks? Local DJs and program directors are being replaced by regional directors or even by voice-tracked or syndicated programming, explaining a marked decrease in the number of people employed in the radio industry. Listeners are losing as well. With an emphasis on cost cutting and an effort to move decision-making out of the hands of local station staff, much of radio has become bland and formulaic.[4]

Less Regulation Has Not Led to Greater Market Competition
The economic argument for the need for increased competition in the radio industry is specious. Prior to 1996, radio was among the least concentrated and most economically competitive of the media industries. In 1990, no company owned more than 14 of the

---

[4] See the following articles for more information about voice-tracking, loss of localism, and regional-based programming: Anna Mathews, "Think Your DJ is Local? Think Again." *Wall Street Journal*, February 25, 2002. Randy Dotinga, "Good Morning [Your Town Here]," *Wired.com*, August 6, 2002. http://www.wired.com/news/business/0,1367,54037,00.html . Denny Lee, "Disc Jockeys Are Resisting Taking the Local Out of Local Radio," *New York Times,* August 25, 2002. Eric Boehlert, "Radio's Big Bully," *Salon.com*, April 30, 2001, http://www.salon.com/ent/feature/2001/04/30/clear_channel/index.html. Greg Kot, "Rocking Radio's World," *Chicago Tribune,* April 14, 2002. Jeff Leeds, "Clear Channel: An Empire Built on Deregulation," *Los Angeles Times*, February 25, 2002. Todd Spencer, "Radio Killed the Radio Star," *Salon.com*, October 1, 2002 http://www.salon.com/tech/feature/2002/10/01/nab/print.html Dale Smith, "Hello Honolulu and Amarillo, my Austin Secret is… I'm Your DJ," *Austin American-Statesman*, July 22, 1999.

10,000 stations nationwide, with no more than two in a single local market. But we found that local markets have consolidated to the point now that just four major radio groups control about 50 percent of the total listener audience and revenue. Clearly, deregulation has *reduced* competition within the radio industry.

More Diversity?

Finally, we raise questions about Steiner's theory that an owner would not want to compete against himself and would, therefore, operate stations with different programming. Our analysis of the data finds otherwise. Radio companies regularly operate two or more stations with the same format in the same geographic market. Using stations' self-reported formats, we found 561 instances of format redundancy nationwide – a parent company operating two or more stations in the same market, with the same format – involving 1,190 stations in Arbitron-rated markets, as of May 2002.[5] This amounts to massive missed opportunities for format variety, which might in turn enhance programming diversity.

Format Variety versus Format Diversity

In addition, we need to be clear about the difference between format variety and format diversity. Often, the radio industry measures diversity in programming by counting the number of formats available in each local market. In our report we show, in accordance with other studies, that format variety counted this way increased for a while after deregulation. But we also find that format variety has become stagnant over the last two years.[6]

Regardless, format variety is a flawed measure that doesn't capture the more relevant concept of programming diversity. A format is just a label – it doesn't necessarily describe the contents or imply that the contents are different than anything else. Increased format variety does not ensure increased programming diversity.

---

[5] Source data: Media Access Pro, BIA Financial Networks, data as of May 16, 2002.

[6] For an analysis of format variety 1996 – 2002 please see "Radio Deregulation: Has it Served Citizens and Musicians?" Chapter 3 pp. 44-48.

We tested this theory by analyzing data from charts in *Radio and Records* and Billboard's *Airplay Monitor*. Using radio playlist data, *Radio and Records* magazine computes weekly charts for 13 categories of music formats. We took these charts from one week in August 2002 – which show the top 30, 40, or 50 songs played on a given format – and calculated the number of overlapping songs between formats.

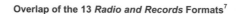

Overlap of the 13 *Radio and Records* Formats[7]

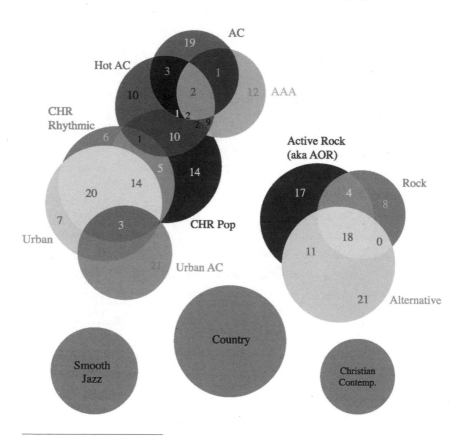

---

[7] Notes: Data from the week ending August 2, 2002. The size of each circle in the diagram is proportional to the size of its corresponding format's chart (charts list 20, 30, 40 or 50 songs. Most of the charts have either 30 or 50 songs – only Christian Contemporary has 20 songs and only Hot AC has 40 songs. Not every overlap between two formats is demonstrated here, but almost all of the largest (five songs or more) overlaps are.

The charts revealed considerable format homogeneity – playlist overlap between supposedly distinct formats. Note that the formats are grouped in clusters. First, there's the pop cluster. It features seven overlapping formats. For example, Urban and CHR/Rhythmic overlap at a 76 percent level. 38 of their top 50 songs are the same. Then, there's the rock cluster. Rock, Alternative, and Album-Oriented Rock overlap considerably, between 36 percent and 58 percent depending on which pair among those three you consider. Only Country, Christian, and Smooth Jazz stand alone.

This high level of homogeneity shows that simply counting format names will overstate programming diversity. Adding a CHR/Rhythmic station to a market that already has an Urban station adds format variety. But it doesn't add any programming diversity. Thus, the radio industry has measured itself – and encouraged policy makers to measure it – with an inadequate statistic. If the FCC or the NAB are sincerely trying to measure "diversity" the quantity of formats is a flawed measure. That's like counting the number of jars on a shelf without taking the time to look inside.

Format Oligopolies
In addition, viewing each format as its own product market, every format category charted by *Radio and Records* is controlled by an oligopoly.

We studied format oligopolies by considering the radio stations nationwide within each format as a separate market. We simply tallied the listener share and revenue share within each format nationwide. As you can see from this chart,[8] every format is controlled by four companies with a 50 percent market share or greater.

---

[8] Source data: *Radio and Records* website, www.radioandrecords.com, and Media Access Pro, BIA Financial Networks, data as of May 16, 2002.

Format Consolidation in the 13 *Radio and Records*-based Categories, by Listener Share

"R & R" Category	Listeners (in Millions)	Top 4 Firms, by Listeners	Top 4 Share
AC	38.5	Clear Channel, Viacom, Bonneville, Entercom	56.3%
CHR Pop	37.3	Clear Channel, Viacom, Entercom, Citadel	69.8%
Country	33.9	Clear Channel, Viacom, Citadel, Cox	52.6%
Rock	28.8	Clear Channel, Viacom, Citadel, ABC Radio	52.3%
Hot AC	19.3	Clear Channel, Viacom, ABC Radio, Entercom	57.9%
Alternative	17.8	Viacom, Clear Channel, Emmis, Citadel	60.5%
Urban	15.5	Radio One, Clear Channel, Inner City, Viacom	64.9%
CHR Rhythmic	14.4	Clear Channel, Viacom, Emmis, Cox	71.8%
Urban AC	13.1	Clear Channel, Radio One, Emmis, Cox	67.1%
Active Rock	9.2	Clear Channel, Viacom, Entercom, Greater Media	65.5%
Smooth Jazz	6.1	Clear Channel, Viacom, Radio One, ABC Radio	69.7%
AAA	3.6	Viacom, Clear Channel, Susquehanna, Entercom	53.8%
Christian Contemp.	2.7	Salem, Crista Ministries, Crawford, Clear Channel	68.9%

The format oligopolies reinforce the homogeneity of the product offered to listeners. They also result in a small number of gatekeepers deciding which musicians have their music played on the air. Importantly, these format oligopolies include many of the same companies. For instance, Clear Channel is one of the top four firms in each of these 13 formats. Viacom is one of the top four firms in 11 of these formats.

In fact, only 15 companies populate this chart of format oligopolies. These 15 gatekeepers determine to a very large extent what programming will reach the airwaves. And this just looks at music. Four companies own a 67 percent share of News format listeners nationwide. Consolidation has not resulted in a greater number of viewpoints represented on the air; instead, it has reduced the diversity of viewpoints considerably.

This final point may be the most critical one as we face an FCC that is poised to deregulate media even further in the next few months. It is time to put to bed the commonly held yet fundamentally flawed notion that consolidation promotes diversity as that radio station owners who own two stations within a marketplace will not be tempted to program both stations with similar formats.

In sum, consolidation has resulted in a small number of dominant companies, not competition; it has resulted in extensive local oligopolies, not localism; it has resulted in format homogeneity, not diversity in programming; and it has resulted in small number of gatekeepers for music and news, not a diversity of viewpoints. Clearly something has gone wrong. From the perspective of citizens and musicians, deregulation has failed to achieve its goals. Radio needs a new direction to restore its status as a live, local, diversely owned and diversely programmed medium.

Where Do We Go From Here?

Over the past year, we have heard concern about radio consolidation expressed by musicians, unions, record labels, consumer groups, religious groups, small broadcasters, current and former industry employees and elected officials. Concern about the loss of local voices. Concern about business practices like "pay for play" that appear to make eligibility for radio play contingent on an artist or label coming forward with huge "promotional" fees. Concern that the local stations that used to provide a platform for public service announcements now turn them away. Concern about the seemingly incessant advertising. Concern that small stations that have programmed an eclectic mix are changing formats or selling out because they can't compete. Concern that elected officials have fewer outlets available to communicate directly with voters. Concern that talk radio stations won't allow questions from callers who "sound old" because it will send the signal that their station is targeted for older consumers. Concern that parents can't listen to the radio with their kids in the car because the content has become so overtly sexual. Concern that alternate models to commercial radio, like community-based Low Power FM, are scaled back because of the power of the broadcast lobby. And concern that musicians who speak publicly about troubling business practices will be in essence signing the death warrant for their careers.

In the end, we come back to this point: radio is a public resource. It belongs to the citizens of the United States. It is not simply a tool for corporations who are interested in maximizing profits.

We do not question that broadcast conglomerates spend enormous resources in attempts to draw the largest possible audience in the specific demographics that their stations are targeting. But is that really how we define serving the public interest? Huge ratings?

We need to return to the traditional priorities of localism, diversity and competition. Can local artists have a legitimate chance to get on commercial radio in their hometown? Is there not only diversity of format, but also diversity of ownership and, dare we say, diversity of programming targeting populations who may not fall into the most attractive marketing demographics? And is there a competitive environment that allows for the kinds of small, independent stations that tend to focus on local content and genres of music that are rarely seen from the conglomerates?

We have been joined by our colleagues in the music community to raise these questions. In particular, we are greatly appreciative of the support and cooperation of AFTRA – the union that represents on-air talent – the AFM, the Recording Academy, Just Plain Folks, the Artists Empowerment Coalition and the Recording Artists Coalition. On many of these issues, we even agree with the RIAA. But the onus of proof should not fall simply on the complainers. The broadcast industry pushed for these changes, and now they should be able to step forward to fully explain their impact on localism, competition and diversity. To this date, their participation in public discourse regarding the present and future of the radio industry has been sadly lacking.

In the end, it is clear that the broadcast conglomerates have one primary mission - maximizing shareholder value. They maximize value by utilizing the latest research techniques in an effort to build the largest possible audiences in their targeted demographics. Their mantra is that they give the people what they want. They play the hits.

But do they give the people what they want? According to *Duncan's Radio Report*, radio listenership is at a 27 year low.[9] And not one but two companies are now selling a satellite radio service based on the notion that consumers are so disenfranchised with radio today that they would pay $10 a month to subscribe to their service. And what if you don't fit into the demographics they pursue – what if you are old, or poor?

Has the restructuring of the radio industry been a success? This is the crux of the great disconnect. On one side, artists, record labels, consumer groups, religious organizations, community groups, unions, elected officials and music fans say "no". On the other, broadcasters say "yes." But you can't even say all broadcasters, since it seems that an increasing number of those left are expressing concern about their ability to compete in this consolidated marketplace.

Radio is too precious to let this happen. It is universal, and it is cheap. It is part of our culture. And communities are begging for the opportunity to better utilize it for non-commercial means. Thanks in great deal to the efforts of Chairman McCain, roughly 1000 rural community groups, schools and churches are launching Low Power Radio Stations in their neighborhoods or towns. The FCC was stripped of its ability to place these stations in urban areas pending further signal tests, and hundreds of urban groups are eagerly awaiting their shot.

Mr Chairman, the problem is not radio, it's what has happened to radio. We can – we must – do better. I hope that today's hearing serves as an inspiration for citizens around the country to contact you, members of this committee and other members of Congress to inform them of how they would like to see radio better utilized in their community.

Thank you again for inviting me to testify today.

---

[9] "12+ Radio Listening At 27-Year Low" *Radio and Records* website, September 4, 2002.

8 New Audio Media and Localism

The Impact of Satellite and Internet Radio

Satellites and the Internet are homogenizing all radio content and eliminating local services. Satellites and the Internet are providing more local services than are terrestrial radio stations. Depending on whether your focus is political, social, or economic, you are likely to come to different conclusions about these highly successful new technologies even looking at the same facts. Many consumers are against satellite radio because it is not local enough. The radio station industry and the National Association of Broadcasters are against satellite radio because it is trying to be too local.

What is not at issue, however, is that these technologies are having and will have an even greater significant effect on local radio, one way or the other. Writing in *Newsday*, Peter Goodman declared, "Radio is under assault—from the sky, from the computer, even from tiny, low-powered stations that threaten to sneak in under the radar. . . . It may still be called radio in 10 years, for lack of a better word, but that familiar world of transmitters, antennas, and frequency and amplitude modulation . . . appears to be going through changes that will add up to a revolution in how we get food for our ears."[1]

Satellite Versus Broadcast

In mid-2004, NAB president Eddie Fritts conceded that "with the advent of the Internet and satellite radio, there is more competition than ever before for the listener," but he expressed confidence "that [terrestrial] radio will continue to thrive so long as stations retain a commitment to providing local listeners with compelling content."[2] A year earlier, addressing Canadian broadcasters, Fritts emphasized "broadcasting's fundamental commitment to localism." He asserted that "localism is our franchise, and ours alone, and I believe localism will remain the foundation of our success well into future generations. It is that which distinguishes local stations from a cable or satellite channel."[3] Goodman quotes CBS vice president Gil Schwartz's agreement: "The essence of radio is local. These national services piped to you without commercials are not really attractive to radio listeners who are looking for localism." Goodman adds, "That's where local news coverage, local weather, local traffic and local sports come in. It's what local broadcasters have always relied on to win listeners." He concedes, however, that "there's less and less localism on radio today."[4]

Early in 2000, John Eckberg summed up the anticipated impact of new technology in an article entitled "Radio to Change Dramatically."[5] Satellites, he said, would provide dozens of commercial-free channels to automobiles, where more than one-fourth of all radio listening occurs. Pay-to-listen radio would compete with current commercial radio stations, and radio via the Internet would not only grow in popularity, but would also increase in sophistication.

The most immediate dramatic change in radio listening was likely to occur—and did—in automobiles. Modest monthly fees to satellite subscription services bring dozens of music channels without commercial interruptions. Looking ahead from 2000, one broadcasting consultant said, "It will be like [having] all the radio stations in New York and Los Angeles combined."[6]

The satellite industry anticipated the likelihood of its being able to successfully compete with terrestrial radio, given America's penchant for cars and the fact that some 200 million were in operation, and in 1998 Sirius Satellite Radio and XM Satellite Radio, the providers of satellite radio today, obtained rights from the FCC to be "the exclusive providers of clean-signal programming."[7] By mid-2005, XM Satellite claimed to have over four million subscribers. Its president, Hugh Panero, claimed that his company had only "begun to scratch the surface of our market," that XM Satellite was "on our path to reach 20 million subscribers by 2010."[8] In mid-2004, Sirius Satellite Radio passed the half-million subscriber mark. Both companies had reached beyond mobile listeners in cars, boats, and trucks and were providing service to households, as well. Sirius's president was, like his rival satellite radio company, optimistic, stating that "our customers are telling us that Sirius is a service they can't live without." The popularity of satellite radio has grown to such an extent that Wal-Mart added to its line a Sirius "Plug & Play" satellite radio automobile kit and boom box.[9]

Satellite radio has continually extended its music formats, ostensibly the key to its initial success, and has expanded beyond music into other competitive formats. Sirius, for example, added five music channels in July 2004: Elvis Radio, Underground Garage, Boombox (party beats), Area 63 (trance music), and Vacation (including Jimmy Buffett, Bob Marley, and the Beach Boys).[10] Also in 2004, XM strengthened its promotion of a format it had carried since 2002, a Radio Classic channel featuring programs from the so-called golden age of radio such as *The Bob Hope Show, The Shadow, The Jack Benny Show,* and *Gunsmoke.*[11]

Satellite radio proponents compare the service to cable, which developed from being a broadcast-signal repeater to original programming and hundreds of producing networks because viewers were not getting the diversity of programming they wanted from over-the-air television. Several broadcast radio mainstays, among them Howard Stern and Bruce Morrow, have migrated to satellite. Long-time radio professional Jonathan Schwartz has added satellite deejay work to his terrestrial radio work. "Anyone who listens to American radio in any city, large or small, can hear the absence of diversity," Schwartz says. "Anyone with ears can hear the same 37 recordings played over and over again. The industry is run by people with their eyes on the bottom line and not on the CD. This is a tragic American fact of life."[12] XM Satellite Radio, for example, offers over one hundred channels, more than two-thirds of which are music and the rest devoted to news, sports, children's programs, talk, and nonmusical genres such as comedy.[13]

Paul Lewis, co-owner of a low-power FM radio station that is totally oriented to local service is nevertheless enthusiastic about satellite radio—specifically XM in his automobile. He notes that he has a choice of forty channels, including music he can rarely find on terrestrial stations (such as Glenn Miller and other big bands and Frank Sinatra and other crooners) and old-time radio drama and comedy shows.[14]

A Supplemental Service?

At satellite radio's beginning, it was not thought to pose a serious threat to local radio; it would serve as an adjunct or extension, much like early cable did vis-à-vis television. In 2002, shortly after satellite radio made its debut, NAB spokesperson Dennis Wharton said that satellite radio might end up with a small slice of the radio market, mostly to long-distance truck drivers and to music aficionados who either want to sample every music format possible or who want a particular music niche not popular enough for terrestrial stations to play. He stated that satellite radio won't seriously affect traditional radio because it won't have the local service and air talent, such as weather, traffic, and deejays and music styled for a given locality.[15] Emmis Communications CEO Jeff Smulyan believes that traditional radio's local ties will keep it relevant and competitive despite increased competition from other media and new technologies.[16]

Jonathan Schwartz, WNYC host of "The Sunday Show," lauds satellite radio as "the savior of intimate communication. . . . It makes listening to a CD sound like listening to AM radio during a thunderstorm . . . [and] it offers the vastest library of music ever assembled anywhere." But he agrees that "satellite radio is not intended to replace commercial radio. People need local radio. They need local weather. They need to know when the 86th Street cross town bus gets stuck in a tunnel."[17]

When XM Satellite Radio started in 2001, it announced that it had no plans to offer local services to its subscribers. Nevertheless, in 2002 it was putting hundreds of terrestrial radio repeaters throughout the country that, combined with a patent it had obtained, could enable it to transmit locally oriented material to local subscribers. XM insisted that the purpose of the repeaters was only to fill gaps in its satellite coverage. While one arm of the NAB was asserting that satellite radio was not expected to be a threat because it was not carrying local programming, another arm was filing a request with the FCC to bar XM from using its new technology to provide local programs. The NAB complained that "while XM was telling the Commission that it had no plans to use repeaters other than to fill gaps, it was actively developing technology specifically intended to use repeaters to provide locally differentiated material." XM countered, "We are strictly a national satellite-radio service."[18] In March 2004, however, XM launched fourteen new channels with weather and traffic information twenty-four hours a day, each channel oriented to a different metropolitan area.[19]

Terrestrial radio giant Entercom Communications countered with a series of announcements denouncing satellite radio. Bill Pasha, Entercom's vice president for programming, said, "We wanted to tell the story of free radio. Critics say that the main story of free radio in recent years has been one of penny-pinching and canned, cookie-cutter programming. To keep their listeners on board, broadcast radio stations may have to change more than just the image of satellite radio."[20]

An Attitude Shift

The prospect of satellite radio providing local programming changed the tune of many terrestrial broadcasters. Bill O'Shaughnessy, one of the broadcasters opposed to xM terrestrial repeaters, said that local programming services by satellite radio "could unquestionably have a devastating impact on free over-the-air traditional broadcasting as we know it."[21] By 2004, the problem had grown worse. Congressional legislation was introduced barring satellite radio from delivering local programming. NAB president Eddie Fritz commented that the "NAB strongly supports the satellite radio legislation introduced by Representatives Pickering and Green. Localism is the hallmark of our free, over-the-air system and this bill will ensure that satellite companies be held to the standard upon which their licenses were granted. Local stations are the first responders in times of emergency and have an unparalleled record of community service."[22]

At the same time, the NAB petitioned the FCC to forbid both xM and Sirius to broadcast local weather and traffic information. While the satellite-radio companies were allowed to use their terrestrial repeaters to fill gaps in their satellite-serviced delivery, they were not allowed to use them for programming aimed at a particular local market. The NAB petition stated, "This foray into local content is directly contrary to repeated and express promises that satellite radio service would be limited to delivering national programming to serve the unserved and underserved." The NAB also expressed concern that xM and Sirius were developing technology that would enable them to provide locally oriented commercials as well as local news and other local material.[23] The NAB asked the FCC "to evaluate the economic impact of these new satellite services on local broadcasting and the local communities they serve"[24] and to make sure that "satellite radio remains a national-only programming service" and does not impact "local broadcasting and the community it serves."[25]

By June 2004, the battle was joined. xM and Sirius jointly filed in opposition to NAB's position, making it clear that the satellite radio companies did, indeed, intend to provide local programming. Their filing cited 25,000 comments from their subscribers opposing the NAB petition. "They all opposed NAB's position, noting the enormous benefits the traffic and weather service provides them, such as promoting safety by providing alerts to impending severe weather, preventing delays and saving fuel by reporting on traffic congestion."[26] The NAB petition, by the end of June 2004, had the support of forty-five state broadcasting associations, with more coming.[27]

It now seemed like a matter not of whether satellite radio would hurt terrestrial radio, but to what degree. In 2001, when satellite radio began, there was some question as to whether enough subscribers would pay the monthly fee (about $10 at that time) to keep the satellite companies in business. Within a couple of years, it appeared that a sufficient base was there, not only for XM but for Sirius, as well. In 2002, radio programmer Greg Rice warned that "if more people begin switching to satellite radio, less money will be invested in product advertising for smaller, older radio stations. If listeners start switching entirely to [satellite] radio, they not only lose community reporting and local news, but they also decrease the overall constant listener population of AM/FM radio, possibly resulting in less AM/FM advertising investments."[28] This scenario, if played out, could result in the further demise of local, independent stations, the economics of survival forcing them to sell their stations to the conglomerates, thus reducing even more the voices and services of local radio.

Satellite Is Sound

At the end of 2003, the investment research firm of Stifel, Nicolaus and Company released a study of the status of satellite radio. A major conclusion was that both XM and Sirius were doing so well that neither company needed any further equity investment to succeed. Another conclusion was that one of the keys to satellite radio's success was content superior to the homogenized programming, commercial clutter, and censorship found on terrestrial radio stations. The study found that 99 percent of satellite radio subscribers were satisfied with the service and the initial loss-of-customer rate was only one percent; "satellite radio is one of the fastest ever consumer electronic products to reach 1MM subs," and the 108 million daily automobile commuters provide a solid base for growth.[29]

The report also evaluated the impact of satellite radio on traditional radio and found that it is a "slow but legitimate threat": in five to ten years, it "will likely siphon off terrestrial radio's higher income demographic listeners and steal an appropriate share of national advertising dollars." The report suggested that 5 percent of traditional radio's listener base would be lost during that period. The report concedes that satellite radio's current lack of localism is a drawback, but that the FCC will likely authorize satellite radio to broadcast "individualized local market content," at least in the larger markets. In considering other competitive sources, the report broke down the audience listening sites: 39 percent in the home, 33 percent in automobiles, 25 percent on the job, and just 3 percent elsewhere. It dismissed CDs as not having enough variety potential nor immediate access to new music for most listeners. It contended that Internet radio, while a potential competitor to terrestrial radio, would not offer much competition for satellite radio because two-thirds of all radio listening takes place away from home, where most of the accessible computers are.[30]

To what extent might satellite radio force terrestrial radio to reinstate its formerly strong local services in order to compete effectively or, conversely, to abandon localism even more as satellite radio begins to provide it? In November 2004, the NAB dropped its petition against XM providing local weather and traffic programming, but, as the *Radio and Internet Newsletter* concluded, "the issue may not be dead yet."[31]

Cybercasting

While broadband Internet technology has permitted and encouraged many radio listeners to download music for immediate and future use, its impact has been less on local radio stations than on recording companies and musical artists, whose income sales have been allegedly harmed because of illegal pirating. Federal legislation, blocking technology, and legal approaches to music distribution by more and more Internet music companies have ameliorated the situation somewhat. Concomitantly, more and more radio stations are streaming their signals onto the Internet so that if some of their listeners no longer listen to their broadcast signal, many of these listeners continue to hear the stations in cyberspace.

A case in point is the country's largest radio conglomerate, Clear Channel. In 2000, Clear Channel was ready to acquire another radio conglomerate, AMFM. In doing so, it also would be acquiring a substantial Internet radio presence. AMFM began its e-commerce in 1999 as an extension of its hundreds of radio stations, and emphatically not as an alternative. AMFM's executive vice president, Chick Armstrong, explained that "our main job is to extend our radio franchises online as we position radio as the vehicle of choice for consumers and advertisers. Video didn't kill the radio star and neither will the Internet." Five major components made up their marketing use of the Internet: "interactive playlists, customized CDs, personalized web pages tailored to individual listeners, localized home pages for use by community groups, and general e-commerce [to sell] station merchandise, music, tickets and related items." Armstrong stressed that the key to successful radio station streaming on the Internet was localism: "Not only is radio demographically and psychographically segmented, it's geographically segmented. And that's what will give radio a leg up. We are miniportals. We are the local on-ramp. . . . One of the great challenges that we have is to look at e-commerce as an additive, a positive way to extend our brand."[32]

Clear Channel had already entered the Internet milieu, investing in an Internet music network and positioning its stations to provide an Internet audio presence. For small broadcasting stations with limited over-the-air signal reach, the Internet became a special boon, extending their stations not only to national audiences but literally all over the world. For listeners, the same extended reach applied: radio stations from all over the world were instantly available. In addition, many listeners found an element of personalization—if not geographic localism—from many stations. E-mailed requests for plays frequently were answered, unlike many requests going to faceless deejays at conglomerate stations that play homogenized hits.[33] In early 2005, CNet's John Borland wrote that in the previous year Internet radio was "reborn," citing Clear Channel's new approach where its stations will "serve as independent gateways into a network of online services," providing a great variety of program content. He noted, importantly, that advertising could be targeted to local markets.[34]

Bill Goldsmith, who operates a Web site with the title Radio Paradise, says there is no passion left in commercial broadcast music and that a growing number of listeners are tuning out AM and FM terrestrial stations and listening to radio online.[35]

The Web site Radio and Internet Newsletter (RAIN) presents daily indications of the growth of Internet radio. Some examples from just a few days in July 2004: Apple's digital music service, iPod, helped triple Apple's profits in 2003 and helped sell Mac computers. Apple's iTimes Music Store sold its 100 millionth song download. PC magazine predicts a new generation of portable Internet radio boom boxes. Starbucks has equipped 3,100 of it stores with WiFi hotspots.[36]

Webcasting Approaches

It should be noted that there are two major approaches to Internet radio. One consists of radio programming designed for and originated on the Internet. The other is the streaming of terrestrial radio programming onto the Internet. The former can reach their audiences at much less cost than the latter. In a competitive market, which has the advantage?

By 2004, there were thousands, perhaps tens of thousands, of radio stations on the Internet from more than 100 countries, and some 4 million Internet entries relating to Internet radio. A look at even a fraction of what Internet radio offers appears to contradict the skeptics who think that Internet radio is not a threat to traditional radio, whether consolidated or local. One site's homepage says, "Welcome to Live Radio on the Internet. On this site you will find links to thousands of radio stations worldwide, all of which, with the correct (free) software, you will be able to hear via your computer—great if you're living away from home and want to listen to news from your country or *your home town radio station*" (emphasis added).[37]

Another site facilitates access to radio stations on the Web with links to U.S. stations by location, by call letters, and by format, and links to foreign stations by country.[38] Still another enables one to find stations playing virtually any format desired, listing the following major categories:

80s	Alternative	Americana
Blues	Christian	Classical
Electronica	Hip-Hop	Jazz
Latin	Metal	Oldies
Pop	R&B	Reggae
Rock	Talk	Various
World	More[39]	

At *Radio and Records'* annual convention in 2004, webcasting was one of the key topics. In response to terrestrial radio representatives who expressed concern over Internet radio's competition, Jay Frank of radio Web site Launch complained, "I'm tired of all of us (in the new media) being blamed for the problems of the industry. The number one threat is crappy music; it's not technology." David Porter of Live365 lauded wireless broadband transmission, saying, "We're probably two or three years from infiltrating car stereo. We're the biggest threat to terrestrial radio." Napster executive Michelle Santosuosso said, "[Terrestrial] radio has lost its ability to engage the listener in a music experience." Panelists at the conference agreed in general that an eventual change in the differing rules that apply to terrestrial and Internet radio will level the playing field, making it easier for Web radio to compete against traditional radio stations.[40]

Critic Allan Hoffman summed up the feelings of those who have become aficionados of Internet radio: "Internet radio explodes the boundaries of radio broadcasting, opening up a universe of stations offering far more diversity than what is available on the traditional radio dial. Once you start listening to Internet radio, the limits of AM and FM—a limited number of stations, within a limited geographical area—seem like a throwback to another era. Net radio provides possibilities for listening well beyond the advertising-soaked sameness of the commercial stations available."[41]

A study by Ben Compaine and Emma Smith of MIT suggests that in terms of service and organization, terrestrial radio and Internet radio may not be so far apart. The study found that Internet radio is, like terrestrial radio, essentially controlled by "a small number of players. The top two owners (NetRadio and ABC Radio) deliver more than 50% of Internet radio listening across the country." In addition, the study contends, "Internet radio broadcasting may lead to a decrease in the availability of local programming such as news, local-issues talk shows, traffic and weather." Major content is either very general or targeted to a few of the larger markets. "To the extent that government regulators continue to expect localism from radio license holders in the United States, Internet-only radio broadcasters may not further that goal." Compaine and Smith's principal thesis, however, relates not only to localism but to the key issue of ownership regulation as a factor for localism—a service that they note is a cornerstone of policy and practice. They point out that "Internet radio is adding substantial diversity to the radio broadcasting industry" through the variety of program formats and an increase in separately owned stations and that it "complement[s] traditional radio and provide[s] more overall diversity to audiences." They conclude that "if the Internet is adding significant diversity to the radio broadcasting universe, regulators could further relax the ownership rules that currently govern the radio industry in many countries."[42]

Questions and Opinions

Will Internet-only radio stations replace, substantially or in part, the traditional radio station? If so, will all localism disappear? Will a substantial number of listeners turn to cyberspace instead of the radio dial for their listening? If so, will the traditional stations all stream onto the Internet, thus retaining their presence but with an additional means of distribution? Can Internet radio, as its proponents claim, provide local content and services? Is local the same as personalized, more readily possible through the interactive qualities of the Internet and less and less possible with local stations that have been consolidated into a distant headquarters? Are local stations no longer feasible in a climate of economic consolidation and opportunism? Are local stations no longer necessary in light of satellite radio, Internet radio, and other emerging technologies that have yet to make their mark? Or, as some critics suggest, do these new media simply complement, not replace, traditional media?

We asked our panel of interviewees how they thought the new and evolving audio technologies were impacting the existence of local radio. While all agreed that the new technologies could affect local radio, not all believed that they necessarily would do so negatively; some felt that the increase in generic network programming through satellites or voice tracking might encourage listeners to seek a return to local programming. Others conceded that while technology may have an effect, the key to local programming will still be content.

Christopher Sterling states that "easier and better means of recording make it easier to rely on music and centralized programming (and its re-use), as opposed to usually live programs. Additionally, voice-tracking pretends to be local, but assuredly is not." Lynn Christian says, "Currently, Internet web sites operated locally by schools, churches, government agencies and public service organizations are starting to impact local radio's nearly exclusive service to listeners in need of information on weather, school closings, road repairs, sports events, meetings, and organizations' date books for meetings. As of this writing, satellite radio minimally impacts local radio (except for music listening); however, new services to be provided by major communications companies such as AOL, Microsoft, Cingular and T-M Washingtonobile via wireless cell phones, PDAS and pocket PCs will further erode local radio's current advantage in providing local services."

At the end of 2004 and the beginning of 2005, satellite companies Sirius and XM announced an increasing number of programming coups that boded ill for terrestrial radio. XM signed Dr. Laura Schlesinger and Gordon Liddy, two stalwarts of terrestrial radio, to contracts. XM also announced that it will carry almost all Major League Baseball daily games on sixteen channels in 2005. Sirius countered with a contract to distribute the Associated Press's "Sports Power," which covers all professional and college sports, including information on state and regional sports. Representing the growing use of both satellite and the Internet as competition to terrestrial radio, the text will be delivered by satellite and the audio through the Internet.[43] Further, Sirius obtained rights to broadcast the NCAA men's basketball tournament from 2005 to 2007,[44] and in November 2004, provided the only live coverage of the Heisman Trophy awards ceremony of college football.

Jay Allison believes that it is necessary for stations to stress local programming to prevent new technologies from affecting the stations negatively, declaring "Internet and satellite radio are young, but their impact will be large. . . . Localism is [the] only draw to counter the pull of these technologies." Mike Adams thinks the cost of subscribing to some of the new technologies, such as satellite radio, may limit their use to affluent listeners.

Ed Shane says that the new technology facilitates local radio stations moving to network programming. He gives this example.

About five years ago our company helped KIKK-AM in Houston into "Business Radio 650," with reports and talk shows on business, finance and money management. When that station launched, live operators were required to switch from network to network and from network to local origination. In contrast, just last month [in 2004] we launched WVNT, "The Valley's News-Talk Leader" in Parkersburg, West Virginia. I helped to assemble talk programming from Jones Radio Networks (Neal Boortz and Clark Howard), Westwood One (Bill O'Reilly and Jim Bohannon), Dave Ramsey's self-syndication and a collection of shows from TRN, Talk Radio Networks. All of these networks are automatically switched from one to another, including from one satellite to another when needed. There's only one point in the day when a local operator has to physically record a show for playback later. That's how quickly the technology—and the price of technology—changed.

Christopher Maxwell believes that technology can help localism if used properly. Maxwell says that one "can provide 'additional content' on the website that is an extension of that provided on the analog broadcast. We can provide City Council meetings on the Subcarrier Audio Channel and send that to micro rebroadcast units for each neighborhood." Michael Brown feels that the new technologies may become so profound that listeners will long for local radio once again. He says that "the pressure is on. I have an XM satellite in my car so I no longer have to listen to re-runs of Rush Limbaugh as I drive across isolated parts of Wyoming. I have 35 music channels that come with my cable television. I listen to Tuvan throat-singing from Mongolia through the Internet. In the end, this might ultimately drive radio back toward increasing localism because it is the one area not being served by the new technologies that deliver other kinds of programming."

Valerie Geller believes that the new technologies offer more choice but result in less local radio. She argues, "Satellite radio will provide huge variety and choice for listeners, but it's national programming, not local, although with the all-weather channel and all-traffic channels coming on both XM and Sirius satellite radio, they are heading in a direction that consider a localized audience."

Donna Halper and Rollye Cornell believe that the new technologies can affect the stations superficially, but content is the basis for any real change. While technology may make the stations less local and more impersonal, the stations themselves can maintain localism if they wish by maintaining local program content and services.

Halper says,

Personally, I think these alleged new technologies don't affect the life of the average listener very much. The new technologies may be exciting for engineers to discuss, and they are great to display at conventions like the NAB; and yes, I know there is a small group of very wealthy folks who like to be the first to own the newest whatever. But how has the average person benefited from streaming video or the IPod? I think new technologies such as the ultra-versatile automaton devices, while they have helped owners to staff their stations even at times when they can't find good help, the downside is automation and voice-tracking have only made radio stations more impersonal, since there are few local personnel with whom you can interact.

Cornell says,

Technology is forever changing, but the human condition is largely static. While social mores and outwardly acceptable or attractive behavior change with the times, the underlying psychological needs of an audience probably haven't changed since the days of Plato and before. Programming seen as relatable and entertaining, regardless of the elements that make it so (such as type of entertainment or reasons for relatability) will always have a place in society. From the news criers of the middle ages to the Internet today, people hunger for information. From the earliest writings to the latest DVDs, people are captivated by a compelling story. As long as radio can accurately reflect the needs, interests and wants of its audience, it will be a vibrant part of the spectrum.

Enemies at the Gate

Numerous developments in satellite and Internet radio in the mid-2001–2010 decade (some in XMS and Sirius's programming were noted earlier) indicated the continuing weakening of terrestrial radio in face of strengthening competition. Perhaps most indicative of the trend was *Radio Ink*'s story of the year 2004: former president and CEO of Viacom Mel Karmazin, who was considered responsible for taking Infinity Broadcasting and Westwood One to leadership positions in terrestrial radio, became CEO of Sirius Satellite Radio. Karmazin announced that he joined Sirius "because I want to lead a growth company that can reshape the landscape of the radio business."[45]

Prior to Karmazin's move, Howard Stern, arguably the most controversial performer in radio (and one of the most listened to) signed a five-year contract with Sirius, to begin in January 2006. Stern maintained that Sirius was "the future of radio."[46]

Other Sirius developments that further threatened terrestrial radio included the establishment of a studio on the West Coast to go with its headquarters studio on the East Coast and the introduction of a new radio receiver about the size of a cell phone that can be plugged in to receive its satellite signal. Within a couple of months, XM Satellite Radio also introduced a handheld satellite radio receiver. Sirius growth was punctuated by reaching over 1,143,000 subscribers by the beginning of 2005, exceeding its target of one million.[47] XM announced that it had exceeded its goal of 3.1 million subscribers by the beginning of 2005,[48] and that its 2004 revenue was triple that of 2003. Perhaps the strongest satellite omen of things to come for terrestrial radio was a prediction in the *Kiplinger Letter* that the more than 4 million combined subscribers would double by the end of 2005.[49]

Other developments in the newer technologies included the availability of XM Satellite Radio in portable boom boxes, the increasing incursion into local programming by satellite radio, such as Sirius's real-time updated traffic information through in-car navigation systems in at first thirty, then fifty markets,[50] and XM's establishing five additional local traffic and weather channels, despite protests from the NAB, that will provide a total of twenty-one such channels with information available 24/7 in metropolitan areas around the country.[51]

Cyberspace contributed its share of competition to beleaguered terrestrial radio, too, as the decade reached 2005. Yahoo hired media executive Lloyd Braun to help it become a major source of audio and video entertainment.[52] Classical music station WGMS launched an Internet radio station, VivaLaVoce.com, to present opera, choral music, and other classical forms.[53] New York's classical music station, WQXR, also streamed to cyberspace on the AOL Radio Network.[54] Music Choice, which provided music on digital cable, planned to offer "personalized radio stations" and offer other new features on the Internet.[55] "Podcasting," a form of radio Internet service, began to grow. One of the innovators in this new service, Doc Searls, declared that "podcasting will shift much of our time away from an old medium where we wait for what we might want to hear to a new medium where we choose what we want to hear, when we want to hear it."[56]

Both satellite and the Web are increasingly impacting terrestrial radio, sometimes in combination. For example, XM announced that it would begin airing its sixty-eight commercial-free music stations and a number of its other stations to subscribers on the Internet, as well.[57] The *Economist* reported in late 2004 that the record industry might soon bypass other media, including terrestrial radio, and use the Internet to market their music.[58]

The shift of listeners away from terrestrial radio to satellite and the Internet continues to grow. A survey reported by *Radio Ink* concluded that "[terrestrial] radio was 13 times less likely than the Internet to be used first by those wanting information about their favorite recording artists and the Internet was 10 times more likely than radio to provide 'fun.'"[59] One approach terrestrial radio, led by Clear Channel, is taking to counter the loss of audiences to satellite and Internet radio is to reduce commercial loads.[60] Another approach is to provide new formats that were previously available and popular on satellite and cyberspace radio, such as "Jack," "Chill," and "Red," variations of adult comtemporary format.[61]

John Gorman, a veteran radio programmer and columnist, sees "dark days" ahead for terrestrial radio, noting that the departure of Howard Stern, Bruce Morrow, and other personalities to satellite radio may well be the beginning of a "talent vacuum" for an industry already dealing with "hard times."[62] Rishad Tobaccowala, a media innovation expert, suggests that not too far in the future "old-fashioned radio as we know it ceases to exist."[63] Tom Taylor, editor of *Inside Radio*, takes the prognosticating a step further and suggests that it may not be too long before even satellite radio is made obsolete by wireless Internet access and online music. "I'd argue that the technical innovation that's hanging over everything in the media is wireless broadband," he said.[64]

Underlining all this is Wall Street's evaluation of the terrestrial radio industry at the end of 2004: it downgraded radio, noting that by that point the industry had lost 20 percent of its public value.[65]

What can terrestrial radio do? One answer is obvious: sacrifice short-term financial gain for long-term survival and profits by returning to the roots of its popularity and prosperity—local programming and service.

9 Tuning the Alternatives

Community Radio and Pirate Broadcasts

Low-power radio is, by definition, local radio and, essentially, community radio. Its limited power contains its signal within a given area, usually from a radius of a few miles to perhaps ten or more, depending upon terrain and antenna height. Wattage of low-power radio is currently defined as one hundred watts; at one time it was as low as ten watts. The circumscribed audience reach limits its ability to obtain capital and operating funds as well as audiences. Because it doesn't reach as many potential customers as do higher-power stations, low-power stations cannot attract any appreciable underwriting support unless they are located in high-density urban areas. Even then, given the frequently alternative, sometimes narrow goals of low-power-station programming, underwriters are reluctant to identify their products or services with what may be considered by many to be controversial subject matter.

Low-power radio, with few exceptions, is necessarily highly local. It provides a voice for civic, political, social, racial, ethnic, religious, and other community groups traditionally excluded from access to the major network and station-controlled airwaves. Its issues are local. Low and sometimes nonexistent budgets require that its personnel are local, most often dedicated volunteers. Low-power radio, therefore, has been touted as a practical alternative to the increasing consolidation and national homogenization of radio.

Rise of the "Lows"

Low-power radio is not new. As noted in the opening chapters of this book, early radio was perforce local, limited by the available technology. Even after advancing technology permitted expansion into higher power and audience reach, many stations retained their commitment to localism. In the 1960s and 1970s, Lorenzo Milam, concerned that all commercial radio was coming under corporate control not only in terms of ownership and operations but in terms of programming for the community, became the guru of community broadcasting. He either established or helped establish more than forty community radio stations around the country. His goal was to obtain access to the airwaves for those denied a voice by the mainstream media. Some of the stations he founded were not low power, but the priority of all was service to the local community. His legacy is in great part responsible for the efforts by current community activists to lobby the government to provide more low-power stations today.

Low-power radio fell into two general categories: hundred-watt stations, the low-power assignment today; and ten-watt stations, used by colleges, other nonprofit educational institutions, and nonprofit organizations established by community groups. While commercial broadcasters concentrated their objections on hundred-watt low-power stations, it was the so-called educational or pubic broadcasting organizations that sought the dissolution of ten-watt stations. Even these nonprofit noncommercial broadcasters adopted the mantra that bigger is better and that national service is more important than local service. Most ten-watt stations operated at that low power because they could not afford the equipment required for higher power. They were the poor relatives in the field of noncommercial broadcasting. For example, many licensees of ten-watt stations were to predominantly black colleges in the South, whose budgets were so limited by donors or discriminatory legislatures that they simply could not afford higher-power stations. In the late 1970s, the FCC, under pressure from both commercial and public broadcasting, eliminated the ten-watt station license. Neither the Corporation for Public Broadcasting nor National Public Radio nor the National Association of Educational Broadcasting tried to save these highly local stations. They all went off the air, and the poorer licensees could not move to hundred-watt station categories, their local voices silenced.

Macro Opposition

With the growth of high-power conglomerates, the demise of local and low-power stations, and the refusal of the FCC to authorize more low-power stations, community activists in the 1990s established their own low-power local stations—without benefit of FCC licenses. These microstations, as their operators call them—or pirate stations, as the FCC calls them—increased in number following the passage of the Telecommunications Act of 1996. They will be discussed later in this chapter. Following the 1996 deregulation, a number of consumer organizations asked the FCC to authorize a low-power, hundred-watt radio station category. One such group, Americans for Radio Diversity (ARD), wanted the FCC to legalize the existing microstations, stating, "In most cases, a hundred-watt station can serve a community. But the Federal Communications Commission, with the support of the National Association of Broadcasters, is cracking down on these guys [microstations]. We think micro-power is at least a partial answer to giving a voice back to the communities."[1] With the prodding of other groups and the support of the majority of the FCC (at that time a majority of whom, including the chair, were Democrats and supportive of community access and services), the FCC issued a Notice of Proposed Rule Making in early 1999 to establish a low-power radio service.

Europe had already demonstrated the importance and desirability of local radio. Increasing national control of the medium in Europe and the attempts to break down artificial barriers within member states of the European Union resulted in more national and international programming and less local programming. Unlicensed stations went on the air in droves during the 1960s and 1970s. As in the United States, no sooner was one located by the government and taken off the air than another one or more went on the air. In the 1990s, European countries coped with the situation by licensing hundreds of local stations. The national radio system in the given country operated the local stations and preempted the national system's programming for local programs that provided important local services.[2] In Latin America today, even the smaller countries have hundreds of low-power radio stations that, according to a Rockefeller Foundation report, "serve rural and urban communities with content that is appropriate to the local language, culture and needs." The same local radio development is taking place in other parts of the world, with many stations going on the air unlicensed in order to meet local needs.[3]

It looked like legal licensing of low-power radio would be the solution in the United States, too, and in January 2000, the FCC authorized low-power radio stations of ten, one hundred, and one thousand watts. Many of the advocates represented the needs of minority and other media-disenfranchised groups. For example, the Native American Navajo nation wanted low-power radio stations to serve their rural members "with broadcasts in the Navajo language tailored to concerns like health (diabetes is a major issue), education and culture."[4] As one station manager put it, "radio is one of the cheapest forms of communication you can find. Homeless people don't have nothin', but they have a radio."[5]

Commissioner Gloria Tristani summarized the FCC's actions.

> Consolidation among radio broadcasters following passage of the 1996 Telecommunications Act has resulted in ownership concentrations in both national and local markets unknown since the inception of radio. The 1996 removal of national radio ownership caps has caused the number of radio station owners to substantially decrease while the total number of stations has actually increased. With recent merger activity in the radio marketplace, control of broadcast radio has become concentrated in even fewer and fewer hands. . . . So how can the FCC operate an effective federal policy that ensures access to the airwaves by diverse voices? We can only do this if we exercise our affirmative duty to take action to ensure the public's interest, while preserving the marketplace of ideas. Broadcast consolidation means the shelves are stocked by too few hands. The loss of local content and local participation, and the rise of national play lists, syndicated programming and generic issues reporting arise from the loss of access to the airwaves by local residents. Loss of local control and limitations on community access may prove intractable in the not too distant future. The public's interest includes maintaining a diversity of voices.[6]

As it turned out, the reality depended on congressional politics. The effective pressure of the National Association of Broadcasters, the corporate media industry, and even from public broadcasting's National Public Radio, turned the desire for low-power licenses into a wish and a prayer.

While FCC chair William Kennard supported the FCC's action, saying that "we cannot deny opportunities to those who want to use the airwaves to speak to their communities simply because it might be inconvenient for those who already have these opportunities," NAB president Eddie Fritts vehemently opposed it, saying, "The proposal will likely cause devastating interference . . . to broadcasters." The FCC received more than three thousand comments on its proposal to establish low-power radio, more than ten times the average number filed on proposed rule making. Virtually every listener and citizen organization was in favor of low-power stations, while virtually every broadcaster and broadcaster association was against them. Representative Mike Oxley introduced a bill in Congress, the Radio Broadcasting Preservation Act of 1999, that would "prohibit the FCC from establishing rules to authorize new low-power FM radio stations."[7] Republicans, in general, supported the bill; Democrats opposed it.

The FCC commissioner who voted against low-power radio argued that "you'll have to prove there's a relationship between diversity of ownership and diversity of viewpoints." Representative Billy Tauzin, chair of the House Telecommunications Subcommittee, said, "The LPRS [Low Power Radio Service] will allow skinheads to get stations and threaten struggling public radio stations." Senator Conrad Burns, chair of the Senate Telecommunications Subcommittee, declared, "We don't need all these little [LPRS] radio stations. I've had about the all diversity I can stand."[8]

National Public Radio (NPR) joined commercial radio broadcasters in opposing low-power radio on the grounds that "it is neither self-evident nor established" that low-power radio would provide a "diversity of media voices." NPR contended, too, that low-power radio would cause even more interference, that "the broadcast spectrum in many portions of the country is now severely congested." As for diversity, NPR argued that the goal of diverse content is provided by the Internet.[9] FCC chair Kennard commented on the NPR stance: "I'm particularly disappointed that National Public Radio joined with commercial interests to stifle greater diversity of voices on the airwaves. I can only wonder how an organization that excels in national programming could fear competition from local programming by these tiny stations operated by churches, schools, community groups and public safety agencies." Kennard also upbraided commercial broadcasters: "Why in the midst of all this opportunity for broadcasters have you chosen to muster your considerable power in Washington and around the country to deny churches and schools and community-based organizations just a little piece of the broadcast pie?"[10]

Democratized Air

The *Boston Globe* editorialized that radio is the most ubiquitous medium in the world and that the FCC's low-power proposal "could open the airwaves to the public-spirited and the quirky, to those with something to say but not much money with which to say it. The FCC should not let the power of established broadcasters stifle this opportunity." A *Radio World* editorial supported low-power FM, noting that existing broadcasters are afraid that their bottom lines will be damaged by new competition, but that could happen only if "existing stations don't serve their audiences well" and it is not Congress's job to "protect the economic interests" of selected broadcasters. The editorial suggested that new low-power stations "will benefit communities, schools, and other groups who can create voices of their own" on the air, create more radio jobs and strengthen the radio marketplace.[11]

The Media Access Project issued a description of low-power radio and its benefits. It noted that the service would be "intensely local" and "would be available to entrepreneurs, community groups, high schools, labor unions, and churches, and anyone who would like to reach out to a small geographically-concentrated group of individuals." It stated the need for diversity, that when "media become divorced from their local surroundings, we become more disenfranchised from our government and from our communities." The Media Access Project stressed that "consolidation weakens our democracy" and that "without locally owned and programmed outlets, citizens" will not get the information they need about their communities to enable them to effectively "participate in civic life."[12]

In spite of the public approval, the House of Representatives passed the Radio Broadcasting Preservation Act in April 2000, cutting out about 80 percent of the low-power stations that would have been possible under the FCC authorization. Shortly afterward, the Senate voted to support the House, and eight hundred of the potential one thousand new local voices of radio went up in smoke. FCC chair Kennard said, "Special interests triumphed over community interests."[13]

The FCC did go ahead with the greatly reduced number of LPFM stations permitted by Congress and issued guidelines for applicants.

> LPFM stations may operate with 100 watts or less. The approximate signal reach is a radius of about 3.5 miles.
>
> LPFM stations are available to noncommercial educational entities and public transportation organizations.
>
> LPFM stations must protect authorized stations on the same channel (co-channel) and on the three adjacent channels to the given LPFM's frequency.
>
> Where two or more applicants seek the same available channel (mutually exclusive or MX situations), selection will be based on the organization's presence in the community, commitment to be on the air at least 12 hours per day, and the number of hours of locally originated programs.[14]

The FCC established varying filing periods for groups of states, but not in terms of geographical region. For example, Alaska, California, District of Columbia, Georgia, Indiana, Maryland, Oklahoma, Rhode Island, and Utah were in the same filing period.

The FCC began accepting applications in 2000, and in 2004 there were one thousand LPFM stations licensed to operate—far fewer than the two thousand sought by applicants.

In late 2000, Congress held up the FCC's further implementation of low-power assignments. Senator John McCain, chair of the Senate's Communications Subcommittee, differed with his Republican colleagues and cosponsored a bill with Democratic Senator Patrick Leahy authorizing the FCC to license low-power stations. Their bill was based on a study by the Mitre Corporation for the FCC that found that low-power stations "do not pose a significant risk of causing interference to existing full-service FM stations." McCain said, "I look forward to hearing more local artists, local news, local public-affairs programming and community-based programming on low-power FM radio stations throughout the country."[15] The NAB's response was that "it is unfortunate that Senator McCain is relying on the deeply flawed . . . study in supporting the authorization of more low-power FM stations. Local radio listeners should not be subjected to the inevitable interference that would result from shoehorning more stations onto an already overcrowded radio dial."[16]

When the FCC's Powell launched his Localism Task Force in 2003 in response to massive criticism of the FCC's June further deregulation of ownership rules, most critics were skeptical of both his motives and his sincerity. One aspect of that initiative, however, struck a positive chord with low-power station advocates. Powell promised to expedite the processing of LPFM applications, and praised low-power stations as an excellent way to achieve broadcast localism in communities across the country. Up to then, he had made low-power licensing a low priority at the FCC.[17]

Low-power FM radio got another boost in 2004 when the FCC officially released the Mitre Report to Congress with its (the FCC's) recommendation that the three-adjacent-channels restriction on LPFM stations be eliminated, opening up the broadcast spectrum for more low-power stations. *Radio World,* the industry magazine, called the Mitre Report "the seventh wonder of broadcast engineering—the data is deep and exhaustive."[18] The NAB continued to insist that the study was flawed. As this is being written, in July 2004, the Senate Commerce, Science, and Transportation Committee just approved a bipartisan bill by Senators McCain and Leahy to allow low-power stations to operate on the third adjacent channel to a full-power FM radio station. If approved by the entire Congress and signed by the president, this bill will make possible a greatly increased number of local radio voices. NAB reaction to the bill was sharp and quick, its president, Eddie Fritts, declaring that the passage of this bill would subject "millions of American to aggravating interference" and that "hundreds of LPFMS are broadcasting and hundreds more are awaiting final authorization without rolling back needed interference protections."[19]

Micro Movement

Low-power radio stations called microstations or pirate stations, depending on whether one supported or opposed them, have been the epitome of localism, frequently no more than one or two watts in power reaching a radius of a few hundred yards or a couple of city blocks. They are not new, historically or recently. In the early days of radio, prior to mandatory licensing and even after it, anyone with the ability to construct a radio transmitter could put a station on the air. Many did, some for experimental purposes, some for potential commercial gain. With the establishment of the Federal Radio Commission, as noted earlier in this book, all stations were ostensibly removed from the air and only those that met the FRC's new criteria were allowed to go back on with formal licenses. The principal purpose of establishing a regulatory agency for radio, it should be remembered, was to end the chaos on the air, with frequency interference creating what media historian Erik Barnouw called a tower of babel. Nevertheless, throughout the years stations went on the air without licenses. These illegal stations, usually of low power barely sufficient to serve a targeted audience in a limited geographical area, went on and off the air, some because they weren't able to continue because of lack of funds or personnel and others because of government crackdown through the FRC and, later, the FCC. Those pirate broadcasters, as they were called by officialdom, who were caught were usually fined and their equipment confiscated.

In more recent years, microradio stations have come to the fore as political tools, used by those who for reasons of location, lack of money and facilities, or both, have been unable to apply for or receive a license from the FCC. Local political organizations, community groups, minorities, religious and church societies, and similar entities, including individuals with a cause, have all from time to time established illegal microstations. The major dramatic use, however, has been by those with alternative or dissident political views who have had no other way—until the advent of the Internet—to air their views, having systematically been barred by the predominantly conservative media from access to the airwaves. This is particularly true in times of conservative governments that increasingly limit civil liberties with the cooperation of the mainstream media.

During the past twenty years—beginning in the mid-1980s and accelerating in the early years of the twenty-first century—microradio become a movement. Ted Coopman describes the rebirth of microstations as follows:

> The modern microbroadcasting movement began on November 25, 1986, in a public housing development in Springfield, Illinois. Put on the air for about $600, the one-watt station broadcast openly on 107.1 FM as Black Liberation Radio (now Human Rights Radio). The operator, Mbanna Kantako, a legally blind African-American in his mid-thirties, started the station because he felt that the African-American community in Springfield was not being served by the local media. Kantako felt that because the African-American community had a high illiteracy rate, radio would be the best way to reach this community.[20]

Arguably the best-known microradio station of recent years has been Free Radio Berkeley, or FRB, established in 1993 by Stephen Dunifer. The thirty-watt station, with an optimum signal reach on a good day of about ten miles, has become a poster-station for others throughout the country. Doing for microstations what Lorenzo Milam did for licensed low-power radio several decades earlier, Dunifer published a how-to book, *Seizing the Airwaves,* on setting up unlicensed microstations. The goal of the microradio movement, according to Dunifer, is to establish so many unlicensed microstations throughout the country that it would become impossible for the FCC to enforce a ban against them.[21]

In what was regarded a test case, shortly after FRB went on the air the FCC fined it for illegal, unlicensed use of the airwaves. An initial federal court finding stated that the FCC had not proven that Dunifer and FRB had interfered with and harmed licensed broadcast operations. But that victory for microradio was short-lived, with the decision overturned on appeal.[22] Nevertheless, the die was cast and hundreds of microstations began to spring up throughout the United States, with the FCC striving with only some success to shut them down. Even as some were taken off the air, other new ones went on the air, and by 2005 it was estimated that over one thousand illegal microstations—or, if you will, pirate stations—were in operation.

Countering Consolidation

Kate Coyer summarizes the development of many of these stations as a counter to consolidation:

> In 1996, a wave of media ownership consolidation was let loose in the States by Congress and the FCC. American radio piracy transformed . . . to being an act of civil disobedience against the corporate domination

of media. By . . . the late 1990's, there were close to a thousand pirate operators in the U.S. Some of these pirates formed the Prometheus Radio Project, which has engaged the government and helped to create a new set of rules allowing community radio for the first time in twenty years in the U.S. Drawing on this early success, Prometheus joined the movement against new regulations creating unprecedented corporate power in media. This culminated in a historic federal court lawsuit that blocked the impending wave of media mergers and sent the Bush administration back to the drawing board.[23]

A number of lawsuits have resulted from the FCC's shutting down and fining of unlicensed microstations. The legal filing in one of those cases, on behalf of New York City's "Steal This Radio" against the U.S. Department of Justice, clarifies some of the arguments in favor of microradio. The filing asserted the right of the plaintiffs and the organizations supporting them "to hear the political, educational, and cultural information broadcast over this forum for the diverse community in which they live" and to provide "an important outlet for individuals and groups in that community to share their views and disseminate local news and information." The filing further noted that "because radio is uniquely pervasive and portable, it reaches many persons who lack access to other electronic mass media, including those who cannot afford to subscribe to cable television service, own a personal computer, or access the Internet. Radio is thus vitally important to the economically disadvantaged in society, including the homeless, who rely solely on this medium for critical news and information."[24]

The filing goes on to state that this audience is one of the key targets of microstations and that "microradio developed in response to a dearth of local programming—programming that covers community issues from a diverse range of viewpoints—on licensed broadcast radio stations . . . [and] provide minorities with programming that commercial radio stations will not air . . . [and] also play music that cannot be heard on local commercial music stations because of rigid formats and tight playlists."[25]

The filing included constitutional arguments against the FCC's actions and in favor of microstations' rights, including the following First Amendment considerations.

The spectrum dedicated to radio broadcasting is an electronic public forum of virtually unlimited character in which they [the plaintiffs] have a First Amendment right to "speak." . . .

. . . The current broadcast licensing scheme is not a reasonable time, place, and manner regulation but rather an unnecessarily broad restriction that burdens substantially more broadcast speech than necessary to adequately serve the government's interest in preventing radio interference and ensuring public safety. . . .

. . . The licensing scheme is an impermissible prior restraint on speech to the extent that it gives the FCC virtually unfettered discretion—under a vague and amorphous "public interest" standard—to decide who may and may not speak in the electronic public forum, and under what circumstances. . . .

. . . The licensing scheme impermissibly allows certain speakers to monopolize expression in the electronic public forum dedicated to radio broadcasting by authorizing the FCC to grant broadcast licenses to exclusively use assigned frequencies. . . .

. . . [The FCC] violates plaintiffs' First, Fourth, and Fifth Amendment rights as microbroadcasters—and sanctions impermissible prior restraints on speech—to the extent that it allows the government to seize their expressive instrumentalities without the procedural safeguards constitutionally mandated to minimize the risk of censorship of protected expression, prevent unreasonable searches and seizures, and endure due process of law.[26]

The filing further notes that "for many years, the 'public interest' standard under which first the FRC and then the FCC awarded broadcast licenses was interpreted and applied to require broadcast stations to provide air time for community views and voices as a condition of license renewal." The current licensing approach allows the FCC to give exclusive use of frequencies "to a relatively few broadcast radio stations, which are collectively owned by even fewer media companies [and] allows a select group of favored speakers to monopolize and therefore limit speech in . . . radio broadcasting."[27]

As consolidation grew, resulting in less and less local service, so did the number of unlicensed microstations, resulting in more and more local service. The more the FCC and the broadcasting industry, through the NAB, fought to rid the air of microstations, the more the microradio movement grew, with the assistance of organizations such as the Prometheus Radio Project, founded in 1998 to help new unlicensed stations with legal, technical, and organizational advice on how to get on the air and, for those stations busted by the FCC, to get back on the air.[28]

Pirating for the Public

Operators of pirate stations have been called modern-day buccaneers, ostensibly stealing spectrum space from ships legally plowing the ether. They have been described otherwise by those who use the label microradio as "an eclectic mix of radical, conservative and, for the most part, selfless individuals who are filling a niche in countless communities throughout the United States. The programming they offer, often on a part-time basis and but a few hours a day or week, is diverse, edgy, educational or just plain fun." Freedom Forum's Paul McMasters calls microstation operators "the broadcast equivalent of the old anonymous pamphleteers or alternative newspapers."[29]

The FCC has cracked down on these local pirate stations, not only putting hundreds out of business each year, but, with the cooperation of the Department of Justice, levying sanctions against their operators, as well. For example, the owners of Black Liberation Radio, a fifteen-watt unlicensed station in Illinois that has been shut down and gone on the air again in different locations, have been fined and imprisoned as well as having had their equipment confiscated. A farmer in North Dakota who set up a microstation to broadcast right-wing talk shows was shut down after complaining about his treatment from "Big Brother."

A case study of how pirate stations are born occurred in Minneapolis in the late 1990s. A group of local deejays wanted to bring dance music to the city, a format that was missing on the increasingly consolidated stations in the market. They explored the legal options first. They couldn't compete with the conglomerates in buying an existing station. They weren't able to get any of the existing stations to change their format. They couldn't afford to buy a block of time on any of the stations for a dance music show. There were no frequencies available to permit them to start their own station (low-power FM had not yet been authorized). Broadcaster Alan Freed, who led the fight to get a dance music format for the Twin Cities area, said that because there were no other legal options, they had no choice but to establish an unlicensed microstation—which they did, in Freed's home. It was called "Beat Radio." It wasn't long before the FCC showed up at Freed's home, seized the equipment, and closed down the station.[30]

In the Detroit area, Ron Goodsight described himself as a pirate, openly operating an unlicensed low-power station prior to the FCC's authorization of LPFM. He said he'd prefer to operate a legal station, "but the law says I can't. It's currently illegal to have low-power stations—so if I wanted to run a radio station, I had no choice but to do it underground."[31] The frustration for would-be legal broadcasters turned pirate became so great, heightened by incessant raids on their facilities by the FCC, the FBI, and local police, that in 1998 a group of microstation operators went to Washington in a protest march at the FCC and NAB headquarters. The pirate protesters claimed a citizen's right to affordable access to broadcast time in order to fill the gap in commercial broadcasting offerings—"alternative music, talk, intensely local news and public affairs shows broadcast from garages and bedrooms . . . [with] signals [that] can cover anywhere from a few blocks to several miles."[32]

Free and Local

As noted earlier, a leading voice in the contemporary battle for low-power radios has been Stephen Dunifer, who founded unlicensed microstation Free Radio Berkeley in 1993. Dunifer has cited low-power operations in Canada as a model for the U.S., showing that possible interference with existing stations is greatly exaggerated and a spurious argument by the FCC. In Canada, aboriginal communities established unlicensed low-power stations with no negative impact on other broadcasting facilities but, in fact, used their stations to provide services and information that even helped save many lives.[33]

Microbroadcasters have defended their unlicensed stations as the only local programming alternatives to what have largely become terrestrial distributors of satellite-fed automated content from a distant source. Their supporters point out that they've "covered high school sports, broadcast city council meetings and church services, and given airtime to local musicians; they have trained teenagers and retirees to be broadcast engineers, sponsored concerts and parties, coordinated flood relief, and exposed local corruption and crime." As one critic wrote, "Even the worst micro stations have a ragged vitality that most of their legal competitors can't touch."[34]

When the FCC finally approved low-power stations, one might think that the pirate station operators would be pleased to finally be able to obtain legal permission to operate their stations. It didn't quite work that way. First, Congress banned anyone who had operated an unlicensed microstation from applying for a legal low-power station. Some of the disenfranchised microstations supported the FCC's rule making. The Prometheus Radio Project, organized by some of the people whose unlicensed stations has been shut down, held workshops throughout the country for potential applicants for LPFM licenses. Others, including microstation leaders Stephen Dunifer and Mbanna Kantako, argued that the FCC's authorization was merely damage control, a sop to the nationwide protests. They reminded supporters of microbroadcasting that Congress had reduced the number of licenses that would be made available to LPFM stations from about a thousand to one-fifth that number. They complained that the FCC had given no recognition to the role the "free station" or microstation movement had played in forcing the FCC to take action on low-power stations. Dunifer urged that localism can only be truly achieved by "putting hundreds and thousands of free stations on the air."[35]

As Susan Douglas wrote, "When social movements and radio have intersected, previously forbidden and thus thrilling listening possibilities have emerged. . . . With the 1996 Telecommunications Act sanctioning corporate greed and the squelching of localism and diversity . . . micropower pirate radio stations have sprouted up around the country, arousing the ire of the FCC. . . . The growth of pirate radio suggests a new insurgency is afoot."[36] And indeed it was.

Ethereal Battlefield

A victory for the unlicensed broadcasters came about in 2002 when a U.S. District Court found that the congressional action in 2000 barring former microbroadcasters from being eligible for LPFM licenses was unconstitutional, a violation of First Amendment rights. Victories for the FCC and Congress against unlicensed broadcasters continued after LPFMs went on the air. The lack of an adequate number of low-power stations left most parts of the country without a local voice, and the pirate stations tried to fill the void. They suffered for it. One example was San Francisco Liberation Radio (SFLR), which had been broadcasting without a license for more than ten years. As a local alternative voice to the conservative news and right-wing talk shows that dominate consolidated and even most independent radio in the United States, SFLR openly criticized Bush administration policies and the war on Iraq. In October 2003, five FCC agents, ten Department of Justice agents, and ten San Francisco police raided the SFLR studios. They had a battering ram and guns and searched the studios for two hours. They confiscated all the station's equipment and put SFLR off the air. Ironically just two months earlier, the San Francisco Board of Supervisors passed a resolution in support of SFLR and local service and diversity in programming and had instructed the city's police not to harass or attack the station.[37]

On the other hand, some political jurisdictions have advocated strong action against pirate stations, and the state of Florida (perhaps not unexpectedly) actually passed a law, effective July 1, 2004, with great acclaim from the state's commercial broadcasting industry, that superseded FCC jurisdiction. The law makes it third-degree felony, subject to fine, seizure of equipment, and jail, to run an unlicensed radio station in the state.[38]

In the middle of the first decade of 2000, raids continued on pirate stations. On an early fall morning in 2004, U.S. marshals with guns drawn rousted residents out of bed in a co-op house in Santa Cruz where a pirate station was broadcasting. The station was providing twenty-four-hour music and local activism programming not otherwise available in the community. It was reported that "residents, programmers, friends of alternative radio and enemies of corporate media were joined by two city council members, one council candidate and two congressional candidates" in support of the station. Despite this, the U.S. marshals shut down the station and hauled away its equipment.[39] At about the same time, U.S. marshals did the same thing in Tennessee, shutting down the Knoxville First Amendment Radio station.[40]

The issue became significant enough for people to prompt NBC to present in the fall of 2004 a television special entitled "LPFM: The People's Choice." Promotion for the program noted the importance of radio localism, promising that the program would detail how "low power FM radio is bringing diverse peoples closer together and giving new life to declining communities, new strength to neighborhoods and new voices in the marketplace of ideas." The program was produced by the United Church of Christ Office of Communication and was supported by proponents of low-power radio, who said, "LPFM is a low-cost service designed to promote diversity and localism and to encourage voices from the margin." They also noted the NAB's opposition to LPFM on the grounds that "low power stations interfere with their larger signals [but] an independent study ordered by Congress has concluded that this is patently untrue."[41]

Is unlicensed microbroadcasting a solution to restoring a local voice in radio? Is an expansion of legal low-power FM a solution? Is a reversal of the Telecommunications Act of 1996 and divestiture of multiple stations by their current owners desirable or even possible? Are more congressional laws and FCC rule making a way back to radio localism? The next chapter looks into the present state of affairs and what some broadcasters, critics, and citizens think should be done.

10 **What, If Not Local?**

Globalism, Localism, and Public Interest

Traditionally, the mass media have been local, serving local audiences with material of local interest. Even when that material has transcended local issues and events—national and international news, for example—the media have conscientiously tried to orient it or add to it in terms of local concerns. The managing editor or program director's dictum to the young reporter in almost every movie about journalism, "find the local angle," is true in real life. When that program director is hundreds or thousands of miles away and the radio station is largely automated, there is no one to judge what the local angle is as well as no one to find it. As we have tried to show in this book, that problem applies to the selection of music and other formats as well as to news.

No one, not the consumers or the radio station managers or the executives of the conglomerates that own the stations, deny that localism is the key to broadcasting's responsibility—and financial success. The problem is in the definition of localism—and here the consumers and the conglomerates part. Technology has bred globalism. Many of us believe that global awareness is essential to the world's future and, at any given time, to an avoidance of war, hunger, and pestilence. Life on a small planet requires understanding, tolerance, compassion, and cooperation among all the peoples and their political entities if any are ultimately to survive. Most of humankind has consistently sought the ideal of interdependence, even in the face of some of humankind's efforts to shatter such notions through wars and other exploitative means for political, economic, or religious gain. The nineteenth and twentieth centuries' technological developments, principally in the areas of energy, transportation, and—in terms of the focus of this book—communications, have made it possible for global attempts to reach the ideal through such instruments as the League of Nations, the United Nations, the World Court, and global treaties dealing with environmental protection and nuclear proliferation bans, among other issues. Some countries' leaders, usually for nationalistic or jingoistic reasons, refuse to participate in or pull out of such organizations and treaties. In the early 2000s, the United States was the world's most active nonparticipant.

Globalized Voice

That leads us to what appears to be a dichotomy—but in fact it is not one. Global participation—or lack of it—in international treaties and organizations is not analogous to globalization of corporations and commerce. The United States, for example, backed away and even flouted global participation and cooperation in the early 2000s but at the same time became the world's leader in globalization. While it is important for the media to reach out around the world, bringing countries and peoples together with content relating to common issues, concerns, needs, and desires, what happens when that content becomes homogenized to reflect the beliefs of the global media owners and replaces the beliefs and concerns of the many localities globalized media serve? Although occurring decades later than prognosticated, globalization takes on the aura of thought control predicted in the book *1984*.

Political analyst Richard Flacks suggests that "the globalization of the political economy has undermined the national state" and "corporate elites no longer care very much about the American domestic society," and if this is not changed, "the conditions of life for the majority of Americans will continue to deteriorate." His solution: "Expand community power."[1] Is localism still possible in a global media world?

Is localism in radio still possible in the United States? Consumers and critics tell us that it has all but disappeared because of consolidation. The radio industry—with the exception of the community stations still on the air—tell us that consolidation has resulted in more localism than ever before. The industry continually points out that the economic power of consolidators enables them to provide local services to stations that previously did not have sufficient budgets to meet their community's needs. They also point out that their greater access to a greater variety of program materials makes it possible for them to give individual communities music, talk shows, news, and features oriented to the community's interests that had been unavailable to the local stations trying to obtain this level of programming on their own. Industry spokespeople claim that deregulation has resulted in greater variety, diversity, and localism in radio programming.

Fritz Messere writes in the *Encyclopedia of Radio,* "Even though deregulation and the easing of ownership has increased competition among the top radio stations in most radio markets, critics of deregulation note that the FCC has failed to create a diversity of ownership that mirrors the demographic characteristics of America itself."[2]

The highly politically conservative Heritage Foundation (considered by many to be correct on this point) responded to those who claim that consolidation stifles diversity: "Despite the many mergers in the media industry in recent years, Americans today actually enjoy more diversity and competition in the media than at any other time in history. . . . On the local level . . . Americans in most cities and towns [are] enjoying remarkably more choice of media outlets than ever before. . . . Moreover, the ability to own multiple media outlets can provide substantial benefits to consumers. . . . Owners with several stations each are able to target niche markets with different programming on each station. . . . The number of radio station formats increased after ownership limits were relaxed in 1996."[3]

An NAB study in 2004 concluded that commercial radio and television stations provided $9.6 billion in public service to their local communities in 2003, through airtime and funds. NAB president Eddie Fritts lauded the local contributions: "This census confirms again that local, over-the-air radio and television stations are collectively the number one provider of public service in America. Local broadcasters can stand proud for the enormous pro-social contributions stations make in bettering the lives of listeners and viewers."[4]

Conversely, consumer groups and critics say that the opposite has, in fact, occurred. An editorial in the Syracuse, New York, *Post-Standard* stated that "ever since the government in Washington became obsessed with 'deregulation' and the cable industry became so monopolistic, this nation has seen a steady decline in the quality and integrity of what it sees and hears on the airwaves. . . . When you have a monopoly like that which is enjoyed by Clear Channel in this and hundreds of markets, you no longer need to have a superior news operation. Just crank up the satellite dish and let some guy in Phoenix or Los Angeles or Hartford spoon-feed the local hicks."[5]

The seemingly endless case histories, some of which are noted throughout this book, repeatedly stress the reduced quality or disappearance of local news and the homogenization of programming. "In the same way that every mall in every city has the same stores carrying the same products," one critic wrote, "you can tune in to a Clear Channel radio station in Phoenix and hear the same music that the Clear Channel station in Milwaukee is playing. Sometimes the same announcer, too. Just try calling their request line."[6]

The opponents of consolidation sometimes relate the decline of localism to an even more grievous cause, as asserted by critic Clark Humphrey. He writes that radio is controlled by just a few major players, by

> companies that care naught for local communities or for responsible broadcasting. . . . Their obsessions are with further consolidating their stranglehold on the biz, with cross-division "synergies" and stock-price manipulation, with ruthless cost-cutting and centrally-planned station formats, with payola skimming, and with crushing any would-be challengers to their empires. . . . It's all about . . . the creation of an authoritarian, anti-freedom culture in which everyone will be isolated into advertiser-friendly sub-segments, all obediently viewing/reading/listening to the demographically-segmented branches of the same media combine. . . . It's way past time to take back the airwaves, to bring locality and responsibility back to broadcasting.[7]

It may be that the bottom line, not principle, will decide. In the early 2000s, as the United States suffered an economic recession and an almost unprecedented loss of jobs, radio advertising revenues, like people's incomes, dropped. However, while national radio sales declined precipitously, local ad sales suffered only slightly. Gary Fries, president of the Radio Advertising Bureau, predicted, "Radio will withstand the effects of the current economic slowdown because of its localism. Radio stations across the country serve the needs and tastes of their local communities and generate ad sales from within their marketplace. This will keep radio solvent through the tough national economy."[8] Yet in mid-2004, radio stocks declined 20 percent in two months to precipitous lows and national ad sales continued serious declines. Investment banks downgraded the stocks of six key conglomerates: Clear Channel, Emmis, Cox Radio, Entercom, Citadel, and Westwood One. One reason for the fall, some critics suggest, is that the proliferation of commercial spots not only has negatively impacted listeners but has made many advertisers feel that their own ads are lost in a sea of commercials.[9]

In *The Radio Broadcasting Industry,* Alan B. Albarran and Gregory R. Pitts write that "the advent of television in the 1950s forced radio to reposition itself as a local rather than a national medium. Today, the radio broadcasting industry offers localism as its greatest asset. In the future, localism will continue to be one of the primary ingredients driving the success of the medium." They quote from a *Broadcasting & Cable* magazine editorial: "Broadcasting's edge is localism and tailoring programming to individual markets and listeners." Albarran and Pitts further note that radio broadcasting is "built around the concept of localism or local service" and cite the morning listening hours as an example, when listeners want local news, weather, traffic, and other information that helps them prepare for the day in that particular locality. They state that although each station is supposed to serve the city in which it is licensed, in some large areas with extended suburbs, stations attempt to serve the wider area, moving away from strictly local service. However, "stations in smaller towns have continued to retain a local identity."[10]

Local Realities

Is localism a fact or an omen? Is radio still local enough to be a bulwark against severe loss of income either through a national economic crisis or through increased competition—as is happening currently with the growth of satellite and Internet radio? Or is the advertising decline a warning to radio to reverse what appears to be its current trend and restore and strengthen the medium's local voices? Is local programming the magic elixir that will save over-the-air terrestrial radio? Is radio's salvation likely to be in local orientation and service? Will corporate greed for short-term gain through consolidation kill the goose that has been laying the golden eggs?

Whether local services should be left to the marketplace, where there is a clear difference of opinion between the radio industry and the consumers and critics as to whether localism has grown or been eroded under ownership deregulation, or whether it should be required in the public interest by the federal government is a continuing question. FCC commissioner Jonathan Adelstein raised that question in mid-2004 while commenting on the FCC's upcoming proceedings on localism that aimed to determine what the agency should do, if anything, to see that broadcasters fulfill their public interest obligations by airing news and other programs relating to local concerns. Adelstein contended that it was important to determine whether locally owned stations or distant conglomerate owners did a better job. He noted that multiple-station owners agree that localism is necessary for market success, that stations that don't meet local needs won't be tuned in, while local owners claim that local ownership is the key to knowing what, when, and how to provide local programming and services.[11] Some skeptics doubt that even if it wishes, there is little that the FCC could do in this "after-the-fact" situation.

Fritz Messere, in an *Encyclopedia of Television* article, states that "the Telecommunications Act of 1996 has made it more difficult for the [FCC] Commission to withhold the license of a broadcast station"; the FCC relies on "'marketplace forces' to create competitive programming" and the "Telecommunications Act of 1996 has focused on reducing unnecessary regulation for an industry that is largely regarded as mature." Messere further notes that the industry has exercised strong influence on the FCC, including recent efforts to limit low-power radio. He quotes Supreme Court justices Potter Stewart and Stephen Breyer: "Commissions operate in hostile environments, and their regulatory policies become conditional upon acceptance of regulation by the regulated groups." Messere adds that "critics say both the FRC and the FCC became victims of client politics as these two regulatory agencies were captured by the industries they were created to regulate."[12]

Some have suggested that the concept and principle of localism needs to be revised, that the current interpretations and application do not reflect the realistic state of the market and the service in light of the rapid technological changes that increasingly impact on terrestrial radio. In an address to the International Communication Association, Philip J. Napoli maintained that "the localism principle is sorely in need of being revised and modernized in a way that reflects the recent developments in communications technology as well as the full extent of the principle's underlying rationales." He advocates an expansion of the principle beyond geographical considerations and a concentration on programming considerations. He supports localism per se, as "one of the central guiding principles in communications policymaking," however, not as an end in itself but "as a means of achieving broader social objectives." He cites the dedication of many political leaders and political theories to localism and local participation as a cornerstone of democracy. He believes that both political and cultural localism are essential and quotes a joint statement of former FCC commissioners Kenneth Cox and Nicholas Johnson: "Ultimately, our broadcasting system is premised on the concern that the very identity of local states and cities might be destroyed by a mass communications system with an exclusively national focus."[13]

Media Reform

Robert McChesney and John Nichols ask whether media reform is currently possible, either from the outside, through progressive citizen groups, or through the FCC. They note that those seeking reform usually concentrate on change and improvement through the media that they control, including community radio stations and Internet Web sites. They say that alternative media remain marginal, lending credence to the belief that the powerful corporate media are successful because they give the public what the public wants. The problem with such a belief, according to McChesney and Nichols, is "that it suggests that corporate media have mastered the marketplace on the basis of their wit and wisdom. In fact, our media system is not the legitimate result of free market competition. It is the result of relentless lobbying from big-business interests that have won explicit government policies and subsidies permitting them to scrap public-interest obligations and increase commercialization and conglomeration. It is untenable to accept such massive subsidies for the wealthy, and to content ourselves with the 'freedom' to forge alternatives that only occupy the margins."[14] McChesney and Nichols advocate the building of a national media reform coalition that will seek structural reform of the media through congressional legislation. Among their recommendations:

(a) conduct a formal study and hold hearings on what fair media ownership regulations should be;

(b) restructure and strengthen public broadcasting to make it free of commercial and political pressures and enable it to serve low-income communities and audiences;

(c) give taxpayers a $200 credit for contributions to nonprofit media such as low-power radio and TV stations to enable them to provide serious news coverage and cultural programming;

(d) eliminate political advertising on the media or, conversely, require stations to provide equal advertising time for all bona fide candidates at no cost;

(e) require stations to provide an hour a day of commercial-free news, as opposed to competitive sensational news, with a news budget based on a percentage of the station's revenues;

(f) eliminate or reduce advertising to children under twelve;

(g) revise copyright laws to give greater protection and viable income to creative producers.[15]

McChesney and Nichols think a national coalition is needed to counter the lobbying strength of the corporate media. In advocating a grassroots movement, they quote a long-time labor activist, Patty Allen, who became aware of the significance and state of the media: "We go around with all this frustration over media. But most of us think it's just something that happens to us. When I first heard [Ralph] Nader say that we own the airwaves and that we have a right to demand something better in return, I remember how liberating it felt. I was saying, 'Wow, now that I know this, what do I do? Where do I sign up? How can I demand a change? I think there are a lot of people like me all over this country who are ready. But we need a sense that we're not just wasting our time."[16]

Local Prospects

Given the current debate over what is localism, it may seem that any efforts to change the state of radio are tantamount to either preaching to alternative choirs or running in place. Is there a future for localism in radio? Is there a future for radio without localism? We asked our panel of interviewees how local radio can be preserved for future generations of listeners. Their answers ranged from optimism to pessimism to cynicism to the need for commitment and/or political action.

Valerie Geller is optimistic. She says the answer is to just keep doing local radio programming: "Just like grass grows through the cracks in the concrete, creative people who are passionate about producing local programming will find a way. It must be great programming that truly holds up a mirror and reflects local life. If it is boring, it won't make it. So make it better. Local programming should be produced so that listeners in a community cannot live without it."

Most respondents were pessimistic or, at the least, doubtful. Michael Brown states, "It takes a commitment from those large organizations that own the stations. It also takes a commitment by the FCC to support localism. I think the LPFM was a weak attempt to compensate, but the stations can't compete at the level of large commercial stations. I am somewhat pessimistic about the future of local radio."

Ed Shane answers the question of "how can local radio be preserved?" succinctly: "Hmmmmm. Maybe by doing some?"

Rollye Cornell suggests that technology requires a new approach to and understanding of localism:

I am not sure anything can be preserved for future generations nor am I sure it should be. When discussing local radio programming in this context, we are really quibbling about the delivery truck, not what's on it. When someone buys a new set of furniture and the truck pulls up in the driveway, no one says, "gee, look at this swell truck." They want to see the stuff that comes off it. Ooh and aah are reserved for the couch and table, not the truck that brought them. Radio is really no different. Beyond the one axiom—they will not listen if they cannot hear you— everything else comes down to content. Programming is the furniture. Radio is the truck.

Most members of our interview group recommended action by broadcasters, by citizen groups, and by government as necessary to preserve localism in radio. Former NAB executive Lynn Christian states that radio must become "more actively involved in all aspects of local life. The people who work at the radio stations should be compensated for spending a number of hours each week actively participating in community service organizations, on local government committees, with ethnic support groups, and with city or county non-profit organizations."

Mike Adams suggests, with more than a touch of cynicism, that we have a choice between political change ("socialism") or "education": "those wanting 'local content' will have to learn how to use the Internet, how to receive low-power community stations."

Donna Halper recommends political action: "Let's reverse some of the excesses of the Telecom Act of 1996. Let's work with Congress to fix it, and make localization more of a priority. Also, let's bring back the class D stations—those ten watt educational FMs that could give disenfranchised groups a real voice."

Christopher Maxwell believes the solution is through low-power local stations: "Ensure half-a-dozen LPFMs per market. And encourage LPFMs to carry different programming. Put a fund into place that would fund LPFMs only if they committed to programming that was not substantially duplicated by any other station, programming serving music, news and view that are dramatically different from the other stations in that market. In addition, note that NPR has repeatedly pointed out that FM receivers did not sell in mass quantities until after the FCC 'forced' stations to stop repeating the AM programming on the FM channels."

Sean Ross puts the responsibility on the owners.

Owners have to use localism for more than lip service. Every year, small-market broadcasters have been trotted out at the National Association of Broadcasters convention to espouse localism and to represent NAB's opposition to satellite broadcasting, but they're not typical anymore. It's hard for the broadcasters of America to trumpet localism at the same time they're filling up their airwaves with syndicated morning shows.

Ironically, because many syndicated shows feature edgy content, it may be the current FCC climate of intolerance that encourages broadcasters to go back to the local show, not because of a love of localism.

All Politics Is Local

Political solutions to retaining and/or reestablishing localism in radio reflect the entire spectrum of political philosophies. Interestingly, in some instances the far left and the far right agree. For example, as discussed earlier, some of the operators and proponents of "pirate radio" not only distrust the FCC's LPFM initiative, but find it a Trojan Horse and advocate local initiatives and control in establishing unlicensed radio stations as determined by the people in individual communities. They cite First Amendment rights as a basis for telecommunication freedoms. Their approach has been categorized as coming from the politically left. Operators of pirate stations that represent moderate to extreme right-wing political philosophies have found common ground with the left in relation to locally operated and programmed low-power radio. In the late 1990s and early 2000s, pirate radio stations representing both philosophies sprung up, following the FCC's abolishing low-power radio in 1979. Representatives of the left and the right both condemned the FCC for shutting down their stations and jointly pressured the FCC to allow them freedom to establish and operate their unlicensed radio services.

Milton Mueller of the Cato Institute, which traditionally has represented far right political philosophies, two decades ago similarly advocated a withdrawal of government from communications regulation. He argued that the Communications Act of 1934 needed to be revised, and he offered two approaches. In one, the government would retain central planning powers, which he said would require continual revision and amendment and be subject to continuing special interest pressures. He did not find this approach to be a satisfactory one. A second way, he suggested, would be for the government "to withdraw altogether from the business of shaping the telecommunications industry" and "Congress should apply First Amendment and free-market principles" to telecommunications.[17]

While the left and right might appear to agree on some aspects of telecommunications regulation, basic differences exist. Lawrence Soley, in his book *Free Radio*, also states that there are two approaches to consider. Both of his solutions, however, are oriented toward consumer control, unlike Mueller's strategies, which are oriented toward corporate control. Soley thinks one method to reassert local control is for the people to seize broadcasting stations as revolutionaries have done in many countries. That solution, however, would be short-lived, with the government certain to quash the takeover and give the corporate-owned media the opportunity portray the pro-consumer activists as "thugs and hooligans" rather than as those seeking media freedoms.

The other method, which Soley advocates, is to establish "free radio stations." He lists five advantages of establishing such stations. One is that such stations would demonstrate how FCC policies favor the corporate rich through the current financial qualification requirements while free stations have traditionally operated on shoestring budgets. A second advantage, Soley states, is that "free radio stations represent a form of nonviolent civil disobedience against discriminatory government policy." Third, "free radio stations allow opponents of FCC and corporate censorship to deliver their messages directly to the public, circumventing the media's elaborate filtering system, which distorts the content of the opposition's political messages." (The 2004 documentary *Outfoxed* exemplifies how one network successfully presents to the public as news material that is, in fact, biased editorial comment.) Soley's fourth point is that "free radio stations are one of the few avenues available for community members to freely express their grievances against the governing and owning classes." And fifth, "free radio stations are a community organizing tool. A free radio station can inform citizens about public hearings, boycotts, meetings and protests. . . . Free radio stations can reach hundreds or even thousands of people in seconds with almost no efforts." Solely believes that free local radio stations are a key to the FCC and the media serving the public, as opposed to the corporate, interest.[18]

That ownership rules constitute the basic issue behind diversity and localism was emphasized in mid-2004 when, despite the FCC's Localism Task Force, a coalition of members of Congress, unions, and FCC commissioners Copps and Adelstein called on the FCC to hold full public hearings on reconsidering its elimination of restrictions on media consolidation.[19]

The question comes down to whether we really need localism and, if we do, how do we go about preserving it. The media used to cover all local programming needs and issues, including politics. With increased globalization of virtually all endeavors, we frequently think of politics, as well, only in national or international terms. We tend to forget the late Speaker of the House of Representatives Tip O'Neill's dictum that "all politics is local." Since deregulation began in the late 1970s and especially since its acceleration in 1996 and 2003, more and more consolidation has resulted in less and less local political coverage.

Could it be otherwise, with local stations being run from central head-quarters hundreds or even thousands of miles away by people who have little or no knowledge of the interests or issues in the community in which a station is located? Since music and talk became the staples of radio after the advent of television forced radio to reinvent itself, ideas, information, and news have become more and more critical in any given community.

All our observations and conclusions are based on what we think we know. And what we think we know we get from the media. Where once there were multiple newspapers with at least some differing views available in any community, now many communities have only one newspaper or none at all. Radio—along with other mass media—is supposed to fill that gap. We—hopefully—look for honesty and integrity in the information we receive. How do we find it? For most of us, all that we know is what the media tell us. For example, in the 1952 presidential race, the media spin masters discovered that it was far more effective to switch Dwight D. Eisenhower's television campaign ads from describing his stand on the issues to personal feature profiles of the candidate. Adlai E. Stevenson's media advisors continued, in a losing cause, to present TV ads dealing with the issues.

A 1990s Hollywood feature film *(Wag the Dog)* comes too close to reality for some in its portrayal of a president who uses the media to make the public think we are in a justifiable war in order to distract them from the truth about his personal scandal shortly before a presidential election. Without objective, diverse, and critical political information, we lose the tools that enable us to maintain a political democracy. Local service goes beyond music and entertainment as a cornerstone of our way of life.

Should localism be the responsibility of terrestrial stations, satellite radio, the Internet—or all means of real-time audio distribution? If terrestrial radio remains a key factor, should localism be the province of licensed low-power FM stations, unlicensed pirate stations, or all AM and FM stations of any power? And once we decide, what can we do about it? The political information and knowledge discussed above is a key to the answer. Only two things can create change that we approve of or stop change that we disapprove. One is the economic bottom line. If audiences tune out of terrestrial radio and tune in to alternative systems such as satellite and the Internet, or low-power or pirate stations that by their very nature are local, the consolidators will be forced to reorient their programming and services to serve the needs of their audiences. The second thing is political action. The president nominates the members of the FCC; the Senate confirms them. Congress changes or makes new communication law. Whoever we elect—from the local level on up—will decide what Congress and the FCC will do about consolidation and localism. And localism, it would appear, may turn out to be the only means of saving terrestrial radio.

As this book goes to press in the spring of 2005, it appears the industry once again is preparing to go on a consolidation spree as investment bankers are getting increased calls from conglomerates interested in expanding their holdings. Meanwhile, localism in radio appears to have been rediscovered, at least in theory if not in fact.

With the erosion of terrestrial radio's listener and advertising base by new media such as satellite, Internet, and iPods, terrestrial radio companies launched a $28 million campaign in early 2005 to promote over-the-air radio. Almost every radio group joined in to air thirty-second spots by popular artists on the theme of "Radio: You Hear It Here First." David Field, president and CEO of Entercom Communications, summed up the industry's promotion of local service as the hallmark of terrestrial radio: "Fundamentally, the role of each local programming director is to find the most compelling local, national and international music to bring to our listeners. We are proud to note that local radio introduced thousands of new songs and artists to the public every year."[20]

The handwriting on the wall included increasing evidence and prognostication that terrestrial radio was not providing the personal, local needs of its potential audience and that more and more listeners were turning to other forms of distribution. *USA Today* reported that the Internet appeared to the most logical source of new music to replace terrestrial radio.[21] Advertisers and marketers appeared to be paying more attention to Internet radio. Lehman Brothers cut their ratings for several radio companies in the expectation that satellite radio will erode the listeners to in-car terrestrial radio.[22] And Emmis CEO Jeff Smulyan stated that "despite the buzz surrounding satellite radio, I believe iPods are a bigger threat."[23] NAB president Eddie Fritts, a strong opponent of low-power local radio and a strong supporter of consolidation, now maintains that "whether it's playing regional music or providing news during times of crisis, local radio has its finger on the pulse of the community. It is a bond that no satellite service, cable channel, or MP3 player can ever hope to duplicate."[24] Big radio and the NAB were temporarily stopped in their drive for increased conglomeration as the federal courts threw out the FCC's 2003 rules that facilitated even greater consolidation.[25]

The tide seemed to be turning, at least on the surface, at the FCC, as well.

In March 2005, the commission issued an order and proposed rule making that could facilitate the further development of low-power FM stations by extending the time for construction of LPFM stations and for filing time-share proposals with competing applicants, allowing operation even when there may be possible interference with second- or third-adjacent full-power stations, restricting ownership to local entities, prohibiting multiple ownership of low-power stations, and making it easier for LPFMs to relocate their transmitter sites. The FCC order reemphasized the local nature of the service, that the "original intent of this rule was to encourage licensees to maintain production facilities and a meaningful staff presence within the community served by the station."[26]

Congress, as well, appeared to be taking the issue of radio localism seriously with a bipartisan bill "to expedite the construction of low-power stations" by removing "3d-adjacent channel protection to existing full-power stations." The NAB strongly opposed the third-adjacent channel proposal in the bill, the Local Community Radio Act of 2005, introduced by Senators McCain, Cantwell, and Leahy.[27] McCain stated:

> While low-power FM radio stations were authorized five years ago, implementation has been severely hampered by commercial broadcasters' flagrantly exaggerated claims of interference. The most recent obstruction, a two-year study conducted at the behest of broadcasters, cost taxpayers over two million dollars and proved what the FCC and community groups have known for years: low-power FM stations will not cause significant interference in other broadcasters' signals. It is time for broadcasters to stop hiding behind false claims of interference when they are really afraid of the competition from truly local broadcasters.

Cantwell said that "for five years, large broadcasters have tried to block access for low-power FM stations using tired arguments that don't hold up in reality. This is an important fight to ensure that these affordable, community-oriented stations are allowed access to our nation's airwaves." And Leahy added that "for too long now the number of low-power FM stations the FCC could license has been limited by unrealistic and unnecessary rules requiring these smaller stations to search for available frequencies far from any full-power broadcaster. This bill will open up the airwaves to truly local broadcasting."[28]

Notes
Suggestions for Further Reading
Index

Notes

Foreword

1. See Robert W. McChesney and Ben Scott, eds., *Our Unfree Press: One Hundred Years of Radical Media Criticism* (New York: New Press, 2004).

2. See Robert W. McChesney, *The Problem of the Media: U.S. Communication Politics in the Twenty-First Century* (New York: Monthly Review Press, 2004), ch. 3.

1. The Pendulum Swings: Radio's Local Roots and National Ambitions

1. Peter Fornatale and Joshua E. Mills, *Radio in the Television Age* (Woodstock, NY: Overlook Press, 1980), 194.

2. *Communications Act of 1934,* as amended, 47 U.S.C., sec. 151.

3. Bienniel Review of the FCC Broadcast Ownership Rules, Pursuant to Section 202 of the Telecommunications Act of 1996. Docket #98-35, sec. B, p. 39.

4. FCC press release, March 12, 1998.

5. Jerry Mander "Economic Globalization: The Era of Corporate Rule," Annual E. F. Schumacher lecture, Salisbury, CT, October 1999.

6. Neal Lawrence, "Reclaiming the Airwaves for the Public," *Midwest Today,* Spring 1999, http://www.midtod.com/radiopirates.phtml.

7. *Now* with Bill Moyers, PBS, July 11, 2003. Transcript.

8. Ted Turner, "My Beef with Big Media," *Washington Monthly,* posted July 26, 2004, *Washington Monthly* Web site, printed July 27, 2004.

9. "Today's Word on Journalism," October 27, 2004. tedpease@earthlink.net.

10. "NOW" with Bill Moyers.

11. "David Field: Claim of Lack of Radio Innovation in 'Unadulterated Garbage,'" *Radio Ink,* September 6, 2004, http://www.radioink.com/headlineentry.asp (August 27, 2004).

12. "Radio Reform Sadly Means Loss of Local Voice," *Asheville Citizen-Times,* February 11, 2004, http://www.citizen-times.com.

13. Lawrence Soley, Affidavit in Support of Plaintiffs, Free Speech et al. v. Janet Reno et al. (U.S. District Court, Southern District of New York, June 1998).

14. National Lawyer's Guild Committee on Democratic Communications and the Stephen Dunifer Defense Team, "Broadcasting, the Constitution and Democracy" (paper presented at the National Association of Broadcasters convention, Las Vegas, April 6, 1998).

15. "Letter to the FCC about Radio Consolidation and Payola," by Broad Artist Coalition, May 22, 2002. Coalition members included American Federation of Musicians (AFM), American Federation of Television and Radio Artists (AFTRA), Association for Independent Music (AFIM), Future of

Music Coalition (FMC), Just Plain Folks, Nashville Songwriters Association International (NSAI), National Association of Recording Merchandisers (NARM), National Federation of Community Broadcasters (NFCB), Recording Academy, and the Recording Industry Association of America (RIAA).

16. Todd Chambers, "Radio Programming Diversity in the Era of Consolidation," *Journal of Radio Studies* 10, no. 1 (2003): 35–44.

17. Chambers, "Radio Programming Diversity," 35–36, 41–43.

18. *Digital Beat* 1, no. 8 (March 24, 2004), http://www.actlab.utexas.edu/radio/html.

19. Brent Staples, "Driving Down the Highway, Mourning the Death of American Radio," *New York Times,* June 8, 2003, http://www.donswaim.com/nytimes.staples.html.

20. Doug Reece, "KREV Fans Rally for Radio Diversity," *Billboard,* April 4, 1998, http://www.billboard.html.

21. Tom Wilkowske, "Clear Channel Moves to Dump Local Radio Programming," BusinessNorth.com, December 15, 2003.

22. Anthony DeBarros, "Consolidation Changes the Face of Radio," *USA Today,* July 7, 1998, http://www.benton.org/publiclibrary/digitalbeat/db052899.html.

23. Denise Grollimus, "Fighting Radio Titans," *Akron Beacon Journal Ohio.com,* July 13, 2003, http://www.ohio.com/mld/beaconjournal/6288038.htm.

24. "Radio for the Next Millennium," *Digital Beat* 1, no. 8 (May 28, 1999).

25. "Church Advocacy Campaign Will Hold Broadcasters Accountable," *Radio Ink,* July 21, 2004, http://www.radioink.com/headlineentry.asp.

26. "What's Local about Local Broadcasting?," A Joint Report of the Media Access Project and Benton Foundation, April 1998.

27. John Armstrong, "Prospectus," http://www.org/research/doc%20honors/john%20. Undated paper.

28. National Association of Broadcasters, "Always On: A Marketing Guide for America's Local Radio and Television Stations, State Broadcast Associations and Broadcast Groups," Washington, DC, no date.

29. Broadcast Industry Council, "Making Communities Safer." Undated pamphlet.

30. Gregory D. Newton, "Localism, Diversity, and the Public Interest Policy Implications of DAB and DARS," *Journal of Radio Studies* 3 (1995–96): 79.

31. "JRS Forum," *Journal of Radio Studies* 5, no. 1 (Winter 1998): 5–6.

32. Duncan H. Brown, "Not Getting the Policy Agenda: Radio Station Ownership Changes Following the Telecommunications Act of 1996," *Journal of Radio Studies* 7, no. 1 (Spring 2000): 8–9.

33. "Fritts Says: 'No Better Business Than Local Radio,'" *Radio Ink,* October 14, 2004, http://www.radioink.com/headlineentry.asp.

34. *Radio Ink,* May 15, 2004, http://www.radioink.com/headlineentry.asp.

2. An Act of Local Substance: Regulating for the Public

1. Christopher Sterling and John Michael Kittross, *Stay Tuned,* 3rd ed. (Mahwah, NJ: Erlbaum Associates, 2002), 64–66.

2. Peter Orlik, *The Electronic Media,* 2nd ed. (Ames: Iowa State University Press, 1997), 82.

3. Gregory Newton, "Localism in Radio: U.S. Regulatory Approach," in *Encyclopedia of Radio,* ed. Christopher Sterling (Chicago: Fitzroy Dearborn, 2004), 869.

4. Alan G. Stavitsky, "The Changing Conception of Localism in U.S. Public Radio," *Journal of Broadcasting and Electronic Media* (Winter 1994): 19.

5. Robert Hilliard and Michael Keith, *The Broadcast Century,* 3rd ed. (Boston: Focal Press, 2001), 30.

6. Jeffrey L. Stein, "Radio in the Heartland" (paper presented at the forty-ninth annual convention of the Broadcast Education Association, Las Vegas, Nevada, April 17, 2004), 2, 11.

7. U.S. House of Representatives, Communications Subcommittee, Hearings on H.R. 7357, "To Regulate Radio Communication," March 11–14, 1924, *Congressional Record,* 69th Cong., 2nd sess., 1927, 68, part 3:2571.

8. Hearings on H.R. 7357, p. 36.

9. Lawrence Soley, *Free Radio: Electronic Civil Disobedience* (Boulder, CO: Westview Press, 1999), 34–35.

10. Federal Radio Commission, *First Annual Report, 1927* (Washington, DC: Government Printing Office, 1927), 10–11.

11. Sterling and Kittross, *Stay Tuned,* 142.

12. Derek W. Valliant, "Sounds of Whiteness, Local Radio, Racial Formation, and Public Culture in Chicago, 1921–1935," *American Quarterly* (March 2002): 25, 26.

13. Vaillant, "Sounds of Whiteness," 28, 29.

14. Senate Committee on Interstate Commerce, *Hearings on S.1 and S.1754 Bills re: "Radio Control,"* January 8–9, 1926, 69th Cong., part 1, 34.

15. John Armstrong, "Prospectus." http://www.natcom.org/doc%20honors/john%20armstrong%20paper.doc.

16. Senate Committee on Interstate Commerce, *Hearings on S.1 and S.1754 Bills re: "Radio Control,"* *Congressional Record,* 69th Cong., 1st sess., 1926, 67, part 5:5558.

17. *Radio Act of 1927,* sec. 9.

18. Stavitsky, "Changing Conception of Localism," 20.

19. Stavitsky, "Changing Conception of Localism," 21.

20. Newton, "Localism in Radio," 870.

21. Erik Barnouw, *A Tower of Babel* (New York: Oxford University Press, 1966), 208.

22. Thomas W. Hazlitt, "Assigning Property Rights to Radio Spectrum Users," *Journal of Law and Economics* 41 (1998): 541.

23. Sterling and Kittross, *Stay Tuned,* 144.

24. Armstrong, "Prospectus," 13–14.

25. Vaillant, "Sounds of Whiteness," 30, 29, 35–36.

26. Susan J. Douglas, *Listening In: Radio and the American Imagination* (New York: Random House, 1999), 17.

27. "Communication and the Production of Culture," in *Critical Connections: Communication for the Future* (Washington, DC: U.S. Government Printing Office, 1990), 186.

28. Sterling and Kittross, *Stay Tuned,* 207.

29. Sterling and Kittross, *Stay Tuned,* 208.

3. Acting in the Local Interest: Localism and the National Networks

1. Soley, *Free Radio,* 37.

2. Soley, *Free Radio,* 37–38.

3. Sterling and Kittross, *Stay Tuned,* 209.

4. Fritz Messere, "Regulation," in *The Encyclopedia of Radio,* ed. Christopher Sterling (Chicago: Fitzroy Dearborn, 2004).

5. Messere, "Regulation."

6. Federal Communications Commission, "1965 Policy Statement on Comparative Broadcast Hearings," 1 FCC 2nd, 1965, 393–94.

7. FCC, "1965 Policy Statement," 394–99.

8. David M. Silverman and David N. Tobenkin, "The FCC's Main Studio Rule: Achieving Little for Localism at Great Cost to Broadcasters," *Federal Communications Law Journal* 53 (2001): 471.

9. Cited in Robert L. Copple, "Cable Television and the Allocation of Regulatory Power," 44 Fed. Comm. L.J. 1, 11012 (1991), 475.

10. Silverman and Tobenkin, "FCC's Main Studio Rule," 475, 478.

11. 4 Fed. Reg., 2715, 2716 (June 30, 1939), Par. 3.12, Par. 3.30–31.

12. Silverman and Tobenkin, "FCC's Main Studio Rule," 480.

13. "Promulgation of Rules and Regulations Concerning the Origination Points of Programs of Standard and FM Broadcast Stations," 43 FCC 571, 1 Rad. Reg., 91:465 (1950).

14. "Memorandum Opinion and Order," 43 FCC 888, 890 (1952).

15. Silverman and Tobenkin, "FCC's Main Studio Rule," 482.

16. Silverman and Tobenkin, "FCC's Main Studio Rule," 486.

17. Silverman and Tobenkin, "FCC's Main Studio Rule," 477–78.

18. Douglas, *Listening In,* 175, 224.

19. Patrick Burkart, "Radio Shock: Talk Radio Propaganda," *Bad Subjects,* no. 23 (December 1995), http://eserver.org/bs/23/burkart.html.

20. Sterling and Kittross, *Stay Tuned,* 210–11.

21. *National Broadcasting Company v. United States,* 319 U.S. 190 (1943), 217–18.

22. Sterling and Kittross, *Stay Tuned,* 233.

23. Douglas, *Listening In,* 224–25.

4. Changing the Broadcast Landscape: Radio Reinvents, Television Dominates, and an Act Reforms

1. David A. Moss and Michael R. Fein, "Radio Regulation Revisited: Coase, the FCC, and the Public Interest," *Journal of Policy History* 15, no. 4 (2003): 409.

2. Michael C. Keith, *Signals in the Air: Native Broadcasting in America* (Westport, CT: Praeger, 1995).

3. Sterling and Kittross, *Stay Tuned,* 362.

4. Sterling and Kittross, *Stay Tuned,* 369.

5. Douglas, *Listening In,* 225.

6. Douglas, *Listening In,* 225.

7. Marc Fisher, "Print's Weak Stepsister," *American Journalism Review,* June 1998, http://www.newslink.org/airfisherside98.html.

8. FCC, "In the Matter of Editorializing by Broadcast Licensees," 13 FCC 1248 (1949).

9. *Red Lion Broadcasting Company v. FCC,* SC 395 U.S. 367 (1969).

10. Soley, *Free Radio,* 44–45.

11. Sterling and Kittross, *Stay Tuned,* information interpreted from tables in appendix.

12. Newton, "Localism in Radio," 871.

13. Newton, "Localism in Radio," 871. Also see "Notice of Inquiry and Proposed Rulemaking," FCC 2d 457 (1979), 489.

14. Newton, "Localism in Radio," 870.

15. Tom A. Collins, "The Local Service Concept in Broadcasting," *Iowa Law Review* 65 (1980): 566–67.

16. Elliott Parker, "Perceptions of Radio Localism" (paper delivered at the Association for Education in Journalism and Mass Communication [AEJMC] conference, 2003), 3.

17. Parker, "Perceptions of Radio Localism," 3.

18. *Free Speech et al. v. Janet Reno, U.S. Department of Justice, and the FCC;* U.S. District Court, Southern District of New York, Memorandum of Law in Support of Plaintiff's Motion for Preliminary Injunction, July 13, 1998, by Center for Constitutional Rights, pp. 5, 6.

19. Philip M. Napoli, "Toward an Expanded Localism Principle in Communications Policymaking and Policy Analysis" (paper delivered at the International Communication Association annual meeting, Acapulco, Mexico, June 2000), 9.

20. "Media Monopoly," an interview with Nicholas Johnson, Multinational Monitor, May 1995, http://multinationalmonitor.org/hyper/issues/1995/05/mm0595_07.html.

5. In Whose Best Interest? Diversity, Localism, and Consolidation

1. Robert L. Hilliard and Michael C. Keith, *The Broadcast Century and Beyond,* 3rd ed. (Boston: Focal Press, 2001), 291–93.

2. Sterling and Kittross, *Stay Tuned,* 668.

3. "Radio for the Next Millennium," *Digital Beat,* May 28, 1999, http://www.vitalspace.net/newmedia/forum00033.html.

4. National Lawyer's Guild, "Broadcasting, the Constitution, and Democracy."

5. *Wall Street Journal,* September 18, 1997, p. A1.

6. Yon Lambert, "Radio Mergers Source of Static at Columbia, S.C. Stations." *Knight-Ridder/Tribune Business News,* June 22, 1997.

7. Andy Sullivan, "Radio Deregulation No Hit for Listeners, Report Says," Reuters, November 18, 2002.

8. Daniel J. Rapela, "Analysis of the Effects of Consolidation on the Radio Industry" (paper presented to the Department of Theatre, Communications, and Fine Arts, Gannon University, December 2, 1999), 4.

9. Jim Naureckas, "Media Conglomerates Hijacked Telecommunications Policy with Millions in PAC Contributions," *In These Times,* March 4, 1996.

10. Naureckas, "Media Conglomerates."

11. Marc Fisher, "Sounds Familiar for a Reason," *Washington Post,* May 18, 2003, p. B01ff.

12. Fisher, "Sounds Familiar."

13. Fisher, "Sounds Familiar."

14. Anthony DeBarros, "Consolidation Changes Face of Radio," *USA Today,* July 7, 1998, http://www.usatoday.com/faceofradio.html.

15. DeBarros, "Consolidation Changes Face."

16. Inside Radio, December 4, 2002, http://www.InsideRadio.com.

17. Parker, "Perceptions of Radio Localism," 5.

18. Marc Fisher, "Blackout on the Dial," *American Journalism Review* (June 1998), page number missing.

19. Andrew Ferguson, "Why Is U.S. Radio So Terrible? FCC Should Ask," Bloomberg.com, May 27, 2003, http://quote.bloomberg.com/apps/news?pid.

20. Ferguson, "Why Is U.S. Radio?"

21. Bill McKibben, "Small World: Why One Town Stays Unplugged," *Harper's Magazine,* December 2003, 47, 48–49, 54.

22. "Local Media in Battleground States Valuable to Candidates," *Radio Ink,* August 30, 2004, http://www.radioink.com/headlineentry.asp.

23. Patrick Burkart, "Radio Shock: Talk Radio Propaganda," *Bad Subjects,* December 1995, http://eserver.org/bs/23/burkart.html.

24. Molly Ivins, "FCC and Right-Wing Radio Helping U.S. Press Freedom Slip Away," *Salt Lake Tribune,* February 3, 2003, p. 27.

25. Chicago Media Action, article by Karen Young, April 2, 2003, http://www.chicagomediaaction.org/index.php?link=fcc_report.

26. Frank A. Blethen, "Only in Variety Is There Freedom" (address at a public symposium, University of Illinois, Urbana-Champaign, September 8, 2002), http://www.iwantmedia.com/people/people19.html.

27. Steven Barnett, "Changes in the Landscape of Media Ownership Worldwide," Organization of News Ombudsmen, March 29, 2004, http://www.newsombudsmen.org/barnett1.html.

28. An interview with Nicholas Johnson, *Media Monopoly*, 1995, http://multinationalmonitor.org/hyper/issues/1995/05/mm0595_07.html.

29. Moss and Fein, "Radio Regulation Revisited," 411–12.

30. Moss and Fein, "Radio Regulation Revisited," 411; see Ernest Hollings and Byron Dorgan, "Your Local Station, Signing Off," *Washington Post*, June 20, 2001, p. A27.

31. Moss and Fein, "Radio Regulation Revisited," 412.

32. "New Initiative Started by Radio for Peace International-Station to Resume Broadcasts," RFPI press release, February 16, 2004.

33. Rapela, "Analysis of the Effects," 4.

34. Rapela, "Analysis of the Effects," 10.

35. Dale Smith, "Hello, Honolulu and Amarillo, My Austin Secret Is . . . I'm Your DJ," *Austin American-Statesman*, July 22, 1999, http://www.radiodiversity.com/amfmdjsystem.html.

36. Brad King, "Digital Radio: Small Guys' Ruin?" *Wired News*, October 19, 2002, http://www.wired.com/news/mp3/1.

37. King, "Digital Radio."

38. King, "Digital Radio." See Matt Spangler, "Can't Find Nothin' on Radio?" *Radio and Records*, July 31, 1998.

39. Rachel Chong, FCC commissioner, "Remarks at the 1997 National Association of Broadcasters Radio Convention," September 19, 1997.

40. Interview with Nicholas Johnson.

6. Lights Through the Smoke Screen: Ownership Deregulation and Local Opposition

1. David Lieberman, "Relaxing Rules Raises Concerns about Diverse Media Voices," *USA Today*, January 16, 2003, p. 1B.

2. Lieberman, "Relaxing Rules Raises Concerns."

3. "Beware Media Consolidation," editorial in *Business Week* (May 26, 2003): 126.

4. Lisa Bennett, "Feminists Must Speak Out against Loss of Media Diversity," *National NOW Times*, Summer 2002, 16.

5. "Diversity Summit Addresses Racial and Ethnic Diversity in Radio and Television Newsrooms," Native American Journalists Association press release, January 13, 2004.

6. "Clear Channel CEO Visits Capitol Hill," Lordstown, Ohio, Business Journal Online, January 30, 2003, http://www.business-journal.com/LateJan03/ClearChanneltestimony.html.

7. "FCC Should Kill Cross-Ownership and Duopoly Rules, NAB Says," *Communications Daily*, January 3, 2003.

8. E-mail from Andrew Dubber to Michael Keith, June 21, 2004.

9. Barnett, "Changes in the Landscape."

10. Robert W. McChesney and John Nichols, *Our Media, Not Theirs* (New York: Seven Stories Press, 2002), 47.

11. "Media Rules," *Free Press,* http://www.mediareform.net/rules/page.php?n=fcc.

12. Opening statement of Commissioner Jonathan Adelstein, FCC Field Hearing on Media Ownership, Duke Law School, Durham, NC, March 31, 2003.

13. "Media Rules."

14. Michael James, "Cultural Decline?" *ABC News,* June 2, 2003, http://www.abcnews.com/archive.

15. Todd Shields, "Good Copps, Bad Copps," *Mediaweek,* March 17, 2003, 17.

16 Shields, "Good Copps."

17. Robert W. McChesney and John Nichols, "Turning the Tide: It's Time to Fight the Enronization of the Media," *In These Times,* April 15, 2002, 16.

18. John Dunbar and Aron Pilhofer, "Big Radio Rules in Small Markets," Center for Public Integrity press release, October 1, 2003.

19. Larry Queen, "Does Corporate Radio Need to Go," *Charleston (SC) Post and Courier,* August 7, 2003, p. 7F.

20. Ralph Nader, "Giving Our Airwaves to the Media Moguls," *Dissident Voice,* June 2, 2003, http://www.dissidentvoice.org/Articles5.

21. Interview on NPR's "Fresh Air," July 23, 2003.

22. Tom Wilkowske, "Clear Channel Defends Decision to Drop Local Radio Programming," *BusinessNorth.com,* December 15, 2003, http://www.businessnorth.com/viewarticle.asp?articleid=757.

23. Mireya Navarro, "Media: As Univision Looks to Buy into Radio, a Debate Over How Big Is Too Big," *New York Times,* June 23, 2003, sec. C, p. 8.

24. "FCC Sets Limits on Media Concentration," FCC press release, June 2, 2003.

25. John C. Roberts, "Dishonest Communications Reform," June 4, 2003, http://www.chicagotribune.com/news/opinion/oped/chi-030604333jun04,1,4682840.story.

26. "FCC Vetoes Public Interest," editorial in *Madison (WI) Capital Times,* June 3, 2003, p. 8A.

27. "FCC Vetoes Public Interest."

28. Barnett, "Changes in the Landscape."

29. Barnett, "Changes in the Landscape."

30. "FCC Asks Court to Reconsider Ownership Limit Stay," *Radio Ink,* August 11, 2004, http://www.radioink.com/headlineentry.asp.

31. "FCC to Consider 'Localism,'" Associated Press, August 20, 2003.

32. Andrew Mollison, "FCC to Shore Up Local Stations' Diversity, Public Service," Cox News service, August 20, 2003.

33. Andrew Mollison, "FCC to Push for Diversity, Local Service," *Atlanta Journal-Constitution,* August 21, 2003, p. 1F.

34. Jonathan D. Salant, "TV and Radio Stations' Relationship with Local Communities Eyed by FCC," *Manchester Union Leader,* August 21, 2003, p. D10.

35. "McMedia Threatens Local News," *Wisconsin State Journal,* August 24, 2003, p. B2.

36. Editorial in *Madison.com* (website of the Capital Newspapers), August 22, 2003.

37. "McMedia Threatens Local News."

38. Mollison, "FCC to Push for Diversity."

39. "FCC to Consider 'Localism.'"

40. Susan Crabtree, "Powell's Thinking Locally," *Variety,* August 21, 2003, 4.

41. Kathleen Q. Abernathy, remarks prepared for the NAB Radio Show, October 2, 2003 (statement issued by Abernathy's FCC office).

42. John W. Gonzalez, "Local Talents Sing Blues over Deregulation; FCC Hearing Full of Complaints," *Houston Chronicle,* January 30, 2004, sec. A, p. 29.

43. Bill McConnell, "The Public Is Interested: In Heart of Texas Panel Gets an Earful over Lack of Localism," *Broadcasting and Cable,* February 2, 2004, 1.

44. "Court Rejects FCC's Rules on Ownership," *Associated Press,* June 25, 2004.

45. "Court Sends Ownership Rules Back to FCC," *Radioweek,* June 28, 2004, http://www.nab.org/radioweek.

46. *Radio Ink,* June 28, 2004, (Comissioner Copps' statement), http://www.radioink.com/headlineentry.asp.

47. *Radio Ink,* June 28, 2004.

48. *Radio Ink,* June 28, 2004.

49. "Court Sends Ownership Rules Back to FCC."

50. "Chairman Powell: Localism is Core Mission of FCC," *Radio Ink,* July 2, 2004, http://www.radioink.com/headlineentry.asp.

51. "Chairman Powell."

52. "NAB Responds to FCC's Localism Inquiry," *Radio Ink,* July 2, 2004, http://www.radioink.com/headlineentry.asp.

53. "FCC's Copps Asks for Media Ownership Hearings," *Radio Ink,* July 2, 2004, http://www.radioink.com/headlineentry.asp.

54. "Dear NAB Member" (letter from NAB president and CEO Eddie Fritts), July 2, 2004.

55. "Next FCC Localism Task Force Meeting Scheduled for Monterey," *Radio Ink,* June 21, 2004.

56. *Radio Ink,* May 28, 2004.

57. "FCC Localism Hearing Draws Cheers, Boos," *Radio Ink,* July 22, 2004.

58. "FCC Commissioners to Convene Forum on Media Concentration," *Radio Ink,* December 8, 2004, http://www.radioink.com/headlineentry.asp.

59. "FCC Hears from Broadcasters on Localism," *Radio Week,* December 8, 2004, http://www.nab.org/radioweek.

7. Disharmony in the Air: Downsizing Music Playlists

1. Rapela, "Analysis of the Effects," 11.

2. Marc Fisher, "The Great Radio Rebellion," *Washington Post,* June 2, 1998, p. D01.

3. Spangler, "Can't Find Nothin' on Radio?"

4. Spangler, "Can't Find Nothin' on Radio?"

5. Spangler, "Can't Find Nothin' on Radio?"

6. Erika Shernoff, "Alternative Burden: The Importance of Localism and Non-profit College Radio," no date, http://www.cal.jmv.edu/wrigh2kr/hold/shernoff.pdf.

7. Fisher, "Sounds Familiar for a Reason," B1.

8. "Seattle Statement Calls for Radio Reform," June 22, 2004, http://www.[cedipam]SeattleStatementCallsForRadioReform.

9. Bruce Alpert, "Low-Power Radio Stations Proposed; Supporters Tout Greater Diversity," *New Orleans Times-Picayune,* April 20, 1999.

10. Brent Staples, "The Trouble with Corporate Radio: The Day the Protest Music Died," *New York Times,* February 20, 2003, sec. A, p. 30.

11. Jennifer Lee, "Musicians Protesting Monopoly in Media," *New York Times,* December 18, 2003, sec. E, p. 1.

12. "Anti-war Group Claims Clear Channel Rejected Billboard," *Radio Ink,* July 13, 2004, http://www.radioink.com/headlineentry.asp.

13. Brent Staples, "Driving Down the Highway, Mourning the Death of American Radio," *New York Times,* June 8, 2003, http://www.donswaim.com/nytimes.staples.html.

14. Staples, "Driving Down the Highway."

15. Laura M. Holson, "Survey Shows Opposition to Radio Consolidation," *New York Times,* June 20, 2002, sec. C, p. 6.

16. Andy Sullivan, "Radio Deregulation No Hit for Listeners, Report Says," Reuters, November 18, 2002.

17. "Radio Reversity, Not Diversity, Is No Hit for Music Fans and Listeners, Report Says (11-20-02)," SDN News: Nationwide Radio News Archives, no date, http://www.arbitron.com/national_radio/nr_news_archive.html.

18. "Media Ownership: Radio," Testimony of the Future of Music Coalition to the Senate Committee on Commerce, Science, and Transportation, January 30, 2003, p. 13.

19. "Petition for Reconsideration Filed by the Future of Music Coalition at the Federal Communications Commission on the Broadcast Ownership Rules: Docket 02-277," September 4, 2003.

20. *Radio Ink,* July 1, 2004, http://www.radioink.com/headlineentry.asp.

8. New Audio Media and Localism: The Impact of Satellite and Internet Radio

1. Peter Goodman, "Radio Sings a New Tune," *Newsday,* no date, http://future.newsday.com/8/fmon0809.htm.

2. "Edward Fritts: Competition for Listeners Is 'Intense,'" *Radio Ink,* July 8, 2004, http://www.radioink.com/headlineentry.asp.

3. "NAB President Applauds North American Broadcasters' Commitment to Community Service," The Voice Choice of the Nation Private Broadcasting (statement issued by the NAB), November 11, 2003.

4. Goodman, "Radio Sings a New Tune."

5. John Eckberg, "Radio to Change Dramatically," *Cincinnati Enquirer,* March 28, 2000, p. ARC.

6. Eckberg, "Radio to Change Dramatically."

7. Eckberg, "Radio to Change Dramatically."

8. *Radio Ink,* June 15, 2004, http://www.radioink.com/headlineentry.asp.

9. *Radio Ink,* April 22, 2004, http://www.radioink.com/headlineentry.asp.

10. "Sirius to Launch Five New Music Channels," *Radio Ink,* July 6, 2004, http://www.radioink.com/headlineentry.asp.

11. "Media Bay and XM to Promote Radio Classics Channel, *Radio Ink,* July 7, 2004.

12. David Hinckley, "Listening for Change: Lack of Diversity on the Airwaves Is Opening the Door for Satellite Radio," *New York Daily News,* December 29, 2002, p. 22.

13. Tony Lombardo, "Hype over Satellite Radio Reaches Breaking Point with Local Radio," *Iowa State Daily,* August 1, 2002.

14. Paul Lewis, interview with authors, July 17, 2004.

15. Hinckley, "Listening for Change," 22.

16. *Radio and Internet Newsletter* (RAIN), July 12, 2004, http://www.kurthanson.com.

17. Deborah Solomon, "That Old-Time Radio," interview with Jonathan Schwartz, *New York Times,* March 14, 2004, p. 21.

18. Paige Albiniak, "It's Only a Patent, XM Insists; But NAB Fears That New Satellite-Radio Provider Aims for Local Programming," *Broadcasting and Cable,* March 11, 2002, 19.

19. "Satellite Radio Growth Puts Broadcasters on Defensive," *RAIN,* March 23, 2004.

20. "Satellite Radio Growth."

21. Albiniak, "It's Only a Patent."

22. "Fritts Comments on Satellite Legislation," *Radio Ink,* March 26, 2004, http://www.radioink.com/headlineentry.asp.

23. "NAB Presses FCC to Bar Local Content on Satellite Radio," *Radio Ink,* April 20, 2004, http://www.radioink.com/headlineentry.asp.

24. *Radio Ink,* June 23, 2004, http://www.radioink.com/headlineentry.asp.

25. *Radioweek,* June 28, 2004. *http://www.nab.org/radioweek.*

26. *Radio Ink,* June 23, 2004.

27. *Radioweek,* June 28, 2004.

28. Lombardo, "Hype over Satellite."

29. Stifel, Nicolaus, and Company, research report, "Satellite Radio: Content Is King. Get It Now!" (research report), December 4, 2003, 1.

30. Stifel, Nicolaus, "Satellite Radio," 9, 11.

31. *RAIN*, November 10, 2004, http://www.kurthanson.com.

32. Chuck Moozakis, "Broadcaster Turns Up Volume on E-Commerce," *Internet Week 100*, no date, http://www.internetwk.com/100/media.htm.

33. Eckberg, "Radio to Change Dramatically."

34. "Radio and Internet Newsletter," January 7, 2005.

35. *RAIN*, July 9, 2004.

36. *RAIN*, July 7, 12, 13, 15, 2004.

37. http://www.live-radio.net/info.shtml (accessed June 28, 2004).

38. http://www.radio-locator.com (accessed June 28, 2004).

39. The category "More" breaks down into subgenres of the previously listed formats; the site also provides for an open search of any other format of choice (http://www.live365.com/home/index02.live [accessed June 28, 2004]).

40. http://www.kurthanson.com/archive/news/062504/index.asp; also http://radioandrecords.com/Newsroom/2004_06_25/technologyturns.asp.

41. Allan Hoffman, "Net Radio: Tune In, Turn On," Nj.com: Everything Jersey, March 28, 2004, http://www.nj.com.

42. Ben Compaine and Emma Smith, "Internet Radio: A New Engine for Content Diversity?" (paper presented at the Telecommunications Policy Conference, October 2001), 22, 26–27, 2.

43. "Sirius Inks Deal with AP for NFL 'Sports Power,'" *Radio Ink*, August 25, 2004.

44. "Sirius Gets Men's NCAA Basketball Deal," *Radio Ink*, November 30, 2004.

45. "Mel Karmazin Named New CEO of Sirius Satellite," *Radio Ink*, November 22, 2004.

46. "Howard Stern Signs Five-Year Contract with Sirius," *Radio Ink*, October 6, 2004.

47. *Radio Ink*, January 4, 2005.

48. *Radio Ink*, December 28, 2004.

49. "Sirius, XM Subscriber Numbers Expected to Double," *Radio Ink*, December 7, 2004.

50. "Sirius Signs with NavTeq for Real-Time Traffic Data," *Radio Ink*, December 15, 2004.

51. "XM to Launch Five More Local Traffic, Weather Channels Despite Protests from NAB," *Radio Ink*, July 27, 2004.

52. *Radio and Internet Newsletter (RAIN)*, November 10, 2004.

53. *RAIN*, January 7, 2005.

54. "Classical WQXR New York Now on AOL Radio Network," *Radio Ink*, December 3, 2004.

55. *RAIN*, November 15, 2004.

56. "Audiobloggers Aim to Provide Break from 'Predictable Radio' with 'Podcasting,'" *Radio Ink*, December 9, 2004.

57. "XM Satellite Radio to Broadcast on Web," *Radio Ink*, September 17, 2004.

58. *RAIN*, November 1, 2004.

59. "Online Surpassing All Media as 'Favorite,'" *Radio Ink*, October 1, 2004.

60. *RAIN*, August 4, 2004.

61. *RAIN*, January 6, 2005.

62. *RAIN*, October 14, 2004.

63. *RAIN*, December 9, 2004.

64. *RAIN*, August 9, 2004.

65. "Analysts Downgrade Radio Sector," *Radio Ink*, December 27, 2004.

9. Tuning the Alternatives: Community Radio and Pirate Broadcasts

1. Reece, "KREV Fans Rally."

2. Stavitsky, "Changing Conception of Localism," 26.

3. Frederick Noronha, "Community Radio: A 'Most Appealing Tool' for the Common Man," http://www.cityradio.nu/waves.htm (accessed January 29, 2004).

4. Liss Jeffrey (University of Toronto), "Radio for the Next Millennium," *Digital Beat* 1, no. 8 (May 28, 1999).

5. "Radio for the Next Millennium," *Digital Beat* 1, no. 8 (May 28, 1999). Statement by pirate station operator Napoleon Williams.

6. Gloria Tristani, "Civil Rights in the Digital World" (keynote address to the Leadership Conference on Civil Rights, Washington, DC, September 7, 2000).

7. Eric Boehlert, "Battle for Radio Diversity Heats Up on Capitol Hill," *Rolling Stone*, November 19, 1999.

8. "LPRS Solution," http://members.tripod.com/rad4rest-of-us/LPRS.htm (accessed March 17, 2004).

9. "Microradio Proposals at FCC Opposed by NPR and NAB," from report issued by National Public Radio, May 8, 1998.

10. "Kennard Responds to House Vote," Americans for Radio Diversity, http://www.radiodiversity.com/archives/2000_04.shtml (accessed April 14, 2000).

11. "Bring on Low Power," editorial in *Radio World*, March 3, 1999.

12. "Low Power Radio Matters to All of Us," Media Access Project, no date, http://www.mediaaccess.org.

13. "Kennard Responds to House Vote."

14. "Low Power FM (LPFM) Radio Service," FCC information document, March 9, 2004, http://www.fcc.gov.

15. Undated clippings from *Radio Ink*.

16. Undated clippings from *Radio Ink*.

17. Prometheus Radio Project, "One Small Step for Powell—One Miniscule Tiptoe for Low Power Radio," *Free Press*, September 20, 2003, http://www.freepress.org/journal.php.

18. "FCC's LPFM Report to Congress Says More Room for Stations," Mediageek, February 25, 2004, http://www.mediageek.org/archives/cat_radio.html.

19. "NAB's Response to LPFM Decision: Radio Listeners 'Unintended Victims,'" *Radio Ink*, July 23, 2004.

20. Ted M. Coopman, "FCC Enforcement Difficulties with Unlicensed Micro Radio," *Journal of Broadcasting and Electronic Media*, no. 4 (Fall 1999); quoted in Michael H. Adams and Steven Phipps, "Low-Power Radio/Microradio," *Encyclopedia of Radio*, 2004.

21. Adams and Phipps, "Low-Power Radio/Microradio," 886.

22. Adams and Phipps. "Low-Power Radio/Microradio," 887.

23. Kate Coyer, press release for a presentation, "Community Radio and the Battle for the Airwaves" at the University of London, November 25, 2004.

24. *Free Speech, Steal This Radio, et al. v. Janet Reno, U.S. Department of Justice, and Federal Communications Commission*. Filing in U.S. District Court, Southern District of New York, July 13, 1998, by Center for Constitutional Rights (Robert T. Perry, Barbara Olshansky, William Goodman and Daniel Hecht), 1, 2.

25. *Free Speech et al. v. Reno*, 2, 6.

26. *Free Speech et al. v. Reno*, 9–10.

27. *Free Speech et al. v. Reno*, 13, 19.

28. Edward Lewine, "Radio Pirates Drop Anchor Together," *New York Times*, January 10, 1999, n.p.

29. Neal Lawrence, "Reclaiming the Airwaves for the Public, *Midwest Today*, Spring 1999, http://www.midtod.com/radiopirates.phtml.

30. Bill Snyder, "Take Back the Airwaves," *Twin Cities Revue*, June 10, 1999, http://www.radiodiversity.com/press/review1.html.

31. George Hunter, "FCC Tunes In Pirate Radio," *Detroit News*, April 6, 1999, http://www.detnews.com/archives.

32. Frank Ahrens, "Yo Ho Ho and a Battle of Broadcasters," *Washington Post*, October 6, 1998, p. D02.

33. Charles Fairchild, "The FCC and Community Radio," *Z Magazine*, July 1997, http://zena.secureforum.com/znet/zmag.

34. Jesse Walker, "Radio Waves," Reasononline (*Reason* magazine), June 1999, http://reason.com/9906/fe.jw.radio.shtml.

35. Ron Sakolsky, "The LPFM Fiasco," *Lip Magazine*, http://www.lipmagazine.org/articles, June 30, 2001.

36. Douglas, *Listening In*, 357.

37. San Francisco Liberation Radio press release, October 16, 2003 (updated October 24), http://www.liberationradio.net/articles/statements/raid.php.

38. "South Florida Broadcasters Examine Piracy Issue," *Radio Ink,* July 22, 2004.

39. "Agents Raid Santa Cruz Pirate Radio Station," *Radio Ink,* October 1, 2004.

40. "FCC Raids Pirate Radio Station in Knoxville," *Radio Ink,* September 17, 2004.

41. "NBC-TV Special on Low Power FM Scheduled For Sept. 26," *Radio Ink,* September 13, 2004.

10. What, If Not Local? Globalism, Localism, and Public Interest

1. Richard Flacks, "Reflections on Strategy in a Dark Time," *Boston Review,* Fall 1995, http://www.bostonreview.net/BR20.6/flacks.html.

2. Messere, "Regulation."

3. James Gattuso, "The Myth of Media Concentration: Why the FCC's Media Ownership Rules Are Unnecessary," Heritage Foundation, May 29, 2003, WebMemo #284, http://www.heritage.org/Research/InternetandTechology/wm284.cfm.

4. *Radio Ink,* June 16, 2004, http://www.radioink.com/headlineentry.asp.

5. Robert Stockdale, "Radio, TV in a Sad State? Consolidation Has Caused Decline in Broadcasting," editorial in *Syracuse (NY) Post-Standard,* August 26, 2003, p. A11.

6. "Media Consolidation: What Are the Effects?," Changing the Channels, http://www.changingchannels.org/consol2.htm (accessed March 29, 2004).

7. Clark Humphrey, "Radio Silence," http://www.MISCmedia.com, September 6, 2002.

8. "Local Ad Sales Sustain Radio through Nation's Turbulent Economy," Radio Advertising Bureau press release, July 3, 2001.

9. Jill Goldsmith, "Ad Glut Rocks Radio," *Daily Variety,* June 17, 2004, 17.

10. Alan B. Albarran and Gregory G. Pitts, *The Radio Broadcasting Industry* (Boston: Allyn and Bacon, 2001), 174, 175.

11. "Notice on Inquiry on Localism Coming," Benton Foundation, May 25, 2004, http://www.%Benton%27s2oCommunications-related%20Headlines.

12. Fritz Messere, "Federal Communications Commission," in *Encyclopedia of Television* (New York: Fitzroy Dearborn, 2004), 451, 452.

13. Napoli, "Toward an Expanded Localism Principle."

14. Robert W. McChesney and John Nichols, "Our Media, Not Theirs," *In These Times* (Institute for Public Affairs), April 14, 2003, 18.

15. McChesney and Nichols, "Our Media," 18.

16. McChesney and Nichols, "Our Media," 18.

17. Milton Mueller, "Property Rights in Radio Communication: The Key to Reform of Telecommunication Regulation," Cato Institute policy analysis paper, June 3, 1982.

18. Soley, *Free Radio,* 46–47.

19. "Media 'Coalition' Calls on Chairman Powell to Hold Ownership Hearings," *Radio Ink,* July 24, 2004.

20. David Field, "Radio Industry to Launch Campaign to Promote Over-the-Air Radio," January 11, 2005; "Music Stars Sing Radio's Praises in Campaign to Promote Medium," January 12, 2005, *Radio Ink.*

21. *Radio and Internet Newsletter* (RAIN), March 10, 2005; January 19, 2005.

22. "Analyst Lowers Radio Forecast over Satellite Concerns," radioink.com, February 9, 2005.

23. "Emmis" Smulyan: iPods a Bigger Threat Than Satellite Radio," *Radio Ink,* January 19, 2005.

24. Eddie Fritts, "Historic Agreement Propels HD Radio," *PR Newswire US,* January 5, 2005.

25. "White House Drops Effort to Relax Media Ownership Rules," January 31, 2005; "NAB Seeks Supreme Court Review of Media Ownership Rules Today," January 31, 2005; "National Media Appeal Ownership Rules," February 1, 2005, *Radio Ink.*

26. "FCC to Consider Options for Expanding, Strengthening LPFM Service," *FCC News,* March 17, 2005.

27. "Senators Renew Battle for LPFM," *Radio Business Report,* February 11, 2005, http://www.rbr.com/epaper/pages/februaryo5.

28. "McCain, Cantwell, & Leahy to Introduce Low-Power FM Legislation.," *Radio Ink,* February 14, 2005.

Suggestions for Further Reading

Anderson, Robin, and Lance Strate. *Critical Studies in Media Commercialism.* New York: Oxford University Press, 2000.

Bagdikian, Ben H. *The New Media Monopoly.* Boston: Beacon, 2004.

Carpenter, Sue. *40 Watts from Nowhere.* New York: Scribner, 2004.

Chomsky, Noam. *Media Control: The Spectacular Achievements of Propaganda.* New York: Seven Stories, 2002.

Compaine, Benjamine M., and Douglas Gomery. *Who Owns the Media? Competition and Concentration in the Mass Media Industry.* Mahwah, NJ: Erlbaum, 2000.

Croteau, David, and William Hoynes. *The Business of Media: Corporate Media and the Public Interest.* Thousand Oaks, CA: Pine Forge, 2001.

———. *Media/Society: Industries, Images, and Audiences.* Thousand Oaks, CA: Pine Forge, 2002.

Doll, Bob. *Sparks out of the Plowed Ground: The History of America's Small Town Radio Stations.* West Palm Beach, FL: Streamline, 1996.

Gerbner, George, et al. *Invisible Crisis: What Conglomerate's Control of Media Means for America and the World.* New York: Perseus, 1996.

Herman, Edward S., and Noam Chomsky. *Manufacturing Consent: The Political Economy of the Mass Media.* New York: Pantheon, 2002.

Hilmes, Michele, and Jason Loviglio. *Radio Reader: Essays in the Cultural History of Radio.* New York: Routledge, 2002.

Johnston, Carla Brooks. *Screened Out: How the Media Control Us and What We Can Do about It.* Armonk, NY: Sharpe, 2000.

Lessig, Lawrence. *Free Culture: How Big Media Uses Technology and the Law to Lock Down Culture and Control Creativity.* New York: Penguin, 2004.

McAllister, Matthew P. *The Commercialization of American Culture: Advertising, Control, and Democracy.* Thousand Oaks, CA: Sage, 1995.

McChesney, Robert W. *The Problem of the Media: U.S. Communication Politics in the Twenty-First Century.* New York: Monthly Review, 2004.

McChesney, Robert W., and John Nichols. *Our Media, Not Theirs: The Democratic Struggle against Corporate Media.* New York: Seven Stories, 2002.

Ruggiero, Greg. *Microradio and Democracy: (Low)Power to the People.* New York: Seven Stories, 1999.

Schiller, Herbert I. *Communication and Culture.* Armonk, NY: Sharpe, 1976.

———. *Culture, Inc.: The Corporate Takeover of Public Expression.* New York: Oxford University Press, 1991.

———. *Information Inequality: The Deepening Social Crisis in America.* New York: Routledge, 1996.

Starr, Paul. *The Creation of Media.* New York: Basic, 2004.

Index

Abernathy, Kathleen, 91, 98, 100–101
Abrams, Lee, 21
Adams, Mike, 15, 180, 208
Adelstein, Jonathan, 91, 97, 102–5, 109, 133–34, 204–5, 210
advertising, 79, 152, 203, 212; 1920s, 26–27; local, 2, 20, 26–27, 58; refusal to air, 113; satellite radio and, 174, 175, 184
airwaves, public ownership of, 10, 133, 148, 167
Albarran, Alan B., 204
Allison, Jay, 17, 18, 86, 180
alternative media, 82, 206
American Broadcasting Company (ABC), 2, 26, 52, 127; ABC Radio, 178–79
American Federation of Television and Radio Artists (AFTRA), 142, 168
Americans for Radio Diversity (ARD), 12, 140, 141, 187
AM radio, 19, 21, 25, 49, 54, 59, 63–64
AOL–Time Warner, 84, 94
Arbitron markets, 101, 129–30, 149
Armstrong, Chick, 176
Armstrong, Edwin Howard, 49
Armstrong, John, 14, 35, 37
ascertainment primer, 62
AT&T, 29, 84
audience, 83, 152, 169; automobile listeners, 171, 175, 212; importance of localism to, 76–78, 84, 95; minority, 19, 194; music programming and, 141, 144, 154. *See also* citizens
automation, 3–4, 7, 82–83, 104–5

Barnouw, Erik, 28, 36, 192
Baudrillard, Jean, 79
Baumann, Jeff, 89
Benton Foundation, 13, 14, 72, 74
Billboard Airplay Monitor, 149, 151, 164
Black Entertainment Television, 119
Black Liberation Radio, 193, 196
Blethen, Frank A., 7, 80–81

"Blue Book" (FCC), 52–54
book publishing, 110–11, 121
Borland, John, 177
Boyce, Phil, 146–47
Bozell, Brent, 135
Bracy, Michael, 155
Brandeis, Louis, 81
Branett, Steven, 81
Breyer, Stephen, 205
Broad Artists Coalition, 9–10
Broadcast Century and Beyond, The (Hilliard and Keith), 69–70
Broadcasting & Cable, 204
"Broadcasting, the Constitution, and Democracy" (National Lawyer's Guild), 72
Brown, Duncan, 22
Brown, Michael, 17, 20, 86, 181, 207
Burkart, Patrick, 79–80
Burns, Conrad, 189
Bush administration, 97, 109, 111

cable service, 70, 112, 134, 172
Caldwell, Orestes, 30
Cantwell, Maria, 213
Carter administration, 3, 46, 64–65
censorship, 31, 95; of music, 18, 29, 109, 142–44; underreporting of consolidation efforts as, 5, 6, 106, 108, 115, 117–18
Center for Public Integrity, 93–94
chain broadcasting rules, 49–52
Chaitovitz, Ann, 142
Chambers, Todd, 11
Chong, Rachel, 84
Christian, Lynn, 17–18, 86, 180, 208
citizens: letters from, to Congress, 111–12, 114–15; opposition from, to changes of 2003, 89, 91–95, 98–101; support from, for independent and locally owned stations, 151–52; view of, on low-power FM stations, 188. *See also* audience

235

Clear Channel Communications, 5, 7; censorship of songs by, 18, 29, 109, 142–43; claims of diversity by, 75, 140–41; claims of localism by, 90, 95–96; emergency situations not covered by, 77–78; exceeds ownership limits, 93–94; Internet and, 176–77; music concert wing of, 142; percentage of control by, 5, 42, 92, 150, 160; and programming decisions, 13, 18–19, 29, 45, 109, 143; public protest against, 101; refusal to air advertisements, 113
Clinton administration, 4, 109
Collins, Tom, 65
Columbia Broadcasting System (CBS), 2, 26, 41, 51–52
Commerce Department, 1, 27–28, 30, 34
commissioners, 44, 62–63, 84–85. *See also* Abernathy, Kathleen; Adelstein, Jonathan; Copps, Michael J.; Federal Communications Commission; Powell, Michael
Communications Act of 1934, 9–10, 40, 43, 112, 157, 209; as mandate for localism, 4, 46–49, 98, 132–33; NAB opposition to, 41–47
Communications Decency Act, 70
community building, 75–76
community of license, 63
Compaine, Ben, 178–79
comparative broadcast hearings, 46, 66–67
Congress: authority of, over communications, 92–93; changes of 2003 and, 98–100, 135; citizens and, 74–75, 111–12, 114–15; debates in, over Radio Act of 1927, 34–35; Republican control of, 23, 74–75; Special Orders Session, 106–22
consolidation, 5, 22, 72–75, 150–51; effect of, on television, 14; and elimination of public affairs programming, 119–20; globalization process and, 5–6; illegal stations as counter to, 193–95; impact of, on democracy, 6, 78–82, 97–98, 106–8, 119–22; mar-

ket size categories and, 161–62; negative views of, 7, 9–13; positive views of, 7–8, 84–85; share of largest companies and, 159, 160, 166. *See also* deregulation; diversity; localism; music
consumer groups, 74, 95, 98, 101
Conyers, John, 92
Cooper, Mark, 100, 103
Coopman, Ted, 193
Copple, Robert, 47
Copps, Michael J., 23, 89, 91, 92, 97, 99, 102, 104–5, 107–9, 210; statement of, 132–39
Cornell, Rollye, 16–17, 20, 181, 182, 207–8
Corporation for Public Broadcasting (CPB), 64, 186
Couzens, James, 34–35
Cox, Kenneth, 62, 205
Coyer, Kate, 193–94
Cross-Media Limits (CML), 130–31
cross-ownership, 49–52, 90; 2003 changes in, 94, 101, 103, 108–9

Davis, Ewin, 36, 37
Davis, Stephen B., 34
Davis Amendment, 37–38
Delaware Story, The, 2
democracy: clash of ideas as important to, xiii, 13, 107; impact of consolidation on, 6, 78–82, 97–98, 106–8, 119–22; localism as key to, 17, 26, 47, 205; low-power FM stations and, 189–91
deregulation, xi, xiii–xiv, 21, 63–65, 69; during 1980s–1990s, 65–66; goals of, 157–58; importance of understanding effects of, 156–57. *See also* consolidation
DiCola, Peter, 153, 157
digital radio, 83–84
Dill, Clarence, 30
Dirty Discourse: Sex and Indecency in American Radio (Hilliard and Keith), xiii, 44–45
disk jockeys, 12, 57–58, 83
Disney Corporation, 29, 84, 94

diversity, 4, 9, 22, 31–32; changes of 2003 and, 89–90, 129; cross-media limits and, 130–31; debate, 1920s, 32–35; decline of, 72, 75–77, 95, 109; television and, 55, 126–27. *See also* public interest

Diversity Index, 124, 131

Dixie Chicks, 18, 29, 109, 143

Dorgan, Byron, 82, 99–100

Douglas, Susan, 39, 53, 58, 198

Douglas, William, 52

Dunifer, Stephen, 193, 197, 198

duopoly rule, 51–52, 69, 70–71, 94

Eckberg, John, 171

economic depression, 39–42

economic recessions, 65, 203

economics of radio, 7, 8, 19–21, 53, 65–66, 82–83, 168

economies of scale, 158, 162

Eisenhower, Dwight D., 6, 211

election coverage, 13, 79, 89

Electronic Media, The (Orlik), 25

Ellul, Jacques, 50, 79

emergency situations, 77–78, 104–5

Entercom Communications, 8, 173, 212

European radio, 24–25, 187

Fahrenheit 911, 29

Fairness Doctrine, 44, 60–62, 112–13

Fairness Law, 61

Federal Communications Commission (FCC), ix–x, 4, 23, 40; chain broadcasting rules, 49–52; decline of localism and, 49–50; early rulings of, 43–44; Educational Public Broadcasting Branch of, 60; enhanced power of, 44–45; Localism Task Force of, 98–101, 191; main studio rules and, 46–49; Notice of Inquiry (NOI) and, 103–5; Office of Network Study of, 45, 59–60; Policy Statement on Comparative Broadcast Hearings (1965) and, 46, 66–67; prerogatives of, under 1934 act, 46–47; "Public Service Book" ("Blue Book") by, 52–54; radio allocation priorities of, 25–26;

Report on Chain Broadcasting of, 50–52; rule of sevens of, 2, 56, 67; support of localism by, 45, 52–54. *See also* regulations of 2003 (FCC)

Federal Radio Commission (FRC), 1, 30, 31, 192; broadcasting zones and, 35–39; General Order No. 40 of, 37; stance of, on localism, 31–36

Fein, Michael R., 55, 81–82

Feingold, Russell, 145

Ferguson, Andrew, 77–78

Ferris, Charles, 46, 64–65

Field, David, 8, 212

First Amendment rights, 9, 31, 51, 105, 112, 209; microstations and, 194–95, 198; and obligations to air opposing views, 60–61; "Public Service Book" and, 52

Fisher, Marc, 12, 59, 75–76, 77, 140, 141

Flacks, Richard, 201

FM radio, 49, 54, 59, 63–64. *See also* low-power FM stations

formats: Internet radio, 183; oligopolies and, 164–67; satellite radio, 172; Top 40, 57, 59; variety versus redundancy in, 151, 163–64

Fornatale, Peter, 3–4

Fowler, Mark, 46

Fox, 123, 127, 146, 210

Frank, Jay, 178

Franken, Al, 80

Frankfurter, Felix, 52

Freed, Alan, 196

Free Radio Berkeley (FRB), 193, 197

Free Radio (Soley), 29, 43–44, 61–62, 209–10

free radio stations, 210

Free Speech (organization), 66

Fries, Gary, 203

Fritts, Edward O. (Eddie), 22–23, 104, 188, 202, 212; opposition by, to low-power FM stations, 191–92; on satellite radio, 170–71, 174

Future of Music Coalition (FMC), 73; "Radio Deregulation: Has It Served Citizens and Musicians?" by, 144–

Future of Music Coalition (*continued*) 45, 148–53; report to Congress, 145–46; survey by, 144–45; testimony of, before Congress, 143–44, 154–69

Garcia, Robert, 77
Geller, Valerie, 15, 20–21, 87, 181, 207
General Electric (GE), 26, 29, 36, 84, 94, 122
General Order No. 40, 37
globalism, 200–201
globalization, 5–6, 201
Godfrey, Arthur, 57
Godfrey, Donald, 35
Goebbels, Joseph, 79
Goldsmith, Bill, 177
Goodman, Peter, 170, 171
Goodsight, Ron, 196
Gorman, John, 184
government control of radio, 29
"Growing Concentration of Media Ownership, The," 106–22

Halper, Donna, 15–16, 18, 87, 181, 182, 208
Hazlitt, Tom, 36
Henry, E. William, 63
Heston, Joseph, 105
Hicks, Steve, 76
Hispanic Broadcasting Corporation, 96
Hitler, Adolf, 79
Hoffman, Allan, 178
Hogan, John, 95–96
Hollings, Ernest, 82, 92
Hoover, Herbert, 28–29, 30
House Resolution 218, 109
Human Rights Radio, 193
Humphrey, Clark, 203
Hundt, Reed, 148
Hunnicut, Clay, 146

indecency, 44–45, 70, 137
Infinity, 13, 19, 110
information access, xiii, 80, 104–5; and election coverage, 13, 89; and weather and traffic information, 173, 174, 183

Insless, Jay, 117, 118
Internet radio, xi, 70, 134, 145, 170, 212; approaches to, 177–79; formats, 183; and practitioners' viewpoints, 179–81; satellite radio and, 183–84; streaming technology and, 176, 177. *See also* satellite radio
In These Times, 74
iPods, xiii, 177, 212
Iraq war, 29, 142, 143

job losses, 12, 90–91, 117, 122, 137, 141, 203
Johnson, Luther A., 35
Johnson, Nicholas, 62, 67, 81, 85, 205
Justice Department, 52, 194, 196

Kantako, Mbanna, 193, 197
Karmazin, Mel, 182–83
Keith, Michael, 55–56
Kelley, Don, 146
Kennard, William, 4, 13, 76, 188, 190
Kennedy, John F., 45, 46, 59, 60
Kent, Barry, 146
Kimmelman, Gene, 101–2
Kittross, John, 31, 50–51, 56, 57, 71
Knoxville First Amendment Radio, 199

Lambert, Yon, 73
LaPierre, Wayne, 107
Lawrence, Neal, 5–6
Leahy, Patrick, 191, 213
Lewis, George W., 80
Lewis, Paul, 172
licenses: 1920s, 27–28; length of term of, 53, 71; public interest requirement and, x, 14, 16, 62–63; renewal of, 63, 70, 71, 137, 205
Liddy, G. Gordon, 80, 180
Lieberth, David, 13
Liggins, Alfred, 75
Limbaugh, Rush, 16, 20, 80
Listening In (Douglas), 58
lobbying, 43, 44, 74–75
Local Community Radio Act of 2005, 213
localism: in 1950s, 1–4, 56–59; con-

solidation as threat to, 11–12, 17–19; decline of, 3–4, 49–50, 203; definitions of, 65, 200; in early broadcasting, 24–26; during economic depression, 39–42; economics of radio and, 65–66; FCC stance on, 45, 49–54, 98–101, 191; FRC stance on, 31–36; importance of, 21–23, 76–78, 84, 95; industry view of, 14–15; Internet radio and, 177–79, 181; as key to democracy, 17, 26, 47, 205; local vs. distant ownership, 66, 204–5; mandating, 46–49; monopoly vs. diversity arguments, 32–35; political coverage, 210–11; practitioners' views, 15–21. See also low-power FM stations

Localism Task Force (FCC), 98–101, 104–5, 191, 210

Loevinger, Lee, 86

low-power AM stations, 19

low-power FM stations, 167, 169, 185–86, 208; 2005 FCC order and proposed rule making for, 212–13; arrests and fines for, 196–99; audience views of, 152; as counter to consolidation, 193–95; elimination of, 8, 66; FCC approval of, 197–98; hundred-watt stations as, 185, 186; microstation movement and, 192–93; NAB opposition to, 23, 187–89, 191–92; NPR opposition to, 64, 66, 186, 189; pirate protesters and, 196–97

main studio rules, 46–49

Mander, Jerry, 5

markets: Arbitron and, 101, 129–30, 149; definitions of, 93, 101, 128–30; oligopolies and, 150, 161–62

Marsalis, Ellis, Jr., 142

Marszewski, Ed, 80

Martin, Kevin J., 91

Maxwell, Christopher, 17, 19, 86, 181, 208

Mayflower Decision, 60

Mays, Lowry, 90, 95, 140

McCain, John, 95, 104, 169, 191, 213

McChesney, Robert W., 90–91, 206–7

McDonough, Walter, 155

McKibben, Bill, 78

media: lack of reporting about changes in, 5–6, 81, 106–9, 115–18, 121–22; suggestions for reform in, 206–7. See also power of media

Media Access Project, 12, 14, 76, 84, 101, 141, 144, 190

Mediaweek, 92

mergers, ban on, 126

Messere, Fritz, 45, 202, 205

Michaels, Randy, 7, 76

microstations. See low-power FM stations

Milam, Lorenzo, 186, 193

Mills, Joshua, 3–4

minority ownership, 8, 66, 72, 118–19, 125, 137–38

minority programming, 13, 19, 63, 89–90, 194

minority stations, low-power, 187–88

Minot train derailment, 77–78

Minow, Newton, 45, 59–60

Mitre Report, 191

Monks, Edward, 80

monopolies, in 1920s, 28–29, 34–35. See also consolidation

Moore, Michael, 29

Morello, Tom, 142–43

Moss, David A., 55, 81–82

Moyers, Bill, 6

Mueller, Milton, 209

Murdoch, Rupert, 70, 111, 120–21

music, 9–11, 54, 89, 105; audience viewpoint and, 141, 144, 152; censorship of, 18, 29, 109, 142–44; downloading, 21, 176; playlists, 57, 140–41, 150, 152, 177; political programming decisions and, 11, 18, 29, 109, 143; recording industry, 151. See also Future of Music Coalition

Mussolini, Benito, 79

Mutual Broadcasting System (MBS), 2, 51

Nader, Ralph, 65, 95

Napoli, Philip J., 67, 205

narrowcasting, 57–58, 59

National Association of Black Owned Broadcasters, 138
National Association of Broadcasters (NAB), xiii–xiv, 14–15, 17, 22–23, 43, 145; Code of Ethics, 53; opposition to Communications Act of 1934, 41–42; opposition to cross-ownership rule, 90; opposition to low-power FM stations, 23, 187–89, 191–92; petition against satellite radio, 174–76; support of Powell, 103–4
National Broadcasting Company (NBC), 2, 26, 45, 51–52, 127
National Broadcasting Company et al. v. U.S. Department of Justice, 52
National Lawyer's Guild (NLG), 9, 72
National Public Radio (NPR), 64, 66, 186, 188, 189, 208
national radio conferences, 1920s, 28–29
Native American stations, 55–56, 187–88
Nazism, 32, 50
Ness, Susan, 72
network radio, 21; in 1920s–1930s, 26, 40–41; in 1950s, 53, 56–57; control of affiliates by, 50–51; increase in, since 1980s, 66; O&Os, 127–28; Radio Act of 1927 and, 36
NewsCorp (News Corporation), 84, 94, 120–21
newspapers, 31–32, 40, 49, 94–95
news reporting, 77–78, 150; local political coverage, 210–11; O&Os and, 127–28. *See also* power of media
Newton, Gregory, 22, 25–26, 64, 65
Nichols, John, 90–91, 206–7
noncommercial radio, 43–44, 60. *See also* low-power FM stations
notice and comment procedure, 135
Notice of Inquiry (NOI), 103–5
Notices of Proposed Rule Making, 126, 187, 212–13
Now, 6

Office of Communication (United Church of Christ), 13, 63, 199
Office of Network Study (FCC), 45, 59–60

Ohio Story, The, 2
oligopolies, 151, 160–61, 164–67; geographic markets and, 150, 161–62
on-air personalities, 40, 82, 84. *See also* automation; disk jockeys; voice tracking
O&Os (broadcast network owned-and-operated stations), 127–28
Orlik, Peter, 25
O'Shaughnessy, Bill, 173–74
Our Media, Not Theirs (Nichols and McChesney), 90–91
Outfoxed (documentary), 210
owners: characteristics of, 32–33, 61–62; local vs. distant, 66, 204–5; minority, 8, 66, 72, 118–19, 125, 137–38
ownership rules, x–xi, 4–6, 66; 1920s, 27–29, 34–35; 2003 changes in, 93–94, 126–31; above-cap clusters, 131; Internet and, 179; limits on station ownership, 2, 4–5, 10, 56, 67, 69, 70–71; rule of sevens, 2, 56, 67; violations of, 93–94
Oxley, Mike, 188–89

Paley, William, 41
Panero, Hugh, 171
Parker, Elliott, 65–66
Parks, Darryl, 146
Pasha, Bill, 173
payola-like systems, 152, 167
PC magazine, 177
Petty, Tom, 141–42
pirate stations. *See* low-power FM stations
Pitts, Gregory R., 204
Polgreen, Lydia, 83
Policy Statement on Comparative Broadcast Hearings (1965), 46, 66–67
political solutions, 209–12
politics, media impact on, 5–6, 78–82, 106–9, 115–18
Porter, David, 178
Powell, Michael, 88, 91–92, 97–99, 103–5, 109, 153
power of media, 20, 32, 35, 50, 78–82, 97, 109, 132; media failure to report

on, 5–6, 81, 121–22; World War II and, 50–52

presidential campaign, 2004, 79

programming: 1940s, 54; decline in local, 8, 14, 27, 89–90, 119–20; economic concerns, 7, 8, 19–21; minority, 19, 63, 89–90, 113; percentage devoted to public interest, 62–63; politically based, 11, 18, 29, 109, 143; value of, 15–17. *See also* localism

Project Billboard, 143

Prometheus Radio Project, 194, 195, 197

propaganda, 32, 50, 79

Propaganda: The Formation of Men's Attitudes (Ellul), 50

Public Broadcasting Act of 1967, 64

public commentary ignored, 91–92

public interest, x, 4, 27; ascertainment primer and, 62; deregulation and, 63–65; indecency and, 44–45; programming percentage required, 14, 62–63. *See also* diversity

"Public Service Book" ("Blue Book") (FCC), 52–54

Radio Act of 1927, 1, 30, 31, 34, 43; broadcasting zones and, 35–39; Davis Amendment to, 37–38

Radio and Internet Newsletter, 176, 177

Radio Broadcasting Industry, The (Albarn and Pitts), 204

Radio Broadcasting Preservation Act of 1999, 188–89, 190

Radio Corporation of America (RCA), 26, 28, 29, 36, 41

Rapela, Daniel, 74, 83, 84

ratings, 70, 101

Reagan administration, 3, 44, 46, 61, 63

receivers, 24, 59, 183

Red Lion Broadcasting Company v. FCC, 60

Reece, Doug, 12

regulations of 2003 (FCC), 87, 88–89; 2004 reversal of rule changes, 101–4; changes summarized, 93–94; citizen opposition to, 89, 91–95, 98–104, 135, 138; press statement about, 96;

public hearings for, 92–94, 133, 134; reaction to, 94–98; refusal to disclose, 91–92, 134–35; summary of ownership rules, 126–31

Renshaw, Simon, 143

repeater technology, 173, 174

"Report and Order": 1958, 48; 2003, 123–31

Rice, Greg, 175

Rintels, Jonathan, 100

Roberts, John C., 97

Roosevelt, Franklin D., 41, 49

Ross, Sean, 15, 18, 208–9

rural concerns, 37–38

Sanders, Bernie, 92–93, 106–22

San Francisco Liberation Radio (SFLR), 198

Santosuosso, Michelle, 178

Sarnoff, David, 28

Sarnoff, Robert, 41

satellite radio, xiii, 21, 66, 82–83, 212; broadcasters' view of, 173–75; broadcast vs., 170–71; format types and, 172; number of subscribers to, 171, 175, 183; repeater technology and, 173, 174; subscription fee for, 174–75; success of, 175–76; as supplemental service, 172–73; weather and traffic information and, 173, 174, 183. *See also* Internet radio

scarcity principle, 31–32, 52

Schakowsky, Jan, 111–14

Schlesinger, Laura, 180

Schwartz, Gil, 171

Schwartz, Jonathan, 172, 173

Schwartzman, Andrew Jay, 12, 76, 101

Searls, Doc, 183

Seizing the Airwaves (Dunifer), 193

September 11 attack, 11, 15, 142–43

sevens, rule of, 2, 56, 67

Shane, Ed, 21, 86, 180–81, 207

Shernoff, Erika, 141

Signals in the Air: Native American Broadcasting in America (Keith), 55–56

Silverman, David M., 46–49

Sirius Satellite Radio, 171–72, 180, 182–83
small businesses, 131, 138
Smith, Emma, 178–79
Smulyan, Jeff, 173, 212
Smulyan, Susan, 37
Soderlund, Gretchen, 80
Sohn, Gigi, 84, 141
Soley, Lawrence, 29, 43–44, 61–62, 209
Sony, 84
southern legislators, 37–38
Soviet Union, 120
sports programming, 180
Staples, Brent, 12, 142, 143
Stavitsky, Alan, 36
Stay Tuned (Sterling and Kittross), 31, 71
Steal This Radio, 66, 194
Stein, Jeffrey L., 27
Steiner, Peter, 158, 163
Sterling, Christopher, 16, 19, 31, 50–51,
    56, 57, 71, 86, 180
Stern, Howard, 18, 45, 182–83, 184
Stevenson, Adlai E., 211
Stewart, Potter, 205
stock market crash of 1929, 39
streaming technology, 176, 177
Sullivan, Andy, 73
Supreme Court, 51, 52, 60, 112, 133, 205
Swedberg, Gregg, 146
syndication, 16, 18, 21, 76, 146

Taglang, Kevin, 74–75
talk radio, 12, 16, 20, 80, 87, 96, 114
Tauzin, Billy, 189
tax cuts, 121–22
Taylor, Pam, 84, 144
Taylor, Tom, 184
Telecommunications Act of 1996, 9, 11–
    12; aims of, 148–49; assessment of,
    72–75; buying frenzy after, 5, 20;
    changes due to, 69–70; diversity and,
    75–77; industry lobbying efforts and,
    74–75; limits on station ownership
    and, 4, 67, 71, 119; number of own-
    ers and, 76, 119; predictions about,
    157–58. *See also* licenses
telephone call-in shows, 27
television, 2–3, 14, 19, 41, 48, 119, 126;
    impact of, on radio, 2–3, 11, 54, 55

ten-watt stations (class D), 64, 66, 186,
    208
Thomson, Kristin, 73, 153, 157
Tobaccowala, Rishad, 184
Tobenkin, David N., 46–49
Toomey, Jenny, 145–46, 155
Top 40 format, 57, 59
totalitarianism, 120
Tower in Babel, A (Barnouw), 28, 36
town meetings, 107
Tristani, Gloria, 13, 188
Turner, Ted, 7

UHF discount, 128, 136
United Church of Christ, 13, 63, 199
United Kingdom radio, 90
Unity: Journalists of Color, 89
Univision, 96
USA Today, 13, 76, 88, 212
U.S. Circuit Court of Appeals (Philadel-
    phia), 98

Vaillant, Derek W., 33–34, 38
V-chip, 70
VHF stations, 128
Viacom, 92, 94, 110, 119, 127, 150, 160
Video Display Terminal (VDT), 70
voice tracking, 11, 19, 20, 21, 82–83,
    180

Wag the Dog (film), 210
Watson, Diane, 118
*Waves of Rancor: Tuning in the Radi-
    cal Right* (Hilliard and Keith), xiii
Westinghouse, 24, 26, 29, 36
Wharton, Dennis, 172–73
White, Wallace, Jr., 30
Wilker, Jeremy, 12, 141
Wolfe, Kerry, 146
Woolsey, Lynn, 108–10
World War I, 29
World War II, 50

XM Satellite Radio, 171–74, 180, 183–84

Zenith Radio Corporation, 30
Zisk, Brian, 155
zones, broadcasting, 35–39

Robert L. Hilliard is a professor of media arts and the former dean of graduate studies and of continuing education at Emerson College. He has been the chief of the educational–public broadcasting branch of the Federal Communications Commission, the chair of the Federal Interagency Media Committee, and a broadcasting writer, director, and producer. Among his thirty books about media are the classic *Writing for Television, Radio, and New Media,* now in its eighth edition, and the controversial *Media, Education, and America's Counter-Culture Revolution.* He frequently lectures and consults for governments, corporations, and universities globally.

Michael C. Keith ranks among the most prolific authors on the subject of broadcast media, especially radio. He is a member of the communication faculty at Boston College and is the author of some twenty books, including *Voices in the Purple Haze, Signals in the Air, Sounds in the Dark,* and the classic textbook *The Radio Station.* He also wrote the critically acclaimed childhood memoir *The Next Better Place.* He has written numerous journal and encyclopedia articles. He is a former professional broadcaster and is a past chair of education of the Museum of Broadcast Communications. He is the recipient of several awards.

Hilliard and Keith have coauthored a number of media books, including *The Broadcast Century and Beyond,* now in its fourth edition; *Waves of Rancor,* which President Clinton selected as one of twelve books on his 1999 reading list; *Dirty Discourse: Sex and Indecency in American Radio; Global Broadcasting Systems;* and *The Hidden Screen.*